THE RACE FOR PERFECT

Inside the Quest to Design the Ultimate Portable Computer

BY STEVE HAMM

New York | Chicago | San Francisco | Lisbon | London | Madrid | Mexico City
Milan | New Delhi | San Juan | Seoul | Singapore | Sydney | Toronto

The *McGraw·Hill* Companies

1 2 3 4 5 6 7 8 9 0 DOC/DOC 0 1 0 9 8

ISBN: 978-0-07-160610-3
MHID: 0-07-160610-6

McGraw-Hill books are available at special quantity discounts to use as premiums and sales promotions, or for use in corporate training programs. For more information, please write to the Director of Special Sales, Professional Publishing, McGraw-Hill, Two Penn Plaza, New York, NY 10121-2298. Or contact your local bookstore.

Library of Congress Cataloging-in-Publication Data
Hamm, Steve.
    The race for perfect : inside the quest to design the ultimate portable computer / by Steve Hamm.
    p. cm.
    Includes bibliographical references and index.
    ISBN 0-07-160610-6 (alk. paper)
    1. Microcomputers.   2. Portable computers—Design and construction.   I. Title.
    QA76.5.H3528 2009
    004.16—dc22

                                        2008022946

This book is dedicated to my wife, Lisa, my son, Daniel, the memory of my mother, Marian Hamm, and to my father, J.R. Hamm, engineer and farmer.

CONTENTS

Engineers, scientists, and artists create value. Everybody else just moves it around.

—Robert Noyce
Cofounder, Intel Corp.

Introduction

One of the first commercial portable computers ever produced was almost perfect. The U.S. version was called the Tandy TRS-80 Model 100, but fans of the machine fondly called it "Trash 80" for short. I was one of them.

When Tandy sold the Model 100 through its RadioShack stores in 1983, hobbyists and newspaper reporters snapped them up like candy. At a time when most personal computers were the size of picnic coolers, this gadget—which was really a mobile word processor—could easily be slipped into a small backpack or attaché case and taken anywhere. The Model 100 was roughly 8 by 11 inches (203 by 280 millimeters), two inches (50.8 millimeters) thick, and weighed less than four pounds (1.8 kilograms). It was a tablet of beige plastic with a full-size keyboard and a narrow strip of a screen capable of displaying eight lines of text. It had a modem, so you could send what you had written to another computer via the phone lines. You could get eight hours of use out of the machine on four AA batteries. The price: a mere $700.

The Model 100 was a marvel of then modern technology: simple, yet effective. Like most great tools, it did one thing very well. I credit the machine with sparking my interest in mobile computers, which, for many years was nothing more than a mild affection, but which now has blossomed into a full-fledged obsession—and this book.

The Race for Perfect is the inside story of the amazing 40-year effort by some of the most talented people in the computer industry to design, build, and market the ultimate mobile computer. It's a journey of discovery into the very souls of these new machines. I acknowledge my debt to Tracy Kidder's great 1981 book, *The Soul of a New Machine*, about a minicomputer development project at Data General. The trip began in 1968, when graduate student Alan Kay envisioned a portable personal computer for children. It continued through the early 1980s, when computing pioneers built suitcase-size "luggable" computers. And it followed a winding road to laptop PCs, to so-called personal digital assistants like the Palm Pilot, and to smartphones like the BlackBerry and iPhone. This journey has truly been a race—a marathon, but, also, a series of sprints, as one team of designers is pitted against another to come up with the next big thing. Now, the future of a $100 billion mobile computing industry hangs in the balance as visionaries and engineers pack the latest technologies into ever-smaller packages.

This book is a popular history. I don't try to record every twist and turn and every technology advance. Instead, I focus on some of the notable successes, failures, and human dramas in a quest that started before the personal computer existed and goes on today that's every bit as difficult—technically—as the initial effort by America to land a man on the moon. While that journey into outer space took humans on an impossibly long trip through an incredibly hostile environment, this one is an effort to take machines that started off as room-sized behemoths and use all sorts of technical wizardry to squeeze them small enough to fit into your briefcase or pocket—a trip into inner space. Also, the book shows how the design and manufacturing of mobile computers has truly become a global phenomenon—stoking developing economies and empowering individuals in the remotest corners of the earth.

This story is about the convergence of invention, engineering, design, and marketing in efforts to create the most personal of computers. Think of it this way: the personal computer augments human beings, providing the additional memory, number-crunching power, and communications abilities that our own minds and voices can't muster on their own. The mobile computer—whether a laptop or a smartphone—goes one big step farther, freeing us to do our work and keep in touch wherever we are.

At its essence, this tale is as old as humans: it's about the effort to design the perfect thing, whether a delightful electronic gizmo like the Apple iPhone or a palace like the Taj Mahal. This book is about the nature of innovation itself. It profiles the people who create new things, reveals how they conceive new products, and traces their paths as they design and build them, and then bring them to market.

Has any portable computer been truly perfect? People with generous spirits might make that claim. After all, a number of ingeniously designed machines have delighted their owners, among them the first Apple Powerbook laptops, some IBM ThinkPads, the Palm Pilot personal organizer, the BlackBerry e-mail machine, and the iPhone. But, think again. The Powerbooks were under-powered; ThinkPads have always been hampered by their dependence on Microsoft's Windows operating system; the BlackBerry keyboard is just too compressed for people with large thumbs or lengthy e-mails to write; and the first iPhone had stingy storage for music and a molasses-slow wireless Internet connection. Many mobile products do one or two things very well. It's when engineers pile on the features that things can go haywire.

The Trash 80 had nettlesome shortcomings. One of them was the data communications system. You transmitted documents by hooking up a set of acoustic couplers to a telephone handset so the modem could essentially speak in code over the phone to a remote computer. This was an excellent system in theory, but, in practice, it could be enormously frustrating. For one reason or another, these transmissions would often fail—sometimes resulting in hours of tinkering to get the bits and bytes flowing freely.

A reporting trip I took to Las Vegas back in 1987 illustrates both the joys and frustrations of computing with a Trash 80. I was working for the *New Haven Register* and went to Vegas to attend the annual convention of the International Council of Shopping Centers, a huge confab of mall developers and retailers. Like many young reporters of that era, I was a fan of gonzo journalist Hunter S. Thompson, who had painted an unforgettable psychedelic portrait of America's desert oasis in his book, *Fear and Loathing in Las Vegas*. So, there I was, wandering the casinos, loading up at the $8.95 buffets, and hanging around with some of New Haven's high rollers at the craps tables. When it came time to write, I settled in at a table beside a swimming pool at the old Sands Hotel with my Trash 80 before me. The words flowed easily. So did the Mai Tais. But the magic spell was broken when I finished writing and went up to my room to transmit. There, I spent a couple of hours on my knees beside the telephone table trying over and over again to send that miserable 1,000-word story to Connecticut.

As irritating as the Trash 80 could be, you don't begrudge its makers. They were trying something brand new. The machine was the brainchild of Kazuo Inamori, the president and founder of Japan's Kyocera Corp. He was one of those remarkable Japanese entrepreneurs who came of age in the 1950s and helped lead Japan's resurgence as an economic power. Inamori started Kyocera as a ceramics manufacturer in 1959 at age 27 and had built it into a large conglomerate by the early 1980s. He was always looking for new business opportunities. In 1981, he happened to sit next to Microsoft vice president Kazuhiko Nishi on a flight back home to Japan from the United States. They got to talking and Nishi shared with him some of the excitement at Microsoft about the potential of portable computers. Inamori decided to make one. Sure, the machine Kyocera launched first in Japan in early 1982 had its faults. But the important thing was that it had helped awaken consumers—and an industry—to the potential of portable computing. Microsoft founder Bill Gates has called the Model 100 his all-time favorite computer, partly because it was the last one for which he wrote a substantial chunk of the software. "It was the first machine that delivered on the potential of portable computing," he says.

Since those early days, the quest to design ever better mobile devices has consumed many a techie. I spoke to dozens of engineers, designers, and entrepreneurs to prepare this book, and many of them described their interest in portable computing as nothing less than an obsession. They pursued their dreams and fought their demons for decades, and they just couldn't quit. "I am still on the quest for the perfect mobile computer," says Sam Lucente, who designed some of the early portables at IBM in the 1990s and is now head of corporate design at Hewlett-Packard. "It's an elusive prize, since technology and people are always changing."

One of the most dedicated mobile computing pilgrims is John Ellenby. A manager at Xerox's famed Palo Alto Research Center in the 1970s, he went on to produce one of the earliest portables, the GRiD Compass. He was already over 40 years old when GRiD introduced this laptop in 1982. Yet in 2008, when Ellenby was 67, he was still on the portable computing quest. His company, GeoVector, had introduced a revolutionary new mobile computing service in Japan. Consumers could point a smartphone at buildings and, thanks to a Global Positioning System (GPS) and a compass in the phone, they could view all sorts of information about the places. If they pointed at a nightclub, for instance, they'd learn what performers were appearing there that evening.

Very few of the people who pick up this book will have been familiar with Ellenby's name before they read it. And the same will be true of many of the other pioneers of mobile computing. As with science and math, many of the advances in computer science aren't dramatic breaks with the past. Each engineer and designer and visionary builds on what was invented and tried before. As a result, it would be inaccurate and unfair to pretend that a mere handful of people are responsible for the great leaps forward in portable computing. It has required a cast of thousands, and I spread the credit around.

Still, it's important to have a focal point. I chose to track a single contemporary mobile computing project from beginning to end—and to weave that story through the book. The product, from Lenovo Group, was conceived in the summer of 2006 and introduced to the market as ThinkPad X300 in late February of 2008. Lenovo was at the time the fourth-largest PC company in the world—the result of its 2005 acquisition of IBM's PC division. Chairman Yang Yuanqing had bought IBM's PC business primarily for its well-respected ThinkPad line of portable computers. And the ThinkPad development team, made up mainly of Japanese and American designers, engineers, and marketers, had created the X300 to show just how innovative Lenovo could be.

The X300 is an excellent machine. When I first held the computer, in February 2008, I was struck by how thin it is—ranging from 0.75 to 0.93 of an inch (19 to 23.6 millimeters), depending on where you measure. And it's incredibly light—about three pounds (1.36 kilograms). Yet it includes all of the most advanced features you would want in a notebook computer, from a cutting-edge solid-state drive (no moving parts), to an ultrathin DVD player, to radio transmitters suitable for every type of wireless communication.

The X300 is a vast improvement over today's ordinary laptops. And it may well be the ultimate laptop computer, for the moment, for a frequent-flying executive or a nomadic journalist. But it's not perfect. At a price of nearly $3,000, this machine is too expensive for many people who would otherwise like to buy it (including me). So, 40 years after Alan Kay first dreamed of a portable computer, the pursuit of perfection continues. It will, I'm sure, for many years to come.

1

THE QUEST

Just after lunchtime on January 15, 2008, at Lenovo Group's offices in suburban Morrisville, North Carolina, it seemed as if a four-alarm fire had broken out. Peter Hortensius, the senior vice president in charge of the laptop business, stormed through the cubicles on the fourth floor of Building 2 shouting to his secretary: "Phyllis! Get me one of those interoffice mail envelopes!" Phyllis Arrington-McGee ransacked filing cabinets until she found one and handed it to Hortensius, who was waiting nervously in his office with Sam Dusi, the head of laptop marketing. Hortensius hoisted a slim black notebook computer, the ThinkPad X300, off of his desk and slipped it into the envelope. Then he shouted: "It fits! It fits!"

Such is life in one of the most competitive marketplaces on earth: the portable computer business. Hortensius's anxiety attack had been brought on by Apple Inc. chief executive Steve Jobs. During the annual Macworld conference in San Francisco that morning, Jobs had revealed the MacBook Air, which he proudly labeled "the world's thinnest notebook." For dramatic effect, he drew the supersvelte silver machine out of an interoffice mailing envelope. It was like he was pulling a rabbit out of a hat.

That showy gesture could have been a crushing blow for Lenovo. The X300, on the drawing boards since June 2006, had just that morning received the go-ahead for manufacturing in a factory in Shenzhen, China. Like the MacBook Air, the X300 was supposed to cause a sensation with its thinness. Yet it was in danger of being upstaged—even though it was aimed at businesspeople, while MacBook Air was for consumers. So it was a relief to Hortensius that X300 also fit in the envelope.

The same went for David Hill, who headed corporate identity and design for Lenovo. It had been his idea to create a superthin, superelegant, high-end machine. He happened to drop by Hortensius's office right after the envelope incident and laughed when he saw a photo Dusi had taken of the envelope with the X300 poking out of it. What did Hill think of Air? "I'm a bit tired of looking at silver computers. They seem so flashy," he said a few days later. "I'd never wear a silver business suit."

In the hours that followed Hortensius's outburst, it became clear that Air was not a direct hit on the X300. Not only was the Lenovo laptop almost as thin as Air, it was actually lighter—at 2.9 pounds for the lightest version. And unlike Air, it was packed with every piece of advanced technology that a laptop maven could want. That included a bright LED display, a superthin DVD player for movies, a cutting-edge solid-state hard drive made just of chips rather than a spinning disk, and five different radio transmitters. The early reviews of Air were mixed—showing that even a slugger like Jobs can't hit a home run every time. Within three days, news of X300 leaked onto the Internet, and some of the Net's popular gadget blogs were comparing it favorably with Air.

The X300 was no ordinary laptop for Lenovo. The company had invested in it a tremendous amount of creativity, money, and psychic energy. Back in 2005, when China's Lenovo purchased IBM's money-losing $10 billion PC division, the jewel in the battered crown was the ThinkPad laptop business. ThinkPads were the favorites of executives and business travelers. The original design concept, created by legendary design consultant Richard Sapper, was that ThinkPads would be simple, elegant matte-black machines with precise, 90-degree corners. After being introduced in 1992, the ThinkPad went on to become the longest-lasting design franchise in computing history. By 2007, on the 15-year anniversary, more than

30 million had been sold. After Lenovo bought the IBM PC division, it aimed to overcome the negative impression of China as a country that steals other people's designs rather than innovating itself. The goal was to become a respected global brand, and ThinkPad could help take it there—but only if it delivered cutting-edge technology, design, and quality. In the last years under IBM, Hill, the design chief, had become frustrated with the parent company's focus on cost-cutting. So he welcomed the chance to innovate freely once again. For Hill and some of his colleagues, X300—developed under the code name Kodachi—represented an attempt to produce nothing less than the perfect portable computer.

Is X300 perfect? No computer could be. But this kind of effort is all about striving for perfection. Over time, the Lenovo product development team was forced to make a series of compromises. In spite of that fact, their machine was arguably the best notebook computer ever produced for a business executive. Engineers in Yamato, Japan, squeezed a lot of technology into a very small package. Yet, what they had achieved would doubtless be ephemeral. The way the PC business operates, a competitor would be likely to leapfrog their machine in a matter of months. Lenovo had a lot to prove before it could become one of tech's premier global brands. Asked how it stacks up as a competitor, Michael Dell, chief executive of PC giant Dell, was dismissive: "We have bigger rivals to worry about—except in China."

The X300 arrived at a time of upheaval in the computer industry. Portable computing was breaking out. After decades in which desktop PCs dominated, industry analysts expected more laptops to sell in 2008 in the United States than desktops, and they expected the crossover worldwide in 2009. All told, more than 100 million laptops are being sold each year—ranging in price from $500 to $5,000. At the same time, miniaturization of electronics has allowed tech outfits to pack so much into high-end mobile phones that they have become, essentially, small computers.

These happenings were the latest episode in a 40-year quest to fulfill the potential of mobile computing. The effort started in the late 1960s when Alan Kay, a computer science student in search of computing aids to education, envisioned portables for children even before it was possible to build a desktop PC. Until then, computers were tractor-sized monsters harnessed to the military, large corporations, and universities. But that was about to change, and computers would rapidly become smaller, more personal, and, gradually, more mobile. In the 1970s, the three loci of personal computing were the Homebrew Computer Club in the San Francisco Bay Area, where Jobs and Steve Wozniak of Apple got their start; Xerox's Palo Alto Research Center, where Kay and other scientists dreamed up some of the most innovative personal computing technologies, including the graphical user interface and the mobile computer; and Albuquerque, New Mexico, where MITS created the first PC in the form of a mail-order kit and Bill Gates's little company, then called Micro-soft, had its humble beginnings.

These entrepreneurs and computer scientists were able to spark a revolution in science and society thanks in large part to the advent of tiny microprocessors, the size of a fingernail, which were just then replacing large and expensive vacuum tubes. Meanwhile, software such as the Altair BASIC program written by Gates gave the first personal computers something to do other than blink their lights.

Shortly after IBM turned personal computing into a huge business phenomenon with the introduction of its first PC in 1981, the quest to create portable computers began in earnest. Computing pioneers, including the founders of Compaq, produced suitcase-size "luggables" that were so heavy they practically pulled your arm out of the socket when you carried them, but also were tough enough to survive a fall down a flight of stairs. Gradually, the march of miniaturization did its work. With each new generation of technology, more transistors could be packed into a smaller space, and components such as mechanical disk drives for storing information and modems for transmitting messages across telephone lines became more and more compact. The result, by the late 1980s, was a laptop computer with all the capabilities of a desktop machine that was slim enough to slip into an attaché case. The 1990s started off with some portable computing disasters, including the much criticized Apple Newton handheld, but, by the middle of the decade Palm was producing useful pocket-sized handhelds that were excellent tools for keeping track of contact information and schedules.

Innovation has come in waves, aided by advances in technology and the insatiable hunger driving entrepreneurs to discover the next big thing, deliver it to customers, and make millions by taking a start-up company public. Research in Motion (RIM), the long-little-known Canadian company, figured out how to make the handheld computer a powerful tool for e-mail, and produced the BlackBerry. Jobs, the great tastemaker, brought the handheld computer to a new level of delightfulness in 2007 with his iPhone, a Swiss Army knife–like device that handles e-mail, taps the Internet, takes phone calls, and plays music—and does it all with the intuitive touch of a finger. "The more complex the technology and communication become, the best way to deal with it is through simplifying," says Paola Antonelli, curator of architecture and design at the Museum of Modern Art, in New York City.

Nearly two decades ago, during an address at the 1990 COMDEX computer industry trade show in Las Vegas, Gates was worried about a slowdown of innovation in the PC industry. So he talked up his concept of "Information at Your Fingertips." At the time, most PCs were isolated digital islands—not even connected to other computers by wires. Gates envisioned advances during the decade of the 1990s that would make it possible for people to be in touch with all of the digital information in the world not just via their desktop PCs but, wirelessly, via portables. Previous to that speech, Microsoft's goal had been to put a PC on every desktop; afterward it was to put computers everywhere. Computer networking blossomed in the mid-1990s. But it wasn't until Intel, in the early 2000s, made wireless data communications a feature of practically every laptop computer that Gates's vision of having information at your fingertips wherever you may be made the transition from fantasy to reality.

In mid-2008, Gates left his full-time role at Microsoft to focus most of his attention on his charitable foundation. It's the first time since he was 20 years old that he didn't have a full-time Microsoft job. Yet in his continuing role as chairman he remains involved in technologies that will propel portable computing forward. During an interview before he made the transition, he said he had a passion for natural interface technologies, including speech, pen, and touch, and he looked forward to helping out with innovations that would transform computing again and again. Looking back, surveying the sweep of events from the early days of the Tandy TRS 80 Model 100 portable to the Microsoft-enabled tablet PCs of the 2000s, Gates felt a tremendous amount of satisfaction tinged with impatience for progress still to come. "Portable computing has been a mind-blowing success," he said. "The natural input technologies will let us get more pervasive, and very cheap. That's the thing that's still in promise."

It has been a long hard trip, from the late 1960s to the early 2000s, and, in late 2008, it's still difficult to design and build an excellent portable computer. When people design regular computers, they press forward on two vectors: price and performance. But mobile computing is much more challenging. It operates in four dimensions: price, performance, portability, and usability. That makes the tasks of the engineers and designers much more daunting. As devices shrink, they tend to get more expensive and less capable. It's extremely difficult to design a device that is inexpensive enough to be affordable for a mass audience, powerful enough to perform like a desktop computer, with an easy-to-view screen and convenient methods for getting information into the machine, and yet compact enough to fit in a pocket or small bag. By necessity, designers and engineers are forced to make trade-offs to achieve just the right mix of price, performance, usefulness, and portability. Often, their products fail to meet one goal, and sometimes they miss more.

To make matters even more complicated, product developers now have to deal with an additional element: fashion. "When you make things smaller, you make them more personal. And when you make things more personal, you make them more emotional," says Ted Clark, general manager of the notebook computing business at Hewlett-Packard. "Notebook computers are an extension of your personality, almost like jewelry." When you add fashion to the portable formula, you start to understand why many pioneering mobile computers have been flops, a few have been nearly perfect, and most have been essentially knock-offs of devices that preceded them.

Back in 1990, when Gates was making his COMDEX speech, British computer scientist Tim Berners-Lee was working on concepts that would eventually add a critically important dimension to portable computing: the World Wide Web. Berners-Lee, who worked for a European physics research organization, wanted to make the Internet more useful. This interwoven network of computer networks had been created under the auspices of the U.S. Department of Defense and was at that time primarily a tool for scientific researchers. Berners-Lee created a system of interlinked documents that could be accessed via the Internet, making it easier for scientists to share research. Out of that invention came Web pages, "hyperlinks" within a Web page that connected to other Web pages, and, ultimately, Web browsers that allowed people to easily navigate the labyrinth of the Internet.

Advances in computer science come not only in waves but also in layers—with inventors building on top of each other's innovations. So, adding to Berners-Lee's work, young Marc Andreessen and his colleagues at the University of Illinois, Urbana-Champaign in 1993 produced one of the first browsers with an easy-to-use graphical user interface, called Mosaic. Suddenly, information ranging from text to photographs to videos could be presented on a Web page that could be viewed on any computer—no matter what processor or operating system was used, and no matter if the computer was a 20-pound deskbound machine or a one-pound handheld device. Add another layer: Web search engines from the likes of Google and Microsoft, making much of the universe of knowledge readily available in huge digital storehouses. Then add blogs, where individuals self-publish their thoughts on everything from string theory to Jell-o molds, and, every day, the Internet is restocked in unequal shares with genius and junk.

These gadgets and Web sites are constantly connected thanks to a wireless communications canopy that has been strung over much of the world. A half century ago, wireless communications were primarily of the one-way broadcast type—TV and radio stations sending out their signals from antennas on tall buildings and mountaintops. Now, in developed nations, two-way wireless data communications are nearly ubiquitous—whether in office buildings, on city streets, in airports, or even on lonely stretches of highway.

All of these technical advances, wrapped together, have helped to produce a flowering of portable computing 40 years after Alan Kay had first dreamed of a notebook computer for children. The devices are still just in the beginning phases of fulfilling their potential as empowering devices for education (more about that in Chapter 11), but they have already transformed personal and business interactions.

Consider a scene in Davos, Switzerland, during the annual World Economic Forum in late January 2008. The forum is a gathering of several thousand business, academic, government, and nonprofit leaders with the purpose of solving the world's problems. After a panel discussion in the main hall of Davos's Congress Centre, hundreds of people poured into the lobby just outside. While many of them were talking to each other, face to face, the old-fashioned way, just as many were speaking on their cellphones or staring into the tiny displays of their smartphones. The moment they had emerged from the hall and could turn on their handhelds, they were instantly in touch with the world and interacting with it. On the mezzanine, just above the lobby, Robert Scoble, a former Microsoft employee who published the popular Scobleizer blog, was interviewing two technology journalists with a palm-sized high-definition digital video camera. As quickly as the images and sounds were captured in the camera, they were transmitted wirelessly to a nearby antenna and then to a computer 6,000 miles away that was the host machine for his blog. In a flash, Scoble's fans anywhere in the world could view the video through their Web browsers.

Within minutes, the crowd dispersed and took a different shape. Dozens of people stood at counters around the periphery of the lobby or sat at tables in adjoining rooms, where they opened their laptops and began tapping out e-mails or checking Web sites for the latest in business or political news. No doubt, some of them were writing memos to colleagues or they were checking stock prices and making trades. Others probably used a software program called Twitter that allowed them to keep friends or even strangers constantly apprised of where they were and what they were doing and thinking. Some of them probably navigated straight to Scobleizer to get Scoble's views on the conference.

Thanks to wireless digital technology placing the world at their fingertips, these people were producing and consuming information and images, and sharing their experiences with thousands or even tens of thousands of people dispersed around the globe. They were interacting with the marketplace of ideas. Round and round the bits and bytes flew. Think of the ouroboros, the ancient symbol of a serpent swallowing its own tail and forming a circle. It's interpreted as the symbol for consciousness by some people, and infinity by others. Today, thanks to portable computers and all of the technology that surrounds them, information and consciousness are flowing, like the serpent, in an infinite, self-fulfilling loop.

Where will all of this digital alchemy take us? Increasingly, connections between people and ideas will happen effortlessly, and, often, accidentally. People will make decisions ever more quickly. Their choices will be based on abundant information—though its quality will be questionable. Things will happen faster, and sometimes at a dizzying pace. One can imagine all of this connecting and interacting becoming oppressive. People might long to set aside their laptops and smartphones so they can disconnect from the whirl of activity—temporarily at least. Most of the time, though, these devices will be attached to us as extensions of our senses. We'd no sooner give them up than we'd take off our clothes and run naked through the streets. Jean-Louis Gassée, one of the pioneers of portable computing at Apple and now a venture capitalist, sees the portable as the most personal of personal computers—the machine that, in a sense, completes us. "The more portable you make it, the closer to the body, the more personal it becomes and the more it expands your intellectual reach," he says. Portable computing also greatly expands our ability to express ourselves.

In Davos, in my role as a writer for *BusinessWeek* in the era of online multimedia communications, I carried in my small backpack a laptop computer, a smartphone, a high-quality digital camera, a video camera for blogging, and a tiny digital audio recorder. I also carried a sensor-based ID card around my neck that I presented to a reader device at every entrance so a guard could verify who I was. I was wearing all of these devices, yet they put no strain on me.

But why was it necessary for me to carry six gadgets? Wouldn't one or two have been better? That's a question that confounds today's inventors. They're driven not just to make ever-smaller devices but to make devices that do more for people, both empowering them and simplifying their lives. So they're asking themselves what combinations of features will make sense on the portable devices of the future. It's rarely clear exactly what paths technology will take, or how people will use it. Science fiction author William Gibson wrote in the introduction of the 2004 reprinting of his 1984 novel *Necromancer* that he failed in the book to anticipate mobile phones and the transformative effect they would have on communications and society. Instead, he imagined that people who were on the move would communicate in the future via a souped-up version of the public phone booth. That was a big miss. And he's a very smart guy. Ask technologists today what forms mobile computing will take a decade from now and they're refreshingly honest: it's unknowable. They have only a general sense of what will work. "I don't think there's going to be *an* ultimate anything," says Andy Grove, chairman emeritus of Intel. "I don't buy *an* ultimate computer any more than I buy that the TV and PC will merge. What I see is a generation of highly optimized devices that are compatible with one another."

In Davos, Lenovo's chief executive, William Amelio, was carrying two machines that represented the present and the future of portable computing. One was the X300, which he showed to influential people in hopes of creating buzz. The other was a so-called Mobile Internet Device (MID), a small handheld designed specifically for Net browsing that was based on technology mapped out by Intel. It was one of those "optimized devices" that Grove is talking about. Lenovo had designed its MID machine for sale in Asia, and, if demand took off there, the company planned on marketing it in the United States. The X300 was the ultimate refinement of the laptop computer idea, but, at its essence, it was a smaller and portable version of a desktop computer. The MID was a guess about the future.

The contrast of the X300 and the MID shows that in the transition from PC computing to mobile computing, many of the rules that shaped the PC era are suddenly open to debate. During the 1990s, Microsoft had nearly driven Apple out of business. Its strategy of providing Windows, a general-purpose operating system that many computer makers would load on their products, had proved to be more economically powerful than Apple's strategy of controlling both the operating system and the hardware. The X300, which runs Windows, is a highly evolved expression of Microsoft's strategy. Yet, in the era of mobile computing, it isn't clear that Microsoft's approach will work so well anymore. Lenovo's MID runs Linux, a so-called open source software program developed by volunteer programmers from around the world. Linux is cheaper and more adaptable than Windows. And, thanks to Apple's brilliantly designed iPod music players and iPhones, the company and its business model are on the rebound. The more portable the device, it turns out, the more crucial is the smooth interaction of the hardware and the software that commands it. Within six months of Apple's launch of its iPhone in mid-2007, according to market researcher Canalys, it had captured 28 percent of the U.S. market—outperforming phones running Microsoft's communications software. In early 2008, Microsoft made a couple of moves that signaled its uncertainty about the future of mobile computing: It replaced the leader of its mobile communications business and it bought Danger, maker of the popular Sidekick smartphone. No longer would it rely solely on handset makers to propel its mobile communications business forward. Instead, it would control both the hardware and software of the Danger machines.

As the PC era shifts into the mobile computing era, Lenovo faces stiff challenges of its own. Like other PC makers, it does not control its fate, technologically. The vast majority of PCs contain processors designed and manufactured by Intel, and most are loaded with Microsoft's Windows operating system. Any PC company can load Linux onto its machines as an alternative to Windows, and most do. Storage devices, modems, screens, and radio transmitters are produced by a mere handful of major suppliers, who provide these components for all of the PC makers. The basic laptop is becoming a commodity. One is pretty much like any other. So how is a company like Lenovo to differentiate itself from its rivals?

Its answer is design and engineering excellence. When Lenovo bought the IBM PC division, it inherited two valuable assets, the ThinkPad design tradition and an engineering group in Yamato, Japan, that is arguably the best team of computer engineers in the world. The company's goal is to outengineer and outdesign the competition—producing machines that will command a premium because of their durability, reliability, rich set of features, and good looks.

But the company's product developers are battling against a strong current. Cheap laptops designed and manufactured by superefficient Taiwanese companies for Dell and other major PC makers are flooding the market, and corporations increasingly choose price over any other consideration when they buy laptops in high volumes. Joe Formichelli, who ran IBM's ThinkPad business in the mid-1990s and later was an executive at PC makers Toshiba and Gateway, bemoans the plight of the PC innovator. In the last years before he retired from the computer industry, he was discouraged about the prospects for building machines that stood out from the pack. He'd make sales calls to large corporations and find that new capabilities were the last items on their priority lists. They just wanted the machines to work and to be cheap. Formichelli and Amelio worked together at IBM in the 1990s, and the two stay in touch—but some of their conversations can't be encouraging for Amelio. "I tell Bill that corporations just won't pay extra for innovation," says Formichelli.

Lenovo's executives didn't expect X300 to be a huge seller when it went on sale in late February 2008. With prices ranging from $2,500 to nearly $3,000, depending on the version, they saw it as a "halo" product. They hoped X300 would get positive press and buzz on the gadget blogs, and those good feelings would rub off on some of their more affordable ThinkPads. X300 would also be prominently featured at the Beijing Olympics, where Lenovo was a major sponsor. "Kodachi is a symbol of what Lenovo can do," said the company's chairman, Yang Yuanqing, referring to X300's code name. "We want to send the message that if there's a company in the industry that can continuously develop the most inventive and best quality products, with efficiency, it will be Lenovo."

Do design and innovation matter? Time after time throughout the history of mobile computing, product developers have proved that they do. Now the designers and engineers at Lenovo, Apple, Sony, Nokia, Microsoft, and dozens of other companies need to prove it all over again. In the early days of mobile computing, many of the major improvements were driven by advances in miniaturization. It was a brute force exercise, and the tastes and concerns of the human beings who used those machines didn't always matter that much. But increasingly, as portable computers become ever more personal, only the engineers and designers who spend the time and energy to understand human nature—and are willing to completely rethink what portable computing can be—will be able to fashion machines that delight their owners and stand out from the rest.

2

DYNABOOK AND THE LEGACY OF XEROX PARC

When Alan Kay was a teenager, he was skeptical about adults. He wasn't high on traditional public education, either. These feelings stayed with him as he matured into adulthood. (In fact, he says, he never felt like he truly grew up.) Thanks in part to his two early dissatisfactions, Kay became the first computer scientist on record to envision a portable computer. If Kay hadn't done it, somebody else doubtless would. Still, credit goes to him for launching the quest and the story of portable computing begins with him.

In the fall of 1968, Kay, a 28-year-old computer science graduate student at the University of Utah, flew to Boston to visit with Seymour Papert, a professor at the Massachusetts Institute of Technology. Papert was a disciple of educational theorist Jean Piaget, who believed that children could learn better by doing than by listening to lectures from teachers. A year earlier, Papert had designed one of the earliest computer learning programs for children called Logo. During Kay's visit, they toured a classroom where Logo was being tried out by children on large computer terminals wired to a distant mainframe computer. After the classroom tour, Kay and Papert had a long, stirring conversation about the potential for the computer as an educational tool. "This was a transformational experience for me," recalls Kay. "I thought the computer could be the next big thing since the printing press."

On the flight back to Utah, Kay sketched an illustration of a boy and a girl playing a game they had designed themselves on a small notebook-sized computer. This was the birth moment for his vision of a computer that three years later he called Dynabook. Kay's idea was that a small portable computer loaded with educational software could serve as a powerful tool for learning and self-expression: It could be an intellectual amplifier for children. At the time, most computers were massive devices that were used primarily by scientists, weapon builders, and corporate data crunchers—so it was quite a stretch of the imagination to see them as personal mobile companions for kids. Also, the notion of empowering children and freeing them from the domination of the adult world was a radical one. "I felt that adults don't do a good job of bringing up children, so children don't grow up with the richest ideas in their culture," he says. "Instead, they grow up influenced by mundane ideas, and that's hugely dangerous. I thought about bypassing adults with the Dynabook."

Kay himself had lived an unconventional childhood. His father was a college professor who changed jobs frequently. Kay spent some of his early years on a farm in Massachusetts where his grandfather had a collection of more than five thousand books. He was a loner, spending hours by himself in the family library. In his early teens, when the family lived in New York City, he was a frequent visitor to the New York Public Library in Jamaica, Queens. He also enjoyed repairing machines and tinkering with radios. He first got his hands on computers when he joined the Air Force and learned software programming. After his service, he went on to study math and molecular biology at the University of Colorado.

It was as a Ph.D. student that Kay came into his own as an inventor. In Utah, he came upon the work of Ivan Sutherland, who a few years earlier had written a computer program called Sketch-Pad, which was the first software with a graphical user interface rather than just text and numbers on a screen. He saw a demonstration at the Rand Corporation think tank in California where a

Rand scientist wrote with a stylus on an electronic tablet and saw the words appear on a computer terminal screen. Also, he had seen a movie showing computing inventions made by Douglas Engelbart and his team of researchers at SRI International, including the computer mouse, e-mail, and bit-mapped computer display screens. "Englebart is cosmic," Kay told me. With all of these experiences as inspirations, Kay and Ed Cheadle, an aerospace engineer in Salt Lake City, were working on a prototype desktop computer, which they called the FLEX Machine.

So when Kay returned from his visit with Papert he already had some of the ideas that would go into the Dynabook concept. Over the next few days he sketched out designs for a mobile computer—some flat tablets and others like steno pads, with lids that held a flat display. He recalled from his reading that Aldus Manutius, a sixteenth-century Italian printer, had created the concept of the modern book as something that would be portable enough to fit in a saddlebag on a horse. Using a book as a model, Kay taped together a cardboard mockup of what the Dynabook computer might look like, and filled it with lead shotgun pellets until he decided that he had reached the limit of what people would be willing to carry around. The optimal weight he decided on: two pounds.

Some of the earliest computer pioneers had thought of portability as an element of computing. In his prescient essay, "As We May Think," published in the July 1945 edition of the *Atlantic Monthly*, Vannevar Bush, head of the U.S. Office of Scientific Research and Development, envisioned a personal computer, called Memex, which he thought of as an "enlarged intimate supplement to his memory" where the individual would store books, photographs, documents, and communications. Bush pictured a desklike machine including screens, a keyboard, buttons, and levers that could "presumably be operated from a distance." Toward the end of his essay, he suggested that someday information and impressions might be directly transmitted from the human brain into machines. In other words, the person and the computer would be melded together— the ultimate in portable computing.

In 1968, at the same time that Kay was dreaming up the ideas that led to Dynabook, Bill Gates and his buddy, Paul Allen, later his cofounder of Microsoft, were tapping into huge mainframe computers via timesharing accounts at Seattle's Lakeside School. Gates recalls carrying home a General Electric data communications terminal and attaching it to the family telephone using an acoustic coupler so he could dial into the distant mainframe. "It was *kind of* portable computing," he says. Gates wrote a Monopoly game program at home that way. Still, what he had at his fingertips in 1968 was a far cry from a truly mobile computer.

Kay never did make a Dynabook. The digital electronics technologies just weren't advanced enough in the late 1960s and 1970s to shrink a computer down to notebook size. Instead, in his next career stop, as a researcher at Xerox's famed Palo Alto Research Center (PARC) in California, he contributed some of the thinking that went into the Alto machine, which is widely considered the world's first personal computer. Kay called it "the interim Dynabook." He teamed up with a handful of PARC scientists, including Charles Thacker and Butler Lampson, to bring together the knowledge and funding necessary to develop the Alto. The beige Alto, conceived in 1973 and produced a year later, was designed to sit on a desktop and to be operated with a mouse as well as a keyboard. While his colleagues concentrated on preparing the hardware for Alto, Kay designed a software language, called Smalltalk, for programming the computer. It included a graphic user interface—which made it possible for the user to navigate the computer using icons, menus, and overlapping windows containing various programs. Again, Kay had children and education in mind. He knew that children are naturally very visually oriented, and, by using a graphic interface, he hoped to engage them more deeply in computing than a simple text interface could achieve. Using a mouse, they would click on icons and drag them around on the interface, engaging what he called their "caveman brain" and practicing eye-hand coordination. "The big idea was that they would essentially be having a conversation with the computer, and, through the interface, we'd put what the computer was thinking on the screen," Kay says.

In the early 1970s, in the Bay Area, personal empowerment and communalism were in the air. The Free Speech Movement at the University of California at Berkeley, the anti–Vietnam War movement, free love, equal rights for women and minorities, rock music, psychedelic drugs—all of these influences mixed together and created an environment where revolutionary ideas flourished. And the Alto was one of them. What could be more antiestablishment than a computer that could give any individual the same computing capabilities as The Man? PARC was financed by a corporation, and some of the researchers were involved in the U.S. Department of Defense's ARPA program (which brought us the Internet), so it wasn't exactly a hotbed of social revolution. Still, it was very much of its time and place. "PARC wasn't so much *the* counterculture, but it was influenced by it in the most positive way," says Kay.

Though Xerox's Alto was never commercialized, it inspired many a Silicon Valley entrepreneur. Among them, most famously, was Apple cofounder Steve Jobs, who visited PARC in 1979. There, watching a demonstration of the Alto, Jobs was excited by the possibilities of the computer mouse and the Alto's graphical user interface. A few years later, Alto's interface became the inspiration for the breakthrough Lisa and Macintosh computers from Apple, and, later, to Microsoft's Windows operating system.

In 1976, a handful of PARC scientists had squeezed the Alto's electronics into a smaller package called the NoteTaker. Though only a handful of prototype machines were built, this was arguably the first portable computer. Inspired by Kay's Dynabook, the NoteTaker was developed by a team that included Douglas Fairbairn, Larry Tesler, and Adele Goldberg. The device looked like a portable sewing machine. To use it, you would lay it on its side and fold out the bottom, a keyboard, to reveal a built-in display monitor and the opening for a floppy disk drive.

Kay's Dynabook concept had many disciples. Throughout the coming years, a succession of entrepreneurs, inventors, engineers, and designers labored to make his dream of portable computing a reality. "The idea was influential. It was a great science fiction story that gave people something to aim for," says Steve Sakoman, the original engineer behind Apple's infamous Newton handheld computer.

One of the first people to set the goal of building a commercial portable computer was Blair Newman. A Harvard Business School graduate who had worked briefly for Howard Hughes in his Las Vegas underground bunkers, Newman had found his way to Silicon Valley in the 1970s and established himself as a certified Big Idea man. "He came up with an idea twice a day you might want to start a company around," recalls William M. "Trip" Hawkins, an early Apple employee and friend of Newman's who later went on to found computer game giant Electronic Arts.

After graduating from Stanford Business School in 1977, Hawkins met Newman. Hawkins was working as a freelance researcher for a tech market research outfit, Creative Strategies, for which he wrote one of the first major national market research studies on the personal computer industry. Newman was one of his sources. After the study was published in early 1978, Apple's Steve Jobs read it and, according to Hawkins, was upset that Hawkins had reported that Tandy's RadioShack chain had sold more computers at that point than Apple had. Newman gave Hawkins's phone number to Jobs. Hawkins must have impressed Jobs, because, in the summer of 1978, Jobs hired him as one of his early marketing analysts. He also brought on Newman as a consultant.

Almost immediately, Newman started plotting to start a new company. He had several ideas, including building a mobile computer that would come equipped with a package of business applications—one for number crunching that would later be called a spreadsheet. (This was a year before Dan Bricklin and Bob Frankston at Software Arts would produce VisiCalc, the first com-

mercial spreadsheet program, for the Apple II computer.) Newman recruited Hawkins into his schemes. At the time, Hawkins
and Newman shared a tiny ranch house in Palo Alto, just off the
Stanford campus. "Blair drove roommates crazy, but he moved in
with me until he drove me crazy and I kicked him out," recalls
Hawkins. "He'd be up all hours of the day and night and he'd talk
until you shut off the lights." In the apartment and at a Good
Earth restaurant near the Apple campus in nearby Cupertino, the
two stirred up a business plan. The idea was that this would be the
first personal computer designed specifically for business use. Until then, PCs were for hobbyists and students. Their computer
would be sold through retail stores—which would have been another first for a business computer. They didn't think of offering
the idea to Apple, since it was just establishing itself with desktop
PCs for consumers. (Apple had sold only 1,000 computers at that
point.) Hawkins wrote a 15-page business plan and, at Newman's
insistence, went alone to peddle it to one of the most important
venture capitalists in Silicon Valley, William H. Draper III of Sutter Hill Ventures. "He [Newman] saw me as the front man, and
the right socioeconomic model to give the business credibility,"
says Hawkins.

Hawkins had an MBA, but still he was none too sophisticated.
He was only 24 years old and had less than a year of tech-industry
work under his belt at a time when most of the people who were
approaching venture capitalists in the Valley had much stronger
résumés. For his meeting with Draper, Hawkins wore an inexpensive suit he had bought after graduation at Filene's Basement but
had been too lazy to alter—so it had a pin in the waistband to hold
his pants up properly. The Sutter Hill offices were in a high-rise
office building to the south of the Stanford campus, and stuck out
amid the sprawl of tech office parks. Even though he had a business degree, Hawkins didn't feel like he belonged in a corporate
office. He was nervous as he rode up in the elevator and was intimidated by the plush furnishings in Sutter Hill's waiting room.
Finally, he was ushered into Draper's office, which had a window

with a view of the Stanford campus. Draper was a distinguished-looking middle-aged man in a dark, tailored suit.

The way Hawkins recalls this meeting, Draper grilled him casually for a few minutes about his business plan. Then, as Hawkins remembers the scene, Draper dressed him down: "He called me a complete idiot. He told me there was no way businesses would buy a computer from a retail store." Then Draper excused himself and left the office, returning in a couple of minutes with a younger colleague, who attacked the business plan even more aggressively than Draper had. "He was like a Doberman," Hawkins says. "I had never been in a meeting before where there was so much skepticism about an idea. I felt like my cheap suit got shredded."

Many years later, Draper didn't remember this encounter, and he said he wouldn't have been so critical of a young, would-be entrepreneur. Still, he said, he would have been skeptical of a plan involving mobile computing. "Others may have anticipated the mobility of computers back then, but I was not one of them," he admitted.

After the Draper session, a dejected Hawkins sought advice from his boss at Apple, Armas "Mike" Markkula Jr., who was then running marketing. Markkula had heard through the grapevine what Hawkins and Newman were up to and he didn't like it. "He told me it was a really big mistake. I had the opportunity for a good career at Apple. I should drop this thing and get back to work," Hawkins recalls. "So I did." The outcome wasn't so good for Newman. He was fired.

Hawkins went on to eventually become Apple's director of strategy and marketing before quitting in 1982 to launch Electronic Arts (EA). He left EA in 1991 to start 3DO Corp., a futile attempt to knock off Nintendo and Sega as the top video game consoles, and later got into mobile computing for real for the first time with Digital Chocolate, a mobile games publisher.

Newman continued to have groundbreaking ideas. His MetaView Corporation designed a computer-television hybrid in the late 1980s that presaged TiVo's digital video recorders, which came a decade later. Newman ultimately fell into a downward spiral of depression. A habitué of the Well, an early online community, he in 1990 wrote a computer program that deleted every word he had ever written on the Well's pages after he got in a dispute with some other members. A few weeks later, he committed suicide. His friends said he killed himself first virtually, and then really.

While Hawkins and Newman were searching for a foothold in portable computing, other entrepreneurs were comparing notes and inventions at the Homebrew Computer Club. The club is famous for being the place where Apple cofounders Steve Jobs and Steve Wozniak first showed off the Apple I desktop prototype, but it was also a seedbed for portable computing. The club was started in the garage of electronics enthusiast Gordon French in Menlo Park, California, on March 5, 1975. It attracted a host of early computer mavens and swelled in popularity to the point where, in the late 1970s, it held meetings in the auditorium at the Stanford Linear Accelerator Center in the hills above Stanford University. Ultimately, 23 companies were formed by club members. Two of the regulars were Lee Felsenstein, codesigner of one of the first commercial personal computers, the SOL-20, and Adam Osborne, a former Shell Oil chemical engineer who had become a technical book publisher. One of the books he published, *An Introduction to Microcomputers*, inspired many of Silicon Valley's PC-industry pioneers. Felsenstein often moderated the meetings, and Osborne brought boxes of books, which he sold during breaks between sessions. These two combined forces to design and build the Osborne 1, the world's first commercial mobile computer.

Felsenstein had come of age in the 1960s as a New Left radical and a member of the Free Speech movement at the University of California at Berkeley. In fact, he was one of those arrested at the famous "Sproul Hall Sit-In" in 1964, and later wrote articles for a peppery underground newspaper, the *Berkeley Barb*. Throughout the 1970s, he designed computers and components for a handful of Bay Area companies while volunteering with community computing organizations on the side. He was familiar with Kay's Dynabook idea, but, in the earliest days at Homebrew, "Nobody was saying, 'I'm building a mobile computer.' It was hard enough to build one that was immobile," he recalls.

Felsenstein and Osborne hooked up at the West Coast Computer Faire in San Francisco's Brooks Hall in April 1980. They already knew each other. Osborne had hired Felsenstein to do some manuscript editing for him. Osborne had sold his publishing business to McGraw-Hill in 1979 but was still involved in it. At the Computer Faire, he was hawking books at a booth. Osborne called out to Felsenstein when the engineer sauntered past. He wanted to arrange a meeting to talk over computer product ideas. That was an odd request from a publisher, but Felsenstein was running out of money from his last electronics consulting project, and figured whatever Osborne had to say was worth a listen. Back at home, Felsenstein dusted off some product ideas from his files for the meeting with Osborne. But, when they met, he quickly learned that Osborne already had something specific in mind: a portable computer.

Osborne sketched out what he wanted on a piece of graph paper. Like the Xerox NoteTaker, the computer would be carried like a portable sewing machine and would be set up by turning it on its side and opening the bottom—a keyboard—to reveal a small cathode ray tube screen. The machine would run the then-popular CP/M operating system from Digital Research, in Pacific Grove, California; would have two floppy disks; and would have a five-inch screen. IBM already had a machine in the market that it called a portable computer, the IBM Model 5100, but, at 30 pounds and with a separate data storage unit, it was really a desktop machine. So Osborne's would be the first truly portable computer to be sold.

It's not clear exactly where Osborne's concept came from. People who knew him believe he was inspired by Xerox PARC's NoteTaker prototype, but Alan Kay says Osborne was "too narcissistic" to give credit to anybody else. Osborne died in 2003, and in his 1984 book, *Hypergrowth: The Rise and Fall of Osborne Computer*

Corporation, he didn't spell out why he decided to produce a portable. He wrote that he chose the C/PM operating system because he thought it had the best chance of becoming an industry-wide standard. He wanted the computer to be inexpensive so the market would be large. And he wanted the machine to be small. He wrote: "I decided to build the smallest possible package, given the components then available; and thus was born the idea of the 'portable computer.'" Felsenstein loved Osborne's idea. "Adam said there was a hole the size of a truck in the market and he had decided to fill it," recalls Felsenstein. "I said, 'Why the hell not?'" They soon signed a contract. Felsenstein would get $3,500 and 25 percent of the company.

Osborne Computer, the company they formed, introduced the Osborne 1 less than a year later, at the next West Coast Computer Faire. But they packed a lot into those few months. Felsenstein, who was still a freelancer, worked in a shared barnlike space on Berkeley's Parker Street, an industrial area of the city. He had a drafting board set up in a corner, where, from his window, he could see the Palmolive soap plant billowing smoke in the distance. He designed the first commercial portable computer with paper and pencil, and used a slide rule to do his calculations.

His main challenge was fitting everything into a relatively small space. Osborne had told him to size the computer so it could fit under the seat of a commercial airliner. Felsenstein had earlier designed the first PC modem. But that device was too big for a portable computer. So he saw he had to start from scratch and design a smaller one. To save space on the main circuit board of the computer, he decided to combine the memory for the display on the main memory chip. For the brains of the computer, he chose the Z80 microprocessor from Zilog over Intel's 8085 processor because it was already running a handful of machines equipped with the CP/M operating system, which was the leading PC operating system of the day.

As a youngster growing up in Philadelphia, Felsenstein had learned electronics by tinkering. He enjoyed playing around with

radios, and it was his lucky day when a friend of his father's be-
queathed him a half-completed but paid-up correspondence
course in radio and TV repair. His father, a commercial artist, had
another friend who had a collection of radio and TV chassis that
he handed over to Felsenstein, who scavenged them for parts to
use on future repair projects. By the time Lee Felsenstein enrolled
at Berkeley, he had a head start on many of his contemporaries. It
was through a cooperative work study program that he got the full
immersion in electronics—at the NASA Flight Research Center.
He dropped out of school temporarily in 1967, after participating
in a series of antiwar demonstrations, and kicked around the Valley working for electronics firms before returning to school to finish his degree in 1972. His passion was volunteering to help out in
Bay Area community computing projects. He laid out a blueprint
for a computer, which he called the Tom Swift Terminal and he
designed from the ground up, to be added onto by others in the
community. His thinking had been influenced by Ivan Illich's 1973
book, *Tools for Conviviality*, which advocated designing technology products so people could learn about them by tinkering and
modifying them. Ultimately, Felsenstein launched his career as a
freelance engineer.

When it came time to design the Osborne 1, Felsenstein's ability to tinker and invent on the fly made it possible for him to create a machine like none he had ever seen before. "The Osborne 1
was a step into the void, a leap of faith," he says. These days, many
computers are designed and built to order for the top PC brands
by electronics manufacturing firms in Asia. Felsenstein believes
that's antithetical to innovation. "All you get is small variations on
what everybody else is making," he says. "If you want a design to
have any originality, you have no business turning the design over
to a manufacturer."

While Felsenstein was busy with engineering, Osborne, a pro-
moter at heart, was the company's cheerleader and evangelist. He
had a British father and a Polish mother and had spent much of his
childhood in India before going to college in the United King-

dom. Though he had been in the United States since 1961, he had retained his British accent. "Adam was like a character out of a Gilbert and Sullivan musical," recalls Felsenstein. "He was ramrod straight and absolutely confident in himself. He played well on Americans' tendency to be subservient to people with British accents."

Gradually, Osborne hired a small crew of engineers and manufacturing people, and contracted with a Silicon Valley company, Sorcim, to write the software. He gave Felsenstein a deadline of the end of January 1981 to have the electronics design ready. The engineer brought it in a couple of weeks late, but missing the deadline was no big deal. The industrial design was done by Housh Ghorbani, a recent émigré from Iran, who worked on it in his Fremont, California, living room. "It was done on a pell-mell schedule, so we didn't have a chance to step back and ask, 'Are we doing this right?'" says Felsenstein.

It didn't seem to matter at first. When Osborne showed off the first prototypes at the West Coast Computer Faire in San Francisco in April 1981, his booth was mobbed. This was four months before IBM would announce its first PC. In Brooks Hall, people took turns opening and closing the machines and hefting them. The Osborne 1 was far from perfect. These first models had metal cases and weighed almost 30 pounds. Felsenstein recalls that when he carried one of the machines just four city blocks to the hall, he felt as if his arm was going to come out of its socket. Also, the screens, tiny to begin with, had a wobble caused by magnetic interference from the power transformer. Still, the crowd loved them. Afterward, when Osborne and Felsenstein were walking out of the building, Osborne clapped his partner on the back and babbled excitedly. "He told me, 'The product is the company. We'll build it up and sell it off and do a whole string of these!'" Felsenstein says.

Some of the defects were fixed by the time the first Osborne 1 computers shipped out of manufacturing two months later. These machines had plastic covers, so they came in at 23 pounds. Still, that was too heavy for easy carrying, and they were called "lug-gables," rather than portable computers, by the technology press. The Osborne display was still only five inches across, and the data storage consisted of two single-sided floppy disks, which didn't have enough capacity to be of much use to a businessperson. The price was $1,795, which was reasonable for the time. Sales were remarkable initially, with more than ten thousand selling per month at the peak. But the phenomenon was short-lived. Poor manufacturing practices led to inventory shortages and quality problems. And, within a year, Kaypro released its Kaypro II, which had a nine-inch display and twice as much data storage. To Osborne employees, the Kaypro seemed like a junky computer—partly because its metal case tended to get dented. So they didn't take it seriously. Before long, though, Kaypro sales overtook Osborne's.

Adam Osborne compounded his problems in 1983 by prean-nouncing a successor to the Osborne 1, called the Osborne Executive, many months before it was ready to be shipped. That announcement slowed sales of the Osborne 1 to a trickle. His blun-der was so monumental that it gave rise to a term that's still used by some people in the computer industry to warn against prean-nouncing products: the Osborne effect. The company grew to 1,200 people at its peak, but it was so disorganized, Felsenstein says, that, "half of the people were correcting the mistakes of the other half." Osborne stepped down as CEO in 1982 and brought in a soft drink executive to fill the role. But the company spiraled down-ward and filed for protection from bankruptcy in September 1983. A news photographer snapped a picture of Osborne rushing out of the company's offices holding a briefcase in front of his face. Felsenstein resigned at a meeting of the last remaining 30 employ-ees in the company's cavernous offices in Hayward, California.

That was the peak of fame for both men. Osborne later started a company called Paperback Software that sold applications such as a database program and a spreadsheet for as little as $99. The spreadsheet got him in trouble with Lotus, whose Lotus 1-2-3 program it imitated. In 1987, Lotus sued Paperback Software for copyright infringement, and, in 1990, a federal judge ruled in favor of Lotus. The important ruling established the legal principle that software companies could protect the "look and feel" of their programs. So Osborne had created three companies—in books, computers, and software—that helped shape the PC industry, but he died in obscurity in India in 2003 at age 64. Felsenstein went on to design computer hardware, including one of the first "wearable" computers, and to work for Interval Research, the electronics research outfit set up by Microsoft cofounder Paul Allen. Still later, he cofounded The Fonly Institute, a consulting organization dedicated to developing low-cost, locally operated computing systems in developing nations. He had never abandoned his belief in the value of community computing.

Felsenstein learned valuable lessons at Osborne: "The major one is that appearances are not reality. People could be domestic animals, and follow somebody who appeared to know what he was talking about. And I learned that if you grow a company around a product, the company still doesn't know how to put a product into production, and you have a big problem."

With Osborne a bust, the next significant advance in portable computing came from one of Kay's colleagues at Xerox. There was a lot of frustration going around at Xerox PARC in the late 1970s. The lab's scientists there produced one wonderful technology advance after another, including the laser printer, the graphical user interface, the Alto desktop computer, the NoteTaker portable, PC networking, and object-oriented software programming. Yet Xerox brought almost none of it to market. That was particularly galling for John Ellenby, a British economist and computer scientist who had came to PARC in 1974 with the mission of moving the Alto into volume manufacturing so the machines could be tested in real-world situations. It was Ellenby who produced the first truly portable computer.

Ellenby had high hopes when he arrived at PARC from Edinburgh University and Ferranti in the United Kingdom, which was an early maker of mainframe computers. He loved the Alto, but felt it needed to be made more manufacturable, more easily serviceable, and smaller. The first machines actually sat under your desk, so they weren't properly desktop computers. He nicknamed his personal Alto "Gzunda," a play on words, since the computer "goes under" the desk, and is like a gzunda, which was slang for a chamber pot in England.

He was still optimistic about Xerox's prospects in computing in 1977. That was the year he got the assignment of demonstrating the full suite of PARC products-in-waiting, collectively called the Office of the Future, at a Xerox executive retreat at a country club in Boca Raton, Florida. His partner on this project was Tim Mott. The event was called Futures Day, and it was attended by all of the top Xerox executives. The ballroom in the country club was darkened as the executives and their wives mingled while huge audio speakers blasted the theme to *Star Wars*. Ellenby and Mott showed off the Alto II, an upgrade of the Alto, and a color laser printer code-named Pimlico. Afterward, the executives and their wives were allowed to step up to the front and try out the new machines. The women loved them, Ellenby recalls. Many of them were former executive assistants. But the men seemed less interested. "It was a huge problem for Xerox in those days," Ellenby recalls. "Their machines were recommended and used by women, but all of their executives were men."

Still, based largely on the recommendations of the women, a number of Alto IIs made their way into Xerox executives' offices and even into some offices of Xerox customers. Ellenby believed that the only way to produce excellent computers and software was to put early models into the hands of users. A vital part of his job, he thought, was calling on people who were using the prototype machines and getting their feedback. His breakthrough as an inventor came during just such a visit in 1979. The customer, whom Ellenby will only identify as a person who worked in the Executive Office Building, next to the White House, had tried the Alto II, but said he rarely used it because he was usually on the road. What he'd really prefer, he said, was a portable computer small enough to fit in one half of a standard briefcase. That meant the computer would need to have a flat panel display rather than a bulky cathode ray tube, which was in all computers up until that time.

This was a life-shaping moment for Ellenby, and he savors his memory of it. The two men were having lunch in the White House dining room, an elegant place manned by chefs wearing toques. "What he really said," Ellenby recalls, "is, 'I want a real fucking computer in half your case,'" indicating the briefcase that Ellenby had brought with him to the meeting. From then on, Ellenby referred to the portable computer he hoped to build one day as the RFC, but, when people asked him what RFC stood for, he said "real functioning computer."

Ellenby wasn't long for PARC. He had proposed a new version of the Alto, called Alto III, that would be an all-in-one computer like the Apple II, which came out at that time. But the Xerox bosses shot the proposal down. The company was under assault from a handful of aggressive Japanese copier makers, and it was cutting back on lab spending that wasn't focused on its imaging business. All that computer technology that PARC had been inventing would continue to sit on the shelf. So Ellenby decided it was time to move on.

He and Tim Mott planned on leaving together to create a company and build a portable computer. It would be a thin machine with a multitasking operating system, meaning it could run more than one application at once. It would also come with a set of applications, including word processing, spreadsheet, and e-mail. Unfortunately, Mott never got to join the company. Xerox brass made it clear that they'd sue if Mott departed with Ellenby. But, in a short time, a handful of PARC and ex-PARC colleagues joined him, including Glenn Edens, who would run development, and David Paulsen, who would manage hardware engineering. Carol Hankins joined from Xerox to run software development. Ellenby's wife, Gillian, a sculptor, had picked a name: GRiD Systems. The couple had a three-room bungalow in back of their house on Harker Avenue in Palo Alto—a mushroom-colored place that was shaded by an enormous oak tree. This is where GRiD would get its start in December 1979.

Despite the modesty of the facilities, Ellenby lined up some very impressive angel investors. A friend and mentor, Gene Amdahl, founder of the mainframe maker Amdahl Corporation, helped Ellenby land Robert Noyce, a founder of Intel, and Silicon Valley superlawyer Larry Sonsini. Ellenby remembered Sonsini showing up at an early company party in the backyard with a six-pack of beer and two pizzas, which he carried in the trunk of his Porsche.

It was clear to Ellenby from the start that industrial design would play an important role in the machine, which was ultimately called the GRiD Compass. For that, he tapped Bill Moggridge, a British designer who had just moved his family to Palo Alto and was setting up a branch office of his design firm in the Bay Area. The two had met a few months earlier at a party in London. Moggridge, who later went on to cofound a leading Silicon Valley design firm, IDEO, recalls their first encounter. "The thing I loved immediately about him was he was intensely curious. He was just bubbling away," recalls Moggridge. "Most clients I talked to were only interested in their own thing. John was curious about all the different devices and the design process." Ellenby wanted to hire Moggridge as his vice president of design, but since Moggridge didn't want to leave his firm, he brought him on as a consultant. Moggridge recalled that when he and his family arrived in the Bay Area from England, Gillian Ellenby was there to meet them at the airport in a huge Dodge van.

Moggridge and Ellenby got down to the serious business of figuring out what GRiD's portable computer would look like. Ellenby wanted a model he could take around with him to show venture capitalists and potential customers. His concept idea was that this computer would be used by executives. At the time, personal computers hadn't yet become an office tool. Plus, most executives didn't type. They relied on their secretaries to do their typing for them. But Ellenby thought that if they made the GRiD machine compelling enough, they could actually change behavior—convincing corporate bosses to begin using personal computers.

This was a new challenge for Moggridge. He had designed computers before, but mostly they were as big as a table. "As a designer, the place you start a project [is] by looking at the current state of the art," Moggridge says. "But, in this case, we were trying something completely new, so the reference point couldn't be early examples. Instead, it's what people will do with the device and what components are available. You have the freedom to create something that's precedent setting." The initial design dimensions were 8½ by 11 and three inches thick. Moggridge decided to use a clamshell design, so people would tilt up a lid containing a flat-panel display to reveal a keyboard. He had never seen a computer with a clamshell design before, because there had never been one before. Richard Grant, the leader of the model shop in his London office, made a detailed model in a week. The display was painted to simulate what it would look like. It was black on the outside; with a green, white, and blue keyboard; a little touch screen next to the display; and calculator buttons built in.

The next step was figuring out how to fit all of the components of a computer into such a small space. Today, modems are about the size of a matchbox, but, back in 1980, they were closer to a shoebox size. Ellenby and his colleagues approached a modem company, Racal-Vadic, and said he wanted something along the lines of a cigarette pack. Their first reaction: it couldn't be done. But, it turned out that some of Racal-Vadic's engineers had been thinking of ways to reduce the dimensions of their products. They worked with Ellenby's engineers to shrink their modem drastically. Similar improvements were made with other components.

During the early days of GRiD, Ellenby underwent a personality transformation. Normally a gregarious partier, he toned down a lot and he slept very little. "He went into a monklike state," recalls Moggridge.

While those difficult engineering tasks were underway, Moggridge ran some experiments to see how heavy the machine could be and how much impact it should be capable of absorbing. He made up a set of blocks and asked colleagues to carry them around in their briefcases, steadily adding more until they reached the limit of what they could comfortably carry. The limit was eight pounds, and that became the weight target for the Compass. To set durability standards, Moggridge rented an impact recorder and sent it to himself via Federal Express. He found that when the recorder was dropped, the maximum gravitational force (g-force) that was recorded was 60 g's. He would design the Compass so it would withstand that level of impact. Moggridge and the GRiD team decided to use magnesium for the machine's enclosure because it was light and strong and could disperse heat from the electronic components inside. Nobody had ever diecast large flat sections of magnesium before, but GRiD's vice president of manufacturing, Paul Hammel, figured out how to do it. Since then, many laptops and cell phones have included magnesium parts.

A year passed before Moggridge could complete the industrial design. He had to wait for the basic engineering of the electronics to be finished. Ellenby's engineers had done such a good job of shrinking components that the machine could come in at just two inches thick—though it was broader than the original model. Moggridge added little legs that folded down in the back to tilt the computer at a comfortable ergonomic angle when it was being typed on. And he gave it a full-size keyboard. The display was a glowing orange color. "When it was closed, it looked powerful—almost monolithic. When you opened it, it was friendly and inviting and personal," says Moggridge.

Tensions arose between Moggridge and the engineers. Moggridge wanted to create a perfect visual and tactile design, while the engineers were most concerned about their ability to cool the machine and manufacture it rather than the way it looked. For instance, there were latches that held the display in place when the lid was open. Moggridge wanted people to be able to find and use them easily, so he designed release buttons with a complex grip texture made up of lots of miniature pyramids. The engineers thought they were too complex and would be too expensive to engineer and tool. They called them "paranoids," rather than pyramids, because they felt Moggridge was overly concerned about making the latches easily releasable.

Moggridge and Ellenby had differences of opinion as well. Ellenby wanted to make the machines look and feel a bit like a piece of military equipment. (In fact, ultimately, many of them were bought by the military, and several were used on NASA's space shuttles.) Potential customers had told him they wanted serious-looking machines. Investment bankers wanted portables they could take into a deal negotiation meeting that would impress the people on the other side of the table. And they needed devices that were tough enough to be slung into the overhead compartments on airliners. Moggridge favored a more friendly appearance. Not surprisingly, since Ellenby was the boss, he got his way, mostly. "I'm still not comfortable with mobile products that look too jovial," Ellenby explains. "I don't think we want to have computers looking like Hello Kitty"—the cheerful Japanese fictional character that's printed on children's clothing.

One of the most compelling features of the Compass for many people was the orange glowing display screen. Since computers didn't have flat-panel displays at the time, GRiD had to find a company that could supply them. They settled on Sharp, the Japanese electronics company, which was a pioneer in display technology, and convinced Sharp's executives that there would be a large market for such displays. Sharp invested in tooling up a factory production line. It was a risky bet, but it gave Sharp a quick start in the laptop display business, where it has been a dominant player ever since. Everything was brand new then. The basic infrastructure of the PC industry had not been built yet. GRiD was the first American company to visit Sharp and most of the other Japanese electronics companies of the day. So it pioneered what was to become an essential element of the PC industry: U.S. computer companies would build their machines from Japanese components. At the time, few Japanese spoke English and vice versa, so the meetings were long and awkward.

This was an exciting time for the Japanese, as well. A year after their contract was signed, the general manager of Sharp's engineering center asked to be allowed to visit the building where GRiD got its start. It was night and had been raining when Ellenby showed the executive the tiny cottage behind his home in Palo Alto. Raindrops were still dripping from the giant spreading oak tree as they walked through the yard. The Sharp executive didn't speak much English, and he said little at the time, but, later, one of his lieutenants passed along a message to Ellenby from his boss. "He told his staff to tell me, 'I visited your idea and the rain dropped on my head even though it had stopped raining,'" Ellenby recalls. "This was his haiku. The raindrop reminded him of the freshness of our idea. He now had more faith in his decision to build the product line."

Though the display and some of the other features of the Compass worked as anticipated, the design had one major flaw: the preproduction machine was way too hot. Ellenby had set a deadline for shipping the computer in early 1982 and didn't want to delay it by six months so they could complete design of a custom-made chip that would create less heat. Edens disagreed with him. He thought the machines might be hot enough to actually burn the fingers of people who touched them. But Ellenby overruled him, relying on the magnesium case to keep the heat at a manageable level. GRiD shipped a few of the machines on schedule. Years later, Ellenby talked to some U.S. soldiers who told him the early machines were so hot that once, when they were deployed in the desert, they tried to fry eggs on one.

The Compass was launched on April 5, 1982, one year after the Osborne 1 had hit the market. It had all sorts of innovative features, including e-mail, an operating system that allowed the computer to run more than one program at once, and the ability to connect via telephone lines to a server computer called GRiD

Central where documents and data could be stored. In this way, it anticipated the computer networks that became ubiquitous in the 1990s. (In an April 5, 1982 story in *BusinessWeek*, Apple's Steve Jobs criticized the GRiD Compass for being connected to a network: "I don't want to be a link in a chain, but something very independent." This was one case where the maestro just didn't get it. He didn't understand how important networking would eventually be for personal computing.) On the negative side, the early display measured only six inches diagonally and it cost a whopping $8,100. In spite of those factors, there was a lot of excitement when the Compass became available. It was much smaller and lighter than the luggables that were being produced at the time.

Shortly after the Compass was released, Ellenby sat on a panel at a tech industry conference in Monterey, California, with Adam Osborne. Ellenby recalls that Osborne proudly hefted his Osborne 1 onto the table in front of him and nearly vanished behind it. Ellenby already had his Compass sitting on the table. With the lid down, it was hidden from the audience by his name plaque. He lifted the plaque to show them how slim his machine was. "They were stunned. They all rushed up to look at it," Ellenby recalls. "I can remember Adam's face. He was shocked."

For Ellenby and his crew, it was a time to celebrate. They had designed a remarkable machine. On Fridays the company would sponsor official beer bashes, and, often, they'd decamp to a tavern in Mountain View, the St. James Infirmary, where a 25-foot-tall, well-endowed wooden statue of Wonder Woman stood behind and above the bar. After innumerable beers, recalls Ted Clark, later an executive at Hewlett-Packard, who worked at GRiD at the time, GRiD-ites would try to climb up Wonder Woman and put GRiD bumper stickers on some of her more pronounced body parts.

Impressive as the Compass was, though, sales were disappointing. The price doubtlessly had a negative impact, but its biggest problem was IBM. Big Blue had introduced its personal computer in August 1981. Since IBM was the dominant maker of computers at the time, its PC had instant credibility with businesspeople. Many corporations had standardized on its technology, and they wanted PCs that ran the same operating system from Microsoft that powered the IBM PC. The Compass had its own operating system. It was vastly superior to Microsoft's DOS, in part because of its networking ability. But, it didn't matter. GRiD's software wasn't the industry standard.

Ellenby had had an inkling that something big was coming from IBM long before it arrived. Robert Noyce, one of GRiD's angel investors, was running Intel's research and development (R&D) at the time. IBM had chosen Intel's 8088 microprocessor as the brains of its PC. Noyce wasn't allowed to disclose proprietary information about the IBM machine, but still he guided Ellenby away from using Motorola's then-popular 68000 processor, suggesting Intel processors instead. GRiD chose the Intel 8086 chip. Since the Compass had a chip in the same family as IBM's, it was easier to create a version of DOS for use in its machine. Microsoft's Bill Gates agreed to prepare a special version of DOS for GRiD. Still, it wasn't until 1985 that GRiD came out with a fully PC-compatible version of its machine that ran off-the-shelf versions of DOS.

It wasn't enough to make the company a success. The market for an $8,000 notebook computer was fairly small. Compaq had introduced its luggable in November 1982, which was a functional clone of the IBM PC, and GRiD couldn't compete with its price of $2,995. Ellenby tried to make a deal with Toshiba that would have handed off manufacturing to the Japanese company and reduced costs significantly, but his board wouldn't go along with it. At the time, almost all computer companies did their own manufacturing. GRiD was gradually running out of money. It was acquired by Tandy, then the world's largest PC company, in 1988. Tandy's computer business was later bought by PC maker AST, which was still later bought by Korea's Samsung.

Years later, looking back, Ellenby is proud of what GRiD had accomplished. The company produced the first true laptop computer, and other companies paid royalties for using GRiD's patented folding design for years. It created a network computer a decade and a half before that idea caught fire in the post–Internet world. The Compass was the first computer to come with an integrated package of software applications, including word processing and spreadsheet. And Ellenby conceived of the idea of renting software to computer users, a concept that became mainstream 25 years later.

After he left GRiD, Ellenby continued to innovate. One night in 1991, when he and his son, Thomas, were sailing off the coast of Mexico, they made a discovery that led ultimately, years later, to the commercial launch of another invention. Thomas was coming off watch and told his father that there was a ship off in the distance he should keep an eye on. Up on deck, Ellenby found that he couldn't pick out the lights of the ship in the darkness. Thomas mused that it would be handy if somebody built a pair of binoculars with a global positioning system in them. You could place an electronic marker on an object you saw through the binoculars, and then anybody else who used the binoculars would be directed to the same object. Later, Ellenby's other son, Peter, got involved. Ultimately, after much thinking and experimenting, the three came up with a set of technologies and a service that essentially turned the physical world into an interface to information about it. (Think of the world as a giant computer screen, and the cell phone as a computer mouse.) If the technology is embedded in a mobile device, and the user points the device at a building that has been preprogrammed into a database, he or she will see information about the building on the screen. Microsoft's Bill Gates had long talked about his vision of information at your fingertips via mobile computing. Thanks to the Ellenbys, that vision was realized, quite literally, when their company, GeoVector, launched their mobile pointing–based information service in Japan in 2007.

Moggridge's journey alongside Ellenby launched him into a whole new way of thinking about computer design. He recalls that when he got his hands on an early working model of the Compass, he was proud of what he had done. Later, though, he took it home and played around with it, he realized that much of the experience of using a personal computer related to the software rather than the hardware design. He'd had nothing to do with that. Sitting in his house in Palo Alto, he had a revelation. "I was sucked down into the world of software," he recalls. "I realized that if I was going to be serious about designing for people, I'd have to master software interactions, too." Later, after Moggridge cofounded IDEO with the noted designer David Kelley, they made software an important part of their practice. In 2007, Moggridge published a book, *Designing Interactions*, which traces the development of user interface software design to a position of prominence in computers, mobile phones, and Web sites. So, Moggridge had learned what Kay seemed to understand from the beginning: that software would become just as important as the hardware as portable computers evolved and improved. That insight would shape many of the innovations to come.

3

COMPAQ VERSUS APPLE

Power and influence can be fleeting in the computer industry. These days, Hewlett-Packard and Dell are vying for supremacy in the PC realm. Yet, just a few years ago, throughout much of the 1980s and 1990s, in fact, it was Compaq that drove the industry agenda. (A struggling Compaq merged with HP in 2002.) From Compaq's beginnings, it was a leader in bringing new advances in portable computing to the mainstream. Then, in the early 1990s, its leadership was finally challenged by Apple. This chapter tells the story of the rise of two portable computing giants.

The idea that became the foundation for Compaq came to Rod Canion on January 9, 1982. An engineering manager for electronics industry giant Texas Instruments (TI), he was sitting at the breakfast room table in his suburban Houston home late in the morning on that day. The Osborne 1 was already out, and the IBM PC had hit the market six months before. Canion and two TI colleagues, Bill Murto and Jim Harris, had been casting around for an idea with which to create a company—without much luck. Suddenly it came to Canion: What about making a portable computer, like the Osborne 1—but one that was compatible with the IBM PC? That way they could ride on the coattails of mighty IBM, which then was by far the most powerful force in computing.

At the time, there were other computers that, like the IBM machine, used versions of Microsoft's DOS operating system. But the software wasn't identical with what IBM had on its PCs, and the chips on their circuit boards weren't the same, either. As a result, word processing and spreadsheet software programs made by independent software companies had to be rewritten somewhat to work on each computer company's machines. That limitation was inefficient and expensive. Canion decided that he and his partners should build a durable IBM-compatible portable computer aimed at businesses. It was a very big idea that would not only launch their company but also would help create an entire industry.

Canion had grown up in a blue collar suburb of Houston. His father was a salesman at Sears and his mother was a schoolteacher. Like many of the other pioneers of the PC industry, he was always interested in tinkering with mechanical things. When he was in junior high school he bought a tape recorder just to take it apart and see how it worked. Later he fixed up cars and raced them, competing with other youngsters on the newly finished concrete roads in not-yet-finished suburban housing developments. His pride and joy was a 1955 Ford V8 coupe with an overhead cam engine. "In those days, it was Ford versus Chevy, and I was a Ford guy," he recalls. As he grew older, Canion became obsessed with the NASA space program. At first, he wanted to be an astronaut, but his eyesight wasn't good enough, so he set his sights on designing space exploration vehicles. While studying electrical engineering at the University of Houston, he interned two summers at NASA. But that experience turned him off. "I realized that it was government work, not fast-moving exciting work," Canion says. So, instead, he pursued a career in product design at nearby Texas Instruments.

TI was primarily a chip maker, but it was getting into the computer business when Canion joined. Before long, he led the team that designed a data terminal for auto dealerships that connected to centralized computers remotely via the telephone lines. During that project, he befriended two guys who worked for him, Murto and Harris. The three were excited by the tumult in the budding PC industry and frustrated with their managers. So they decided to try to bust out on their own. One Saturday in August 1981 they met around a table at Murto's house and brainstormed about the company they would start. At first they didn't even focus in on a particular product or technology. Instead, they talked about values. "Our goal wasn't to get rich," Canion says. "It was to create a company that was a good place to work and was doing interesting products. We'd focus on quality products and services. We never thought about leading the industry. We just wanted to be part of it."

Once they agreed on their principles, they set out to find a product to make. The first idea they came up with was a disk storage device for the IBM PC. This would be a gadget that businesspeople would buy to plug into their IBM machine to add additional storage capacity. The partners read extensively about doings in the industry and checked out a book from the library about how to write a business plan. They understood that the best way to get a technology company off the ground quickly was to get money from a venture capital firm. The American venture capital industry was still in its infancy at the time, and most of the firms were located in Silicon Valley, but Canion and his partners had heard of a newly formed venture firm in nearby Dallas, called Sevin Rosen Funds. So that's who they targeted with their sales pitch.

If Alan Kay and other scientists at Xerox PARC were the fathers of mobile computing, Ben Rosen was arguably the father-in-law. A longtime securities analyst, last at Morgan Stanley, he was fascinated with gadgets and fell in love with the Apple II when it came out in 1977. When he visited Morgan Stanley clients, he would have an assistant lug along an Apple II and a TV monitor so he could demonstrate the potential of computers. In a sense, he turned the Apple II into the first portable computer. "He was the first person on Wall Street who took PCs seriously," says Mitchell Kapor, founder of Lotus Development, the early spreadsheet software company. Rosen, a gregarious native of New Orleans, published a series of tech newsletters and, in 1978, began putting on technology conferences aimed at educating Wall Street investors about technology. The conferences eventually became gathering points for the entrepreneurs and technologists in the fledgling PC industry. After long days of speeches and presentations, Rosen would entertain his guests with games of Charades and by doing odd tricks, including balancing a chair on his chin.

Eventually, in 1981, he and Texas semiconductor pioneer L. J. Sevin established a venture capital firm and began backing microcomputer companies. One of their early investments was Osborne. Quickly, they would add Electronic Arts, Lotus, and Compaq to the portfolio. "Ben was great at sniffing out things that were going to happen—rather than already happened," says Sevin. Rosen remembers the first time he met the Compaq founders. They came to Dallas for a meeting in late 1981. "We liked the guys but not the product. There weren't enough barriers to prevent other companies from coming into the same business," recalls Rosen. "We told them, 'We really like you guys. Come back when you have a better idea.'"

After their disk drive was rejected, the partners went back to the drawing boards. They were still working for TI at the time but decided to quit. That was a risky move. But they felt they had to commit totally if they were to turn their dream of starting a business into a reality. Within a few days, they had written up a business plan and called up Sevin and Rosen. The arrangement was for the venture capitalists to travel to Houston for a meeting on January 22, 1982. Canion and his companions knew they'd need a drawing to show, so they called a retired industrial engineer from TI, Ted Papajohn, and arranged to meet him at a Computerland store west of downtown Houston. Papajohn had never designed a computer before, and he wanted to get a sense of the state of the art before he sketched one out. In the store, Canion pointed out the Osborne 1, but said, "It [had] better not look like this." He asked Papajohn to make a keyboard layout identical to IBM's. Then Canion, Harris, and Papajohn walked across the street to the House of Pies restaurant. Sitting together in a booth, Canion and Harris described how they wanted the machine to look, and Papajohn borrowed a pencil from the waitress and turned his placemat over and sketched out a crude drawing. It had smooth edges rather than boxy ones, like the Osborne 1. The screen would be larger than Osborne's, too. And there were doors on the sides that opened to give users access to the guts of the machine.

They were ready to pitch their ideas to the venture capitalists. That crucial meeting took place in a room at the Holiday Inn near Houston's Intercontinental Airport. There weren't enough chairs, so a couple of the men sat on the bed. They showed the rough sketch on the placemat at the beginning of a meeting that went on for two hours. "I loved the idea," Rosen recalls. "Sevin was excited too, but he said I looked at the world through 'Rosen-colored glasses.' He was the skeptic." To Canion, both men seemed a little standoffish. Canion asked them what was bothering them. "Are you doubting that we have the experience to do this?" he asked. That was part of it, Sevin and Rosen admitted. So the three former TIers took turns describing their work experience. Still, Sevin and Rosen weren't ready to commit. They had only been venture capitalists for six months and didn't have full confidence in themselves yet. They had not yet been a lead investor in a start-up. They asked Canion to pitch the idea to John Doerr, a young but experienced venture capitalist at the Bay Area firm of Kleiner, Perkins, Caufield & Byers (KPCB).

Canion was in a hurry, so he arranged that meeting for February 1, just a few days later. He and Harris flew to San Francisco and met with Doerr and some of his colleagues for half a day in their offices on San Francisco's Embarcadero. Doerr warned them that a lot of other companies were starting up and targeting portable PCs. It wouldn't be easy to succeed in such a crowded market. Still, a few days later, Rosen and Sevin called and said they'd invest, and KPCB would, too. Tom Perkins, one of the cofounders of the firm, said years later that investing in Compaq was practically a no-brainer. "We believed. We thought the luggable would be a big thing," he said.

A few days later, Sevin and Rosen led the first-round investment in Lotus. Compaq and Lotus were two of the most successful PC start-ups launched in the 1980s. Their fates would be intertwined, too. Brought together by Rosen, Compaq and Lotus packaged their products together and pitched them to Sears, which became an important early distributor of Compaq's portables.

Originally, Compaq was called Gateway Technology, but the name didn't stick. The founders paid $10,000 to a business naming company, San Francisco's NameLab, which came up with a list of possibilities, including MindSet and Compaq. Rosen liked Compaq because it suggested compactness. Officially, it stood for "*Comp*atibility *a*nd *Q*uality."

New competitors emerged just as Compaq was getting started, but they didn't scare Canion, and he urged his backers not to be put off either. Kaypro launched its portable, but, like the Osborne 1, it ran the CP/M operating system rather than MS-DOS, so it wasn't compatible with IBM machines, meaning that software programs written to run on an IBM PC couldn't run on a Kaypro or Osborne machine. A computer from Hyperion was slimmer than the one the Compaq engineers were working on, but it used 3½-inch floppy disks rather than the 5¼-inch size IBM had adopted. "It was a beautiful machine, but we saw that compatibility with IBM would be foundation of our success. We were fanatical about that," says Canion.

Two things had to be done to make the Compaq portable fully compatible with the IBM machine. One involved chips. A so-called BIOS chip sits on the main circuit board of every PC. It's the intermediary between the hardware and the operating system. Compaq needed to have a BIOS chip that would be the functional equivalent of IBM's, but couldn't copy the chip outright. So Canion set up an engineering team to design a clone of IBM's chip. At the same time, he set out to address a software issue. IBM had licensed MS-DOS from Microsoft for use in its personal computer, and renamed it PC-DOS. And while the guts of MS-DOS and PC-DOS were the same, there were some differences. The result was that software applications written for IBM's PC-DOS wouldn't run on other company's machines. They had to be tweaked a bit to create compatibility. Canion saw that to build a large industry, all of the applications would have to run on all the machines without modifications. He and his engineers talked to Microsoft people about this problem, but didn't make much headway, so Canion decided to talk to Gates directly.

Rosen arranged a face-to-face meeting during the West Coast Computer Faire in San Francisco in the spring of 1982. Microsoft had rented a Victorian house in the city for meetings and parties. Canion waited his turn in the living room and then was ushered into a back room. He had never met Gates before, and was surprised that Microsoft's chieftain was just a kid, still, with scraggly longish hair. "I had heard he was some kind of genius," Canion says. He made his pitch: Microsoft should make a single version of MS-DOS that was compatible with IBM's version, and distribute it to any PC maker that wanted to license it. Gates said he was concerned that if Microsoft did this, IBM would be upset. But Canion argued that Microsoft would sell a lot more software and be less dependent on IBM if they made the two compatible. "Bill agreed to look into it. I could see he liked the idea," Canion says. Gates recalls the encounter slightly differently. He says he had always understood that compatibility between the different flavors of DOS was a good idea. During the meeting, he says, he was trying to get Compaq to do much of the work to make them compatible, and Canion was trying to get Microsoft to do much of the work.

After a few fits and starts, Microsoft and Compaq worked together to craft the new version of DOS. Eventually, their collaboration spawned the growth of the PC clone industry, and, ultimately, wrestled control of the industry from IBM. When IBM realized that compatibility among all the clone PCs meant it no longer dominated the PC business, it tried to switch to new proprietary technologies that would leave the rest of the industry out in the cold. But by then it was too late. Computer retailers and customers had accepted the axis of Microsoft, Compaq, and Intel as the industry's rule-makers. IBM was forced to stick with their standards—or it would be the one left out.

Compaq launched its portable in the plush library of New York's Helmsley Palace Hotel on November 6, 1982. The machine had the same basic design as the Osborne 1. It looked like a portable sewing machine when it was being carried. To use it you would lay it flat on one side, and the bottom would come off to reveal a 9-inch display. The machine weighed in at a hefty 28 pounds. There was nothing beautiful or svelte or even very portable about the Compaq Portable, but it was reasonably priced, at $2,995, and most important of all, it was compatible with IBM PCs. Another thing: This machine was durable. One customer later told of accidentally dropping one of the portables when he was at the top of an escalator in an airport. It bounced down two levels and the keyboard popped off, but, back home, when he plugged it in, it worked. Another machine was backed over by a car and, miraculously, still ran, recalls Canion.

The press conference was pure torment for Canion. Rosen, a master with the technology press, helped gather a scrum of more than 100 print, radio, and TV journalists. At the front of the room, Canion stood at the podium with the Portable under a sheet beside him. As he prepared to speak, all of the TV lights were switched on—immediately blowing a circuit breaker and plunging the room into near darkness. Canion, never comfortable speaking in public, decided to start his introduction anyway. "I had a shaky voice and quivering hands. My heart was beating so fast," he recalls. When the power came back on and the computer booted up, Harris reached over and yanked the covering off and then hastily sat down again. Canion was on his own. But things went smoothly after that. He demonstrated the machine's special features—including its ability to switch the cathode ray tube display back and forth between graphics mode, for spreadsheets, and text mode, for documents.

Canion and his colleagues had set what seemed like wildly aggressive sales goals, but still exceeded them. They had hoped to rack up sales of $70 to $80 million in 1983. Instead, they hit $111 million. That ranked Compaq as the U.S. company with the largest first-year sales in history. Think of it. That amazing record was achieved by an at-the-time no-name PC maker selling a portable computer that would nearly break your arm if you carried it. The reason: businesses executives and salespeople were sold on the idea that personal computers were indispensable, and the ones that traveled extensively insisted on taking their machines with them.

A year after the launch, Compaq faced a potential crisis. IBM announced its first portable in February 1984. In the several weeks leading up to the launch, Compaq's orders dried up temporarily while retailers and corporations took a look at the new IBM model. However, the stall was short. By the end of February, Compaq orders took off again after people decided its product was superior to IBM's.

For the next eight years, Compaq's fortunes soared. It sold a wide range of portable and desktop PCs and achieved a $1 billion revenue mark faster than any other company. The company stayed out in front on portable design by helping to pioneer new technologies rather than just settling for whatever the electronic components makers had in their plans. For instance, Canion spotted entrepreneur Finis Connor when he was an executive at disk drive maker Seagate Technology and invested when Connor started his own company, Connor Peripherals, in 1986, to build tiny 2½-inch hard drives for portables. That won Compaq the first six months of Connor's production. For more than two years, Compaq was first out with the highest-capacity small disk drives. It was the company's dedication to being on the cutting edge of new portable-computing technologies that allowed it to hold its position as the dominant maker of portables for a dozen years.

Just under a decade after he started Compaq, Canion was pushed out by Rosen, who was then chairman. Rosen felt Compaq wasn't keeping up with changes in the PC industry. Canion was devastated at first, but, over the years, he became philosophical about his fate. He remained immensely proud of the role that Compaq had played in the early days of personal computing.

"Our story was a thriller when you think about the risks we took and the decisions we made," he says. "Years later, I'd run into people and they'd still tell me how much they loved that first Compaq portable. It had changed their lives."

But the falling-out was still in the future on October 16, 1989, when Compaq launched a product that would change the game in the mobile computer industry and shake the confidence of one of the pioneers of personal computing, Apple. The Compaq LTE was the first mobile device that packed all of the capabilities and performance of a desktop computer into a slim package the length and width of an 8½-by-11-inch paper tablet. The first so-called notebook computer had been produced a year earlier by Japan's NEC, but the Compaq LTE, with its power and performance, defined what a notebook would be. An article published the next day in the *New York Times* gushed over the LTE and explained: "For the consumer, the new Compaqs mean that computing on the road becomes an almost effortless extension of computing in an office." The LTE was the first portable to include both a hard disk drive and a drive for floppy disks. It weighed in at just 6.2 pounds and cost $2,999.

This was a great day for Compaq's engineers, but, for people at Apple, the LTE was a rude shock. The 7.1 magnitude Loma Prieta earthquake struck the Bay Area the next day, bringing down an elevated highway and a section of the San Francisco–Oakland Bay Bridge, but, for some folks at Apple, the launch of the LTE was the more earth-shattering event. Just weeks earlier, they had introduced their first mobile computer, the Macintosh Portable. The Mac Portable weighed a bloated 15.8 pounds and cost $6,500. "When I heard about the LTE, I said, 'Holy shit!'" recalls John Medica, who was Apple's director of hardware engineering and later went on to hold top executive positions at Dell. "It was just embarrassing."

This was a turning point for Apple. The Portable disaster launched the company on an effort to rethink design that resulted, two years later, in the introduction of the PowerBook line of notebook computers. PowerBook was to become one of the most durable franchises in computing history.

The fall guy for the Portable was Frenchman Jean-Louis Gassée. A compact Napoleon with an outsized personality, his ambitions produced a computer that was out of sync with the market. Gassée had worked for Hewlett-Packard before becoming head of Apple France in the early 1980s. He recalled later that the first time he laid eyes on a portable computer was when Bill Gates brought a Compaq luggable along when he visited Gassée in Paris. "I was impressed. For a geek like me, come on! It was fantastic!" he says. Gassée was promoted to a headquarters marketing job by Apple's then CEO, John Sculley, in 1985, but within weeks after he arrived in Cupertino, California, Sculley and the board of directors had forced out founder Steve Jobs, who was then running product development. Gassée was pressed into service.

One of Gassée's first acts was to launch a team on the quest to design a portable computer that would be every bit as impressive as the original Macintosh. Released in January 1984, the original Mac had sent waves not just through the computer industry but through the entire society. This machine wasn't designed with corporate office workers in mind. It was a personal empowerment tool for students, artists, and the more creative people within companies and society. It had a graphical user interface and a mouse instead of the text and key-based command system of earlier IBM-compatible PCs. The Mac was introduced with a stunning 1984 Super Bowl commercial directed by Hollywood's Ridley Scott. In the commercial, a beautiful young woman ran through a frightening, futuristic world populated by dronelike figures and defiantly threw a sledgehammer at a video screen, which everyone watching understood to represent Big Brother IBM. Jobs's motto for Macintosh: "A computer for the rest of us." With the Mac Portable, Gassée was determined to produce a *mobile* computer for the rest of us.

To accomplish Gassée's goal, the Portable had to have a screen capable of displaying crisp graphic images. The original Macintosh had caught on immediately with graphic artists and designers, and made it possible for publishing books, magazines, and marketing materials to be handled on a desktop computer. The idea behind the Mac Portable was to allow creative professionals to carry their digital portfolios around with them. That required an active-matrix liquid crystal display (LCD), which consumed a lot of electricity. To provide the charge, Apple's engineers used a bulky and heavy lead-acid battery. That meant this would be a large and heavy portable computer. The product development team, led by Roger Mohme, also wanted to pack the Portable with all of the latest, cutting-edge technology, just like they would with a desktop Macintosh.

The team was in no particular hurry, either; another problem. Jobs had created a culture where no product was shipped before it was deemed ready. "Steve is a design purist and a perfectionist," says Jon Krakower, an engineer on the Portable and PowerBook projects. "He hired people with the same attention to detail and love for simple, elegant design." That meant development projects on new product lines typically lasted two to three years. In the case of the Mac Portable, the project stretched out for four years. One reason for the delay was the difficulty in getting a flat-panel display good enough for the graphical Macintosh user interface, which was black type on white—rather than the white type on black of the early IBM-compatible PCs. Any defects in the displays would show up as small black dots on the Mac screen. Mohme spent a lot of time working with display makers to improve their quality. But, no matter what the reasons for the delays, when the Portable finally arrived, the size and price of the computer were at least two years out of date.

One of the oddities of the Mac Portable was that it was made without screws. This was something Gassée insisted on. He loved showing people how he could assemble the computer himself, snapping into place the main circuit board, the hard drive, and the battery. To him, this signaled precision engineering. But for many people who bought the computer, it just meant that it popped and squeaked when they carried it around.

Gassée had uneasy feelings about the Portable months before it was released. The machine was just too big. But he didn't have the nerve to kill it or order up last-minute changes. One of the ironies of the Portable is that because of the incredibly enthusiastic fan base for Macs, it actually sold fairly well at first, in spite of its obvious flaws. "It sold to the Mac faithful, but didn't go outside the faithful," says Gassée. In fact, sales of the Portable collapsed before its first Christmas.

After the Compaq LTE was announced, Sculley called a meeting of most everybody who had been involved in the Portable fiasco. The atmosphere was charged in a conference room near Sculley's office in the company's headquarters on Saratoga-Sunnyvale Road in Cupertino. Medica, for one, thought heads would roll. "He wasn't kicking trash cans around, but you could see that he was pretty upset," he says of Sculley. Instead of bawling them out, though, Sculley told them that mobile computing was going to be a major piece of the PC industry, and so Apple had to succeed with portables. The failure of its first attempt hadn't wrecked the company. The successors to the original Macintosh were selling well. But Apple had to fix this. "I wasn't down. I was excited," Sculley recalls. "Compaq had validated the market for us. Now we could build our own version of what we thought a portable could be."

Sculley told his lieutenants to return to Apple's three core principles. Steve Jobs had always insisted that Apple product-development projects should start with an assessment of what the customers wanted to do and how they'd like to do it. That may seem obvious, but, at the time, a lot of PC companies were totally engineering oriented. They'd size up the chips and disk drives and other components that were becoming available and they'd pack all of that gear into boring beige plastic boxes. The second core principle: Jobs believed in the power of industrial design. These machines should look and feel good. Third: he preached the value of simplicity. Apple machines had to be easy to use.

During the meeting, Sculley began exploring the idea of reorganizing the company around specific types of products. He thought product development teams that lived and breathed mobile computing alone would do a better job of conceiving and crafting portable machines. Within a few months, he created a new portable division and to run it, he chose Randy Battat, one of Apple's top product development executives.

The Portable fiasco didn't get Gassée fired, but, within a year, after a series of product development disappointments, Sculley pushed him out. One source of tension was his advocacy of the idea of outsourcing the design and production of some Apple products to Japanese manufacturers. That sort of thing simply wasn't done at the time. U.S. PC companies designed and manufactured their own computers.

Once the portable division was set up, the next order of business was figuring out what they'd build. Even though Mohme had run the ill-fated Mac Portable project, he was still in his bosses' good graces. He cherry-picked some of the best engineers and set off on a new path—developing a product code-named Companion that was supposed to be one of the smallest and lightest notebook computers ever made. The target weight: just 3.5 pounds. Another product development manager, Jon Sedmak, was assigned to explore other concepts.

One of those concepts was actually already under development—in a manner of speaking. It was a Skunk Works project started by engineer Krakower. A Hewlett-Packard veteran with two engineering degrees from Stanford University, Krakower's specialty at Apple was system integration—fitting all of the components from different suppliers snuggly onto a circuit board and into a computer enclosure.

When he was growing up in Fort Worth, Texas, his first job was packing groceries in the checkout section of a supermarket, so this kind of task came naturally to him. He was also good at explaining technical matters to nontechnical people. He had gone along with the publicity team when the Mac Portable was introduced in New York City. During a series of press briefings in hotel conference rooms ahead of the launch, computer press reporters told

Krakower that the Portable was too heavy and too late. Just being a Macintosh wasn't going to be enough. As soon as he got a break from the briefings, Krakower rushed back to his hotel room with a handful of Mac Portable marketing brochures. With a pair of scissors, he cut out some of the photographs of portables and re-fashioned them into a revolutionary new design that eventually became the standard way of laying out the user interface on portable computers.

At the time, the keyboards on all laptop computers were positioned at the front edge of the machines. Most people set them on desks, and rested the heels of their hands on the desktop when they typed. The Portable had been equipped with a trackball (an alternative to a free-standing mouse) that could be clipped on either side of the machine—depending on whether the person who used it was right- or left-handed. When people wanted to move the cursor, they'd lift one of their hands off the keys and move it to the trackball. Krakower had a much better idea. Why not slide the keyboard to the back of the computer toward the screen so people using it could rest their hands on a flat surface toward the front? And why not place the trackball in the middle of the palm rest space at the front of the machine, so people could twiddle the trackball with a thumb without taking their fingers off the keys? He tried it out with his own hands on the cardboard model he had built. It would work. One of the things that this design shift made possible was actually putting a laptop computer on your lap, rather than a desk or table. That meant mobile computers really could be useful anywhere from airport waiting areas to the bleachers during a high school football game. Ever since Krakower came up with this idea, virtually every notebook computer has been designed this way.

At the time, Krakower's official job was working on an upgrade of the Mac Portable. The upgrade would add backlighting to the screen to improve the readability on the display, substitute in a faster processor, and increase the capacity of the disk drive. But he stayed at the office late and worked weekends on his own pet project. After the Compaq LTE came out, he bought one, took it apart, and studied the internal design of its electrical-mechanical subsystems. He ran focus groups made up of Apple colleagues and tested out the feasibility of his ergonomic concepts. Then, in December 1989, he built a functional model of the computer he had in mind in one of Apple's engineering labs and began showing it around to people like Sedmak, Mohme, and Medica. "This was one of the great things about the Apple culture," Medica says. "You had folks who were comfortable about reaching out beyond their traditional boundaries and bringing in innovative solutions."

That was Medica's reaction. Others weren't so pleased. "I got a cold reaction from Mohme," Krakower recalls. "I can't remember what he said, but the feeling of it was: 'That's nice, but this is not what you're supposed to be doing.'" Even some of Krakower's colleagues in the engineering ranks urged him to forget about it. The design was just too radical. They already had a black eye from the Portable, why risk getting another one? Still, Krakower's bosses gave him the go-ahead to keep working on his concepts— as long as it didn't interfere with his "day" job.

One of Krakower's allies was Robert Brunner, who had been hired in the autumn of 1989 as design director to beef up Apple's industrial design department. Brunner had grown up in suburban San Jose, the son of a disk drive engineer at IBM. After college, he worked his way up in a couple of Valley design firms before co-founding Lunar Design, which had worked on some Apple projects. Apple's brass hired him partly as a counterweight to Gassée, who had established himself as the final arbiter of design after Jobs was pushed out. "This enigmatic French maniac was driving everybody crazy. They needed a designer inside to help manage him," Brunner recalls. But Brunner didn't want to be just a design traffic cop. He said he would take the job under one condition: that he would be allowed to build up a sizable internal industrial design department. His wish was granted.

Everybody had their own peeve with the Mac Portable. Brunner's involved the industrial design. The people who worked on the Portable had tried to apply design rules conceived for Apple's desktop products to the first portable one, and it simply hadn't worked, in Brunner's view. Since the mid-1980s, Apple had used a unifying design language called Snow White. It got the name because when Jobs and some of Apple's early industrial designers set out to achieve a consistency in design, they had asked a handful of top design consultants to make proposals for the appearance of Apple's next seven projects, each of which would be named after one of the Snow White fairy tale's seven dwarves. Ultimately the designer who won the contest was Germany's Hartmut Esslinger and his firm, frog design. Though he was officially a consultant, Esslinger became Apple's de facto design director, and the design language he mapped out was Snow White. From 1984 until 1990, all of Apple's products shared some core design characteristics, including a white color, rectilinear shapes, and stripes in the plastic that were both decoration and ventilation. Relatively early on, the color was changed from white to a light beige, which was, oddly, called Platinum by Apple's design gods.

Snow White was a triumph, initially. It gave Apple products, from Apple IIs to Macintoshes, a distinguishing look that helped define the brand. But, when it came to portable products, Snow White didn't fit. "It wasn't scalable down to notebooks or handhelds," Brunner says. "The stripes were two big. The white was too light. It would get dirty with handling and look terrible." Also, Snow White didn't look personal enough. It felt too corporate. Brunner brought another important change to Apple, according to Medica—a better balance of design and engineering. "In the earlier days, Steve and Hartmut would tell you what the computers should look like, but they didn't care if you could build it and service it," Medica says. "Bob encouraged a partnership between designers and developers."

One of Brunner's first tasks when he joined Apple was to help shape the next generation of portables. He visited Krakower's cubicle with one of his young designers, Gavin Ivester, to see what he was working on. Brunner was impressed with Krakower's ideas, and he saw this as a chance to modify Apple's design rules. He assigned Ivester to work on the project.

In May 1990, the Krakower project became official enough to get a code name: TIM. A small group that was working on it had filled a whiteboard in one of the Apple conference rooms with jottings, including the initials *TTM*. It stood for *Time To Market*. The new imperative at Apple was developing products quicker. Somebody who came late to the meeting saw TTM, misinterpreted it as TIM, and asked, "What's TIM?" So that became the name of the project that eventually would become PowerBook.

Ivester did a concept design based on Krakower's ideas. Brunner decided not to show the design to a focus group of consumers—which would have been a typical step in product development. His concern was that since this design was so radically different, people would reject it instinctually. At the time, portable computers were based on the look and feel of portable typewriters. "If we had got to a focus group we might never have created the Power-Book," Brunner says. "But we were desperate, and we just plunged ahead."

It was crucial to get the approval of one person: Sculley. Brunner asked for a meeting in Sculley's office and showed him a model of the radical new notebook design. Sculley liked it. "I believed the PowerBook had to be an incredibly beautiful product. The style would be just as important as the capabilities," Sculley says. "I liked the design of the keyboard. The PowerBook wouldn't be some thing you just carried around. It was designed so you could actually use it sitting on your lap."

Even with Sculley's blessing, TIM wasn't in the clear yet. The lion's share of design and engineering resources in the portable division were still being used on the Companion project. Only gradually were some of the engineers reassigned to work on TIM, which was being led by Sedmak. The engineering packaging was just as radical as the industrial design. To make a machine as compact as they wanted to, the engineers had to design in nearly fifty new parts that they ordered up from suppliers. Every detail required attention. One of the key debates was whether there should be an internal floppy disk drive in the machine, in addition to a hard disk drive. Those opposed thought it would add too much thickness and weight. But Brunner and Krakower insisted it was essential, and Krakower came up with a way of fitting it in that required very little space.

The designers and developers spent countless hours refining the trackball. They tried a variety of sizes for the ball itself. If the balls were too small, people couldn't control the cursor on the screen easily enough. Also, since people would be using the trackballs after eating snacks on airplanes, the development team tested them with oily fingers. They found that larger balls could handle oil better than small ones.

Some of the changes rippled through Apple's entire organization. The new machines would be held together with 50 screws, yet the manufacturing lines in Fremont, California, were highly automated, using robots to solder or snap components into place. All of a sudden the manufacturing managers were being asked to set up lines staffed by people with tiny screwdrivers. It seemed like a step backward.

Apple was taking a big risk and relying on another company to design one of the PowerBook models. It had chosen Sony to create and manufacture the low-end version, Model 100, which would not have a floppy disk drive. It was the first time that Apple ever farmed out the design and manufacturing of a computer— and the success of this arrangement set the stage for the entire industry to do so in later years. That kind of corporate handoff required a lot of executive attention. Medica made numerous trips to Japan—so many, in fact, that the staff of the Okura Hotel in Tokyo knew him by name. Brunner recalled one of the first design collaboration meetings at Sony headquarters. The Apple people, who typically wore jeans and T-shirts to work, were tipped off to dress more formally when meeting with Sony's executives. Medica showed up in a pink shirt, yellow sports jacket, jeans, and tennis shoes. This was his idea of business attire. "The Japanese didn't say anything about it. They loved John," says Brunner. "We'd go out to dinner and he'd be the loudest guy in the sushi bar."

The first PowerBooks were launched on October 20, 1991, just two years after the Mac Portable debuted. The three models were compact, squared-off machines that came in a dark gray color. Every element of the industrial design was carefully worked out so it was all one piece. One of the models had a bright, backlit, active-matrix display—the first of its type in a slim notebook. Medica got a chance to be front man for one of the launch events. This took place in the San Francisco Convention Center. The audience was made up of thousands of Apple salespeople, dealers, and retailers. He marched out on stage and asked: "Does anybody here need a notebook?" The crowd "went nuts; it was electric," he recalls. Their enthusiasm was matched by that of computer buyers. Apple sold 400,000 machines in the first 12 months they were on the market, grossing more than $1 billion. For many who had worked on TIM in its early, uncertain days, this reception was an immense relief. "In the months before it shipped, I was utterly convinced it would be a failure and would be trashed. It was such a difficult birth. I thought I'd be fired. The night before the launch, I couldn't sleep," recalls Brunner. "Then, everybody loved it. I got my picture in *Business Week*."

The computing world had been so bitterly disappointed by the Mac Portable that it harmed Apple's reputation. Now the Power-Book would restore the brand's luster. It came at a crucial time. Microsoft's Windows 3.1, the first credible challenge to Macintosh software's superior look and feel, had just come to market. People were asking whether there was anything special in the Macintosh line. The answer came loud and clear: yes, the PowerBook.

A year later, Mohme's Companion came out. It was called the PowerBook Duo, and it was one of the first so-called subnotebook PCs. It had the signature PowerBook keyboard design and the gray color. When you opened the lid, the top edge had a slight curve on it that gave the machine a cute look—something like the visual effect of the compact Volkswagen Beetle. Like the code name indicates, this machine was conceived as a companion to a desktop PC and monitor. The most innovative of the alternatives that Apple came up with for linking to the desktop was a device called the Duo Dock. This machine allowed the folded-up Duo to fit inside it—sliding in like a videotape into a videocassette recorder. Voilà! Your mobile machine became a desktop machine. The Duo Dock concept was the work of Dennis Boyle of David Kelley Design, one of the independent design shops that Apple used during those years.

PowerBook remained a mainstay of Apple's product lineup until it was discontinued in 2006. When Sculley later looked back on the early days, it struck him that Apple's role in mobile computing was more about design than it was about technology. Elevating design decisions to the highest level in the organization was one of Steve Jobs's guiding principles. In fact, Sculley says one of the main reasons Jobs recruited him to Apple was because of his background in industrial design. He had attended the well-respected Rhode Island School of Design and, when running Pepsi, he had shepherded the design of the company's plastic bottle and some innovative merchandizing equipment. What bonded Jobs and Sculley most was their mutual appreciation of outstanding design. After Jobs left the company, Sculley expanded the role of designers to try to fill the vacuum left by his departure. "Designers were first among equals at Apple. I don't know any other high-tech company where this is so true," says Sculley.

PowerBook made some people's careers. Medica went on to become one of the top executives at Dell. After he was hired away from Apple in 1993, he totally revamped Dell's portable product line and started the company on a path that made it the number one mobile PC maker. Brunner and his Apple colleagues created a new design language, Espresso, which allowed much more flexibility for the designers of individual products, but produced one iconic design after another, from PowerBooks to desktop Macintoshes to the Newton handhelds. (More about those Newtons later, in Chapter 9.) His team won more international design awards than any other corporate design department. Brunner left Apple in 1996 to join Pentagram Design Partners. In 2007, he formed his own design firm, Ammunition.

Krakower left Apple in 1994 and later worked for several start-ups, including a biomedical company he launched himself. For him, PowerBook taught universal truths about product development teams. "For a project team to function at the maximum, it's important for the project manager to be intimately familiar with the team members, so he understands their strengths and weaknesses, and puts them in the right places. Find their passion, and let them pursue it," says Krakower. "Listen to the creative people. Let them be heard. On this project, if they had done that from the start, the process would have been a lot easier."

By the early 1990s, Alan Kay's vision of the mobile computer had come a long way. Small portable machines that could perform as well as a desktop PC were available for about $2,500. But the art and craft of designing and building computers that you could carry anywhere and use on your lap still had a long way to go. Apart from the GRiD Compass, most of the early machines were fragile. They broke at the least provocation. Those that were capable of being desktop PC replacements still weighed upwards of 8 to 10 pounds—heavy, if you carried them around a lot. Few notebooks were equipped to send and receive e-mails and documents wirelessly. And they were still relatively expensive. Throughout the rest of the 1990s, notebooks would be continuously improved and refined until they became mainstream devices for office workers and consumers. In the commercial market, some of the pioneering advances would come from a surprising source—IBM, the stodgy maker of mainframe computers and dull-as-bricks PCs. The vehicle for this outpouring of innovation would be the ThinkPad.

4

THINKPAD

To get to Richard Sapper's studio in central Milan, you take a creaking, 100-year-old elevator up to the fourth floor of the apartment building where he and his wife have lived for decades. The elevator compartment still has the original dark wood paneling, and it moves upward at a glacial pace. Sapper warns: "Be sure that when it comes to a stop, you wait to hear a clicking noise. Otherwise, if you try to open the door too soon, you'll be locked inside." So the strong impression on approaching Sapper's lair is of traveling back in time. Which is true. But it's also not true. Sapper, who launched his career in the design shop at Mercedes in the mid-1950s, was one of the pioneers of the industrial design discipline, but he is not stuck in the past. Even at 75, his age when I visited him in 2007, he was still experimenting with new materials and forms. And many of his designs are timeless.

Of the more than two hundred designs of his that have gone into production, none has had more profound and lasting impact than the ThinkPad notebook computer. Sapper came up with the design concept for IBM in 1990, and ThinkPads have been in production ever since they were introduced in 1992. The original idea was disarmingly simple. At the time, most notebook computers were beige, and they typically were curvaceous things with a hodgepodge of buttons, latches, plugs, and vents all over the outside. "I wanted to make a box that looks like a black box of cigars," he says. "It's just a plain box from the outside. And when you open it you see that inside it is completely different. That's the surprise."

In his small studio, when I visited, Sapper, a man clad in blue denim with a hawklike but friendly face, placed one of the original ThinkPads on his work table next to a contemporary one. The original was matte black, about two inches thick, and was rectilinear—all 90-degree angles and smooth surfaces. The contemporary model was matte black, less than one inch thick, and still mainly rectilinear. "You see, it looks so similar," he said. "The computer inside, today, is very different, but the design idea is still the same. In this, the ThinkPad is unique. There is no other laptop that has maintained its line over 15 years."

That was clearly a point of great pride for Sapper, and it was indeed a remarkable achievement in the realm of mobile computer design. In a market where new products are increasingly thought of as eye candy, the equivalent of the latest seasonal offerings on the fashion show runways, this ThinkPad design concept has had staying power.

Sapper's reputation as a design pioneer was already firmly established when he began consulting for IBM. He had grown up in Munich and Stuttgart and studied engineering, philosophy, and economics before finally shifting to design. His first job was at Daimler-Benz, where there was no compromise on quality. But he considered the work boring, since Mercedes design at the time was very conservative. "I made a whole series of proposals about how Mercedes should change the way it designed cars," Sapper recalls. "I gave it to my boss. After two weeks he called me and said, 'Your proposals are very interesting, but naturally, Mercedes will never make cars like this.'" Sapper decided that he didn't want to work in a large bureaucratic organization with lots of bosses, and he wanted the freedom to work on cutting-edge products, so he moved to Milan, which, in the mid-1950s, was a design mecca. It was there that he came into his own as an independent design consultant, making a mark in an incredibly broad array of product types, from lamps and TV sets, to cars and bicycles, and to furniture and kitchen appliances.

The call from IBM came in 1980. Paul Rand, the famed graphic designer who was then IBM's graphics and packaging consultant, contacted Sapper to find out if he'd be interested in replacing Elliot Noyes as IBM's industrial design advisor. Noyes had done a number of products for IBM, most famously its IBM Selectric typewriter, but after he died in 1977, the consulting job had been unfilled for a couple of years. Sapper's answer was yes, but it took a number of meetings in Milan and New York with Rand and IBM executives to clinch the deal.

What Sapper found when he reported for duty at IBM was a sprawling design bureaucracy that he felt an overwhelming compulsion to reform. The huge computer company not only had a corporate design department but also each product group had its own design centers. Even though there was a corporate design recipe book, each location sometimes fashioned products its own way. Also, none of the design department managers were still designing products, so there was a chasm between top-level design thinking and what was happening on the company's drawing boards. "It was an incredible mess," says Sapper. "It was a mess aesthetically, but it was also a mess of duplication. Of course, at the time these things were possible because IBM made so much money from its mainframe computers that it could permit itself any stupidity in the world, and it would always come out alright. For a design consultant, this is not an easy situation."

Gradually, over a period of years, Sapper convinced the company to adopt a set of common design conventions and processes. Much of the duplication of effort was wrung out. And corporate design reviews started to include the actual designers of products, not just design managers.

Sapper's first major project for IBM in 1981 was a typewriter, and it was never built. But it launched him on the first step toward thinking about portable computing. The company wanted an update of its immensely popular Selectric typewriter. Nothing radically different. But Sapper did not oblige. Instead, he envisioned an upright form that took up less desk space and put the paper closer to the typist, which made the type easier to read. An electronic flat panel display was located on the angled front surface of the typewriter. Such displays were just then becoming commercially available from the Japanese, and would soon become standard on portable computers. But IBM's product development executives shot it down. "In one meeting they said the influence of good design or bad design on sales is 2 percent, so why should they spend money and time changing something on this typewriter," says Sapper. "Of course, this was the last typewriter they made. Then came the PC, and the typewriter was dead."

When Sapper began working for IBM, the company had a secret Skunk Works operating in Boca Raton, Florida, where a team of engineers was developing the first IBM PC. Sapper knew nothing of it until the product was introduced in August 1981. And when he finally saw it, he wasn't impressed. A clunky monitor had been taken from a computing system designed for banks and plopped down on top of the PC. "I thought the design was horrible. I disliked everything. I thought it was a stupid boring box," he says.

Almost immediately after the PC came out, IBM started working on portable designs—first luggables and then laptops. The first one, a beige suitcase with a computer packed inside, came out in early 1984, and was priced slightly less than models from Compaq and Kaypro. (In fact, IBM had produced in 1973 a 50-pound prototype, code-named "Scamp," that it called a portable. But it was portable in name only.) The first portable that Sapper designed was the IBM 5140 Convertible PC, which was code-named "Clamshell," and came out in 1986. It looked a bit like Moggridge's design for the GRiD Compass laptop: there was a hinge in the middle of the top of the computer, and the lid folded up to reveal a narrow deck where the keyboard was placed. It sold poorly, but that wasn't Sapper's fault. The main problems were that the text on the display was a bit blurry and the machine was underpowered.

In fact, none of IBM's early portables were particularly successful, which became a source of much frustration to the company's product developers and executives. Part of the problem was that, throughout the mid-1980s, there were rivalries between IBM product engineering teams and designers in Boca Raton, Raleigh, and Yamato, Japan. People were working at cross-purposes rather than collaborating. Relatively early on, Sapper concluded that IBM portables should be black so they would stand out from the competition. But he had no luck swaying the product development bosses in Florida. Finally, Sapper forced the issue. He contacted IBM Chairman John Akers and asked him to look at two designs side by side, one produced by IBM's people in Florida and one by him. The meeting took place in Akers's office in New York. "We asked him to choose, and he chose mine," Sapper recalls. "I think from that point on I was the most hated man in Boca Raton." But, from then on, black became the color of IBM portables. "It was a classy look," says Bruce Claflin, who ran the ThinkPad business early on.

Ultimately, black became the color of *all* IBM computers as Sapper's design principles gradually spread to all of the IBM divisions. By the turn of the century, his ideas had taken on the weight of religion there. He believed in purposeful design—that form should always follow function; the company's products should have an elegant but businesslike aesthetic; that they should be crafted from simple forms, like modern architecture; and that they should not be affected by fashion—no frivolous attempts to decorate. These design principles helped make IBM's one of the top five brands in the world. ThinkPad was a key piece of IBM's brand.

The late 1980s was a time of much disagreement about what form the portable computer would take—not just at IBM but throughout the tech world. Would the clamshell design predominate? How big and heavy should they be to be truly portable? What about tablet PCs? To address these issues, Tom Hardy, IBM's new corporate design chieftain, launched a research project aimed at exploring portable computing concepts and coming up with a handful of formats that could be successful. He assigned one of his lieutenants, Sam Lucente, to head the project. Lucente, who was later to become vice president of design at computing giant Hewlett-Packard, and the Yamato team ultimately came up with a series of 12 models of what the IBM line of portables should look like. They ranged from credit card–size pocket computers to handhelds, mobile phones, tablets, and laptops. The idea was to use a lot of common parts on the different machines, reducing costs and the time it took to bring new products to market.

Lucente had joined IBM in 1982, shortly after Sapper came on as the company's corporate design consultant. Lucente worked closely with Sapper for many years. In fact, Lucente felt, looking back, as though he had "apprenticed" to Sapper in the European trades model. Back in those early days, Sapper would make rough sketches of designs for portables. Then he'd work with model makers who would fashion beautiful wooden models. It was an iterative process.

Sapper and Lucente didn't always see things the same. When Lucente started out on the portable design research project, he worked with Yamato engineers and designers and adopted a Japanese quality discipline called Quality Functional Deployment (QFD), a precursor of the now widely used Six Sigma quality discipline. QFD was supposed to get product developers to pay much more attention to user requirements when they set out to create new things. They'd interview customers to find out what they wanted, make a list of the technologies that were available for the product, and then come up with designs that gave people the experience they wanted. In this case, Lucente even asked 110 computer users to make sketches of what they thought the perfect portable computer should be like, mainly to discover the optimal sizes and shapes. "Richard thought this was absurd," recalls Lucente. "He was a purist. In the Italian design model, the master comes up with a design and everything goes from there." Yet out of this work, called the form-factors project, came that set of 12 models that ultimately became a foundation for the portables IBM created in the 1990s.

Another major influence on the shape of IBM portables was a project run by the Yamato design team led by Kazuhiko Yamazaki. Using simple product models and posing as different kinds of computer users, the designers made a video showing a variety of scenarios where portables would come in handy, including in a car, on an airplane, on a park bench, and on a cluttered desk. The video woke up people in the company to the potential for making ultrathin and light machines.

One of the first products that came out of this conceptualizing was a technical failure and a major embarrassment for IBM. But it accomplished two important things: it set the stage for better portable design and engineering and it gave IBM the name ThinkPad. The project was a tablet PC. The idea was to build a flat, one-piece device that people would write on with a stylus. The product was conceived as a tool for people who worked outdoors or in situations where they needed to fill in lots of information when they couldn't be near a desk—for example, an insurance adjuster. The customer that helped IBM develop the product and served as its tester was State Farm Insurance. IBM was building the hardware and using a pen-based operating system designed by a Silicon Valley start-up called Go Corporation. (More about this company in Chapter 9.)

One of the early debates was over what to call the computer. At the time, IBM products almost always were known simply by their model number. But members of the tablet development group wanted a name with more personality. Denny Wainwright, a senior planner in Boca Raton, is credited with coming up with the ThinkPad name. Wainwright was a buttoned-down guy. While many of his colleagues wore casual clothing to work, he typically dressed in a suit and a tie—the traditional IBM uniform for men. He also was in the habit of carrying around with him small leather-bound pads of paper, designed to fit in a dress shirt pocket, that the company produced for its employees in its earlier days. The pads had the IBM motto, "Think," embossed on the front. IBM founder Thomas Watson Sr. had adopted the motto shortly after he reshaped a calculator and measurement equipment company called CTR into the International Business Machines Company in 1911. He had told employees: "All the problems of the world could be solved easily if men were only willing to think." By the early 1990s, the "Think" motto was seen by many IBM employees as little more than a quaint reminder of the company's distant past. But, for Wainwright, it was still an inspiration to live by. At one meeting when his team was brainstorming to come up with a name for the tablet PC, he suddenly held up his pad of paper and exclaimed: "Let's call it the Think pad!"

The name was a winner, but, ultimately, the pen-based tablet computer was a flop. It was too heavy, at more than six pounds. And, in the field tests, it turned out that people didn't understand how to use the devices properly. Insurance adjusters out at storm and disaster sites would break the computers by handling them too roughly. They would even try to use the tablet as a kneeling pad to protect their pants if they were in a muddy place. When they put their weight on these machines, the screens would crack.

During the 1980s, most of IBM's portable design and engineering was done in Boca Raton, but, as failure followed failure, more and more of the work was shifted to IBM's R&D lab in Yamato, Japan. The company had established the lab there years earlier to develop products specifically for the Japanese market, but, in the late 1980s, it was integrated into the global engineering effort by the PC division. The Yamato engineers had their share of failures, too, but, over time, IBM's executives grew to trust them more than they did the development teams in Florida. The tablet, though it was partly designed in Yamato, added more momentum to the company's resolve to move more of the hardware engineering and industrial design for portables to Japan. The first IBM notebook completely designed in Japan, the PS/55 Note, had been shipped in 1991. While it wasn't a huge seller, it gave the IBM PC bosses faith that the Japanese were up to the task of developing portables for global distribution. That's how Yamato got the assignment of engineering the first true ThinkPad—the one designed by Sapper.

Sapper's concept for ThinkPad had emerged out of a design assignment he had taken on nearly twenty years earlier. In 1976, the Swiss firm TAG Heuer had hired him to design the first digital stopwatch. What Sapper came up with was a small black box with a matte finish and a lid that would tilt back to reveal a few simple controls and a tiny digital display. It looked a bit like a hard Marlboro cigarette pack painted matte black. "That formal treatment is carried on in the ThinkPad," says Sapper.

Hardy remembers vividly the first time he saw Sapper's model for ThinkPad. The scene took place in Sapper's Milan studio during a work session Hardy had arranged with Sapper and Yamazaki. Sapper placed a matte black wooden model of the design on a table for Yamazaki and Hardy to see. It was a simple, elegant black box. Sapper talked about the purity of the form. The laptops would have absolutely no ornamentation on the outside. All you'd see would be the hinges, a latch, and the logo. He opened the lid to show them the insides—again, matte black, with a realistic keyboard. "It was vintage Sapper," recalls Hardy. "Absolute simplicity mixed with an element of surprise." There would be some challenges, though. The model was all 90-degree angles. That would be very difficult to manufacture, and would require expensive tooling in the factory. But the IBMers didn't hesitate. "Let's do it," Hardy said as the meeting wrapped up.

That was the beginning of a marathon effort to design and manufacture a notebook PC, code-named Nectarine, which would eventually be called the ThinkPad 700C, the first in the long line of elegant black laptops. Yamazaki handled the detailed design, collaborated closely with Sapper, and was the liaison with the product engineering team in Yamato. Arimasa Naitoh was in charge of engineering. A short, barrel-chested man who had joined IBM right out of college in 1974, he ended up being known in Japan as the Father of the ThinkPad. The Japanese designers and engineers were on a crusade to build the world's best portable computers. They were masters of collaboration. In Japan, it was all about teamwork. In America, there was a tendency by designers and engineers to try to do things by themselves. They were cowboys.

The Japanese faced a host of design, engineering, and manufacturing challenges. In addition to dealing with the 90-degree angles, they had the difficulty of setting a then-large 10.4-inch color thin-film transistor display, with all of its complex circuitry, in a small space on the lid of the laptop. They also designed a new, full-size keyboard with superior responsiveness to anything that was then on the market. Hard disk drives had very little capacity at the time, but they were improving rapidly, so the Japanese designers decided to make the disk drive replaceable. That meant they had to provide a way for the owner of the computer to get at it. Sapper had decreed that the exterior of the box should be as uncluttered as possible, so the Japanese designers came up with a novel idea: why not make the keyboard double as a door to the inner workings of the computer? They put a latch and hinges on it so people could lift it like a lid and switch out the drive.

In the end, though, the most novel innovation in that first true ThinkPad came from a pair of IBM's American employees, Ted Selker and Joe Rutledge. It was called TrackPoint, and it was a small rubberized nub that stuck up in the middle of a keyboard and allowed the computer user to have pinpoint control of the cursor on the display. In the late 1980s and early 1990s, many laptops had trackballs—little plastic balls that could be clipped on or were set in a housing embedded in the computer chassis that users would manipulate with their index fingers to move a cursor on the computer display screen. These were complex devices that tended to malfunction. They also took up a lot of space within the laptop.

Back in the early 1980s, when Selker was a graduate student at Stanford University, he had designed a small pointing device, which he thought of as a tiny joystick, to be embedded within the keys of a keyboard and operated with the index finger. This was before trackball came into wide use. People then used a computer mouse, attached by a cord to the laptop, to move the cursor. The advantage of Selker's scheme was that users could move the cursor without having to look away from the screen or move their fingers off the keys. Selker kept working on the project when he worked at Atari Research, an early PC and gaming company, until Atari fired its entire research team in 1984. He kept at it as a researcher at Xerox PARC and when he moved over to IBM Research.

Selker and Rutledge were assigned to IBM's vaunted Thomas J. Watson Research Center in Yorktown Heights, New York. Rutledge was an accomplished algebraist. He had started on the ground floor of computing as a programmer on Remington Rand's UNIVAC, the first commercial electronic computer. Both men were rock climbers—they climbed Mt. Rainier together—and had become friends. One day Rutledge wandered into Selker's office and said, "I'm sick of doing math. Do you have anything else we can work on?" After reviewing a couple of big projects, Selker mentioned the pointing device. "Let's do that," Rutledge said. It was September 1987.

Selker's original invention for IBM was a little post that stuck up from the keyboard. Although the idea of an in-keyboard pointing device seemed promising, making a joystick that pointed as well as a mouse was hard work. Over a period of four years, they worked together on TrackPoint, which they originally called Pointing Stick. Their early tests determined that finger pressure was an inefficient way to control a cursor. It was hard to use the pointer accurately. People tended to overshoot their target. But over time, after many experiments and a series of working prototypes, they gradually made the device more and more usable. The project was such an obsession that the two even had long discussions about it when they climbed mountains together in Ecuador. Rutledge handled a lot of the math, but they handed most of the electrical engineering tasks to Bob Olyha. They quickly shifted focus from the joystick idea to using the J key itself as a cursor controller operated by the index finger. Then they shifted back to using a nub, but shortened the "stick" to make it easier to control. They put it between the G and H keys, and, later, between the G, H, and B keys. One of their main breakthroughs was the discovery that if they slowed the movement of the cursor on the screen, people's eyes could track it more easily and they could use the device more accurately.

By late 1989, Selker and Rutledge felt they were really onto something. They prepared a handful of patent applications for the technology. But they had no luck getting anybody within IBM interested. Product development leaders they appealed to wouldn't even return their phone calls. They had just about given up on getting IBM to use their invention. In January 1990, they wrote a paper about their device, which they presented at technology conferences early that year along with a short video they had made to show people how the device worked. By coincidence, Jim Lewis, a human factors engineer working on a laptop computer in IBM's PC division, was attending one of the conferences, saw their presentation, and was wowed by it. He arranged for Selker and Rutledge to demonstrate the technology in Boca Raton. Still, it took a couple more years before IBM put their pointing device into a laptop.

A turning point came on November 11, 1991. James Cannavino, who then ran IBM's PC division, was holding a meeting of his department heads in his office in Somers, New York. Just before the lunch break, Jim McGroddy, who was then the head of IBM Research, asked Cannavino if he wanted to see the Pointing Stick technology. Cannavino said yes, and McGroddy called Selker and Rutledge and told them to get over to Cannavino's office fast. They hastily gathered up all of their prototypes and their boss, Ashok Chandra, drove them in his car. It was 13 miles from IBM Research in Yorktown Heights to Cannavino's office, but they made it in 10 minutes. They demonstrated how Pointing Stick worked and answered questions for about two hours. Cannavino was impressed—so much so that he asked them to make him a keyboard with a Pointing Stick embedded in it for him to use on his regular desktop computer in his home.

The fate of Pointing Stick was now in the hands of the laptop engineering team in Yamato. Selker, Rutledge, and Chandra traveled to Japan and worked with the Japanese human factors engineers Saturo Yamada and Kazuo Tsuchiya to test Pointing Stick against trackballs and other pointing devices. Pointing Stick didn't perform as well as the others in some of the early live tests with users, and Selker realized it was because it took some practice to get the knack of it. So he urged the Japanese engineers to toss out the results from the first half minute of each test for purposes of comparison. Pointing Stick did better after that. Another issue was comfort. Selker thought the nub needed to have a hard top to make the cursor easier to control, but Toshiyuki Ikeda, the ThinkPad product manager, held up his index finger to Selker after he had been using the device for a few minutes to show him an indention in the skin of his fingertip. "This hurts," Ikeda said. He told Selker to make the device easier to use and asked him to soften the surface of the nub. The deadline: two weeks. Rutledge flew to Japan, and the two worked furiously to improve Pointing Stick.

There was a lot to do. They were staying in a hotel in Tokyo and taking a one-hour train trip to the Yamato lab each day. So they even worked on the train. They made quite an odd sight. On a rail car packed with Japanese commuters were these two huge Americans (Rutledge is six feet, six inches tall and had a beard) sitting together with their tools tinkering with a tiny mechanical device on their laps. They even had a battery-powered grinding tool for shaping the cap. They tried different materials for the tip, including sandpaper, latex, and cork, and the material that's used on the surface of Ping-Pong paddles. That stuff had just the right combination of give and grip. At the end of the two weeks they had improved the performance of people using Pointing Stick by 15 percent during the first 30 seconds of use.

Sapper had already seen Pointing Stick. He was at the corporate design offices in Stamford, Connecticut, and Hardy had arranged for Selker to present his concept. Sapper wiggled the nub and tried to draw a circle using it—which failed abysmally. Selker and Rutledge had concentrated on making a device that worked well with text and they had ignored drawing. So, while they were in Japan, they also refined the device so it could be used for making a sketch. The next time Sapper tried it out, he liked it. Later, he made a recommendation that became part of the essential design language of ThinkPad. Why not make the Pointing Stick nub red? It made a nice contrast with the black. Red wasn't one of the official colors allowed in the IBM design palette for control buttons at the time, so the designers recorded it as magenta, even though it was really red. The red nub became part of the surprise that Sapper wanted people to experience when they opened a ThinkPad. Ultimately, it was also used in the ThinkPad logo, as a red dot on the top of the *i* in ThinkPad.

When Selker and Rutledge returned from Japan there were still many important details to take care of, for instance, what material to use for the nub. How the computer user's finger gripped the top of the nub was very important. It had to be easy to control. Selker traveled to the IBM typewriter plant in Lexington, Kentucky, to talk to scientists there about materials. They argued against using latex or rubber. Instead, they suggested a melding of rubber and plastic called Santoprene. "Santoprene felt too slimy to me, but they said it was the grippiest stuff they knew," recalls Selker. Back at his hotel, he called his father, Alan Selker, who was a materials scientist, to ask his advice. Eventually, he convinced his bosses to let him hire his father as a consultant on the project. After much experimenting, his father recommended chlorinated butyl rubber. That meant that they would not be able to easily recover the waste in the manufacturing process, since rubber can't be revulcanized, but it had better gripping properties. When ThinkPad launched, the TrackPoint nub was made of Santoprene, but, after customers complained about a slimy feel and breaking, within a couple of weeks, IBM switched to rubber.

While Selker and Rutledge were improving the Pointing Stick, Naitoh and his Yamato team were overcoming one engineering challenge after another. With each victory, they became more confident. "In those days not many executives at IBM believed in the notebook business," recalls Naitoh. "It was like the very early days of airplane," he says. "You'd try something and crash; try and crash. Nobody thought it would stay in the air. The ThinkPad's success was a surprise to all of us, even myself."

Meanwhile, back in the United States, a debate was raging over what the laptop would be called. ThinkPad had been an okay name for the tablet PC, because it was an electronic pad, but the product development people in Boca Raton and Raleigh, North Carolina, thought they should return to IBM's traditional naming conventions for the next generation of laptop computers. The man who saved the ThinkPad name, and, even more importantly, the whole notebook initiative, was Bruce Claflin, a gifted marketing executive, who was brought in as the general manager of the mobile computing group in mid-1992.

Claflin didn't know much about engineering. He had graduated from Penn State in 1973 with a political science major and went straight to IBM in the typewriter division as a salesman. Over the next few years he climbed the career ladder into sales management. His big break came in 1981 when he was selected by then CEO John Opel to be his assistant. He later became the assistant of John Akers, who would succeed Opel, when Akers was waiting in the wings as president. As a reward for his good work, Akers appointed him to run the entire Asia-Pacific region except Japan in 1989. That was a big job. He was running a division with $3 billion in sales and 10,000 employees. So he was stunned when Cannavino asked him in the spring of 1992 to return to the United States and run the portable business. It was, in a sense, a demotion. The portable unit was in a miserable twelfth place in the market for laptop computers and was a money loser. Claflin didn't want the job, and he asked for a chance to appeal directly to Akers. They met in Akers's office at headquarters in Armonk, New York. Akers told him that portables would be vital to IBM's future, and he wanted Claflin for the job partly because of his experience in Asia. He figured Claflin would know how to handle the Yamato engineers. He looked me in the eye and said, 'You're a great guy, this is a great opportunity for you, and we really want you to do it,' " recalls Claflin. "I said, 'Yes, sir.' "

When Claflin reported for duty, he had a prototype of ThinkPad from Yamato on his desk. He liked the looks of it, and he loved the ThinkPad name, so he insisted that they keep the name. But there wasn't much support for the project among his lieutenants. "Morale was horrible. Every product was late, and they sold terribly," Claflin recalls.

That set up the defining moment. During the summer of 1992, Claflin attended a product planning meeting where the financial team projected that they would only sell 30,000 of the first ThinkPad. At that rate, they couldn't make money on it. So they recommended abandoning the project. Claflin thought the proposition over for a minute and then instructed them to change the sales projection to 50,000 to allow the project to go ahead. One of the top salespeople refused to raise his forecast, saying, "I nonconcur," Claflin recalls. That was IBM lingo for disagreeing. Sometimes, if one person "nonconcurred," a whole project would shut down. Claflin was furious. He blurted out: "I don't recognize that word. If you nonconcur, I'm laying everybody off and shutting down the division." After that, everybody concurred. By insisting on the higher forecast, Claflin took complete responsibility for what happened with the product, and that gave the others the protective cover they needed to go along without further protest.

But, still, there were hang-ups. Executives above Claflin had to give ThinkPad the go-ahead. Shortly before the ThinkPad 700C was supposed to go into production in the factory, Sapper heard through the company grapevine that Cannavino wasn't convinced they had the right formula of technology and design. The rumor was that Cannavino might kill the project. "I wrote him a letter and said don't do that, please, because there are people who are interested in good design and having nice products," Sapper says. "I don't know if I convinced him, or somebody else convinced him, or he was already convinced, but the project went ahead."

The first ThinkPad, the 700C, was launched in October 22, 1992. Selker was invited to participate in the launch at IBM's building at the corner of 57th Street and Madison Avenue in New York City. In the interim, some of the product marketers had had rechristened his device EasyPoint, but at the last minute somebody had noticed another product with that name, so a new one was required instantly. In a search, the naming folks discovered that IBM already owned the rights to TrackPoint. It has been used for a trackball on a laptop produced in 1991. "We didn't like the name, but since we didn't have a better idea, we couldn't do much," says Rutledge. Before the launch event, Selker tested out the machines that were on hand and discovered that some of the TrackPoints didn't work right. The cursors raced too fast when he pressed the nub to move them to the left. So he personally removed those machines from the stage. But the launch went off without a hitch. "I felt like I had died and gone to heaven. I was so proud," he says. "As a researcher I do a lot of things, so it's nice to see a project that you put a lot into actually make a difference."

For hundreds of IBM engineers, designers, marketers, and executives, the launch of the ThinkPad laptop ended a decade of frustration with portables and began fulfilling their dreams of making the company into a major player in the mobile computing business. Rather than selling 30,000 or even 50,000 ThinkPad 700Cs, they sold hundreds of thousands, and some later models sold in the millions. The hoopla about ThinkPad was loud enough that even then president George H.W. Bush got swept up in it. Jim Steele, who was John Akers's assistant at the time, received a call on December 18, 1992, from Akers's secretary telling him Bush was on the phone. He wanted a ThinkPad for his wife, Barbara, for Christmas. Within seconds, a nervous Steele was talking to Bush. The president told him that Barbara was planning on writing a book about their dog, Millie, and had asked him for a laptop. He wanted it shipped to the White House. He was willing to pay. Time was the issue. ThinkPads were in short supply, but Steele scrambled and got one to the White House on time. So that's how Barbara Bush's memoir, *Millie's Book*, came to be written on a ThinkPad.

IBM's strategy around ThinkPad was to innovate like mad—to keep pushing the latest technology out ahead of the other PC companies. For this strategy to work, they'd depend on inventors like Selker and Rutledge and others. "I fell in love with Ted Selker, the madman of research," says Claflin. "He had a passion. He was hugely innovative. He was right about the TrackPoint when others wanted to kill it."

But keeping the ThinkPad business on track was never easy. Some of that was due to external events. In the late 1980s and early 1990s, IBM's fortunes had shifted radically. Its expensive, room-sized mainframes were being supplanted by smaller and less expensive computers. Akers was in trouble. He came up with a plan to break up the company into several pieces, but he never got a chance to implement it. In January 1993, the board pressured him into retiring, and a search began to find his successor. Never had IBM been in this kind of trouble before. Mainframe revenue, which stood at $13 billion in 1990, was expected to plunge to just $7 billion in 1993. If something dramatic wasn't done—and quickly—the company might actually fail. IBM, one of the greatest companies ever created, might cease to exist—brought down by a combination of hubris, complacency, and rapid technology change. The search for Akers's successor was followed on Wall Street like a soap opera. Who would replace him? Big names were floated, including GE's Jack Welch, Motorola's George Fisher, and even Microsoft's Bill Gates. But the man the board chose was Louis V. Gerstner Jr., who had formerly run RJR Nabisco and American Express. He knew little about the technology industry, but the board saw him as a fearless and decisive leader. When he arrived on the job in March, he felt that there was perhaps only a one in five chance that IBM would survive. But he was determined to save it. He quickly threw out the idea of breaking up the company into big chunks. "When I got to IBM we were losing billions. We had a lot of businesses in trouble," he says. "When I got there I said we're going to try to fix every business we've got."

Gerstner was a formidable presence at IBM. He thought in bold strokes. Everything at IBM was under review—its future uncertain. Gerstner even kept outsiders on tenterhooks. George Pataki, the former governor of New York, recalled years later that when he became governor in 1994 he visited several CEOs of large New York–based companies, and Gerstner was one of them. In Gerstner's office at IBM headquarters in Armonk, the CEO told Pataki that he wanted to take as many IBM jobs as possible out of the state because of the costs of doing business there. He showed Pataki a map of the area around his headquarters and explained to him that the company had land not just in New York but in neighboring Connecticut as well. Pataki got the point. "I promised we would reduce New York regulations and taxes, and he said he'd stay in New York," recalled Pataki. "Lou was frank with me, and I was open with him, and we both kept our promises." Gerstner didn't hold back when it came to straightening out his own business and his own lieutenants, so there was a lot of fear in the executive offices of IBM. People worried that their businesses would be sold or shut down, and they'd be fired.

Claflin was especially nervous. ThinkPad got rave reviews from the tech magazines, and he sold every one he could make. One reason was Claflin's decision to price it 20 percent below the high-end Toshiba notebook. But there was a major problem. He couldn't make nearly as many as he could sell. The main issue was the flat-panel display. This was a new size and new display technology, and a joint venture set up by IBM and Toshiba had trouble producing them in sufficient quantities, so ThinkPads were perpetually in short supply. Some people worried that Gerstner might even shutter the portable business. A Gerstner confidante told Claflin, "Gerstner doesn't like you. You have to fix things fast." Who knew if this rumor was true? But Claflin realized he was vulnerable. His immediate boss, Bob Corrigan, had just been let go, so he had lost a protector. He wanted Gerstner to understand why he couldn't ship enough ThinkPads, so he wrote him a five-page memo laying out all of his problems.

In retrospect, it's clear that Claflin's fears were overblown. Gerstner says he doesn't remember having negative feelings about Claflin or the laptop business. The top priorities were fixing the company's large-computer businesses—but he also wanted to shore up the PC business. He had no thought of getting rid of portables. "I was unhappy we were losing money, but it would have been unlikely for me to consider getting out of the ThinkPad business," Gerstner says. "We tried to fix the PC business."

In the end, rather than being fired, Claflin was promoted. He was chosen to run the entire PC unit. He knew that the only way he could succeed in that role is if the ThinkPad business thrived. And, for the ThinkPad business to thrive, he would have to hire somebody to run it who could whip manufacturing into shape. He needed an operations specialist. He found one in Joe Formichelli, who had earlier in his IBM career manufactured motherboards, the electronic guts of PC and, later, the PCs themselves. He ran operations for the PC division for several years, then was given a business unit of his own to run—monitors and related products. "I'm the Darth Vadar guy who cuts costs and gets things running," Formichelli says. "I was the guy to get things done."

Still, Formichelli was surprised and a bit intimidated when one of the top executives in the personal systems division called him up to tell him he had landed the ThinkPad job. This was in September 1993. A few weeks after he got the job, he was summoned to Armonk to brief Gerstner on the status of the program. Formichelli got word of the meeting on a Thursday and was told to be in Gerstner's office on a Monday morning. He had been told that Gerstner was concerned about the display supply problem. "I didn't sleep or bathe for four days. I made a dozen foils. (IBM used overhead projectors at the time for all presentations.) All the way on the drive from Somers to Armonk I was ready to fling myself out of the car," Formichelli recalls. With him was Mark Loughridge, who ran finance for the ThinkPad division and later became IBM's chief financial officer. During the drive, Loughridge advised Formichelli about the things he should be sure *not* to say to Gerstner. By the time they arrived at headquarters, Formichelli was in a state of near panic. There to meet them outside Gerstner's office was Jerry York, an executive Gerstner had brought in to cut costs and reorganize the management ranks. York sorted through Formichelli's foils. "After a few minutes, he shouted, 'Formichelli!' and I jumped up and practically saluted," Formichelli recalls. "He said, 'Do you know how much a color foil costs IBM?'"

Formichelli survived his brush with York, and the meeting with Gerstner went well. Gerstner talked to him about branding and said that ThinkPad was one of IBM's important brands. Then Gerstner said: "My friends tell me they can't get a ThinkPad." That was hurting the IBM brand. Gerstner and Formichelli agreed that laptops would be an extremely important product type, and IBM had to be a major player. At the time, it trailed Compaq and Toshiba. To move up in the rankings, IBM would have to solve the display supply problem, which Formichelli promised Gerstner he would do.

IBM and Toshiba had set up their display joint venture, Display Technologies Inc. (DTI), a couple of years earlier in anticipation of huge demand for screens for laptop computers. The two companies collaborated on the design—then each did its own manufacturing. These so-called thin-film transistor displays were like big semiconductor chips. They were costly to manufacture and, inevitably, some of the tiny transistors in a display would fail. A failed transistor would show up as a dot on the screen. So they had rules for how many transistors could fail on a display before it was declared unusable. The color displays on the early ThinkPads were 10.4 inches measured diagonally—larger than the typical size at the time—so it was even more difficult to get a high yield of usable displays through manufacturing. Formichelli recalls that the yield on those screens was about 40 percent when he got involved.

He traveled to Japan in late 1993 to try to sort things out. DTI was located in Hemeji, far from Tokyo and out in Japan's sticks. Formichelli was looking for a quick fix when he went out for late-night cocktails with one of the top Toshiba engineers. Formichelli asked what would happen to yields if they raised the permissible number of bad transistors on a display from 25 to 35. The answer: yields would go up to 50 percent. A few days later, when Formichelli discussed the possibility of changing the quality specifications on the displays with IBM's Japanese quality control managers, they were furious at him. Quality was a core IBM value. "I told them, 'We're not making enough, and the chairman wants me to get these things manufactured!' " he recalls. Back in the United States, he made his case to one IBM executive after another. Finally, it was agreed; they would temporarily lower the bar on quality to raise yields. Meanwhile, they'd work on improving the manufacturing process so there wouldn't be so many bad transistors.

Throughout the early 1990s, the ThinkPad development teams in Boca Raton, Raleigh, and Yamato competed not just with other companies but among themselves to see who could design the best laptops. Gradually, as more of the engineering tasks were handed to Yamato, the American teams became resentful. Starting in 1992, a product development team in Raleigh overseen by Nick King began working on a new model that they hoped would prove they could perform every bit as well as the Japanese. Ultimately, the product would be called the ThinkPad 701C, and it would be known as "Butterfly," the most famous ThinkPad ever made. The goal was to build one of the world's lightest and smallest laptops. Yet they still wanted it to have a full-size keyboard. At the time, several manufacturers produced small laptops, called sub-notebooks, but customers were frustrated by their small keyboards, which measured about nine inches across rather than the 11.5 inches of a full-size keyboard. But how could you put an 11-inch keyboard into a nine-inch box?

The answer came from an IBM researcher named John Karidis. Though he worked at the company's labs in Yorktown Heights and had a Ph.D. from Penn State, he was a hands-on engineering type of guy. He had grown up just south of Pittsburgh and his father was a mechanical engineer at Westinghouse. His dad had a shop in the basement where Karidis built go-carts and bicycles. Once, when he was just 15 years old, he designed a bicycle with pedals that went up and down rather than around a fulcrum. It didn't work. He had used levers connected to the back axle. The levers flexed too much and there was too much load on the chain. But Karidis had enjoyed trying out a brand-new concept. That was the kind of guy he was.

At IBM, he managed a group that invented technologies for printers and test robots, and had recently started to branch out into keyboards. He had always had a knack for solving problems in dreams or while taking a shower or just sitting around in his office. He could envision how designs might work in his head— something he called his "3-D imagination." The idea for the Butterfly keyboard came this way. In late 1992, he had been thinking about the subnotebook keyboard dilemma on his own, separate from the discussions that were going on in the PC division. At the time, his daughter, Amy, was three, and she had a set of wooden blocks. Some of them were triangular shapes made by taking a rectangular block and cutting it from corner to corner. One day, sitting at his desk in the office, Karidis was daydreaming about how to make a better keyboard for a subnotebook computer when his big idea came to him. Why not divide the keyboard into two pieces like the two triangular blocks that combined to make a rectangle, and slide them together to stow them in a computer case that had smaller dimensions? He envisioned stowing the two-piece keyboard inside the laptop when the lid was closed and having the two pieces shift out beyond the sides of the computer when the lid was lifted.

Over the next few days he tried out the idea until he was satisfied it would really work. First he made a bunch of photocopies of a full-size IBM keyboard, and, sitting on the floor of his office, he tried cutting the papers diagonally in different places. It looked like the best way to cut was from the *F4* key at the top of the keyboard in a jagged diagonal line past the *4*, *T*, *H*, *M*, and *Alt* keys. He glued the photocopies to pieces of Plexiglas and tried it out. Then he got Michael Goldowsky, one of the engineers in his group, to explore different mechanisms for moving the keyboard parts. Soon they went to a shop in the lab and had technicians cut an actual keyboard into two pieces along that line and put the pieces in a mechanical frame so they could demonstrate how the concept worked—folding out like the wings of a butterfly.

A few months later, in April 1993, Karidis had a chance to show his concept to a group of PC division executives. Claflin, Formichelli, and others gathered in a conference room in Somers to look at new design ideas for ThinkPad. They were a tough audience. When Karidis first showed them his contraption, he had the keyboard compacted. Then he turned his back to them and shifted the two sides into their extended positions. He was later told that while his back was turned, Formichelli whispered, " 'What an asshole!' " He didn't understand where Karidis was going with this demonstration. (Formichelli remembers things slightly differently: "I don't think I called John an 'asshole.' I think I said something like, 'Let's stop wasting our time with this tinker.' ") When Karidis turned around and showed the extended keyboard, they were all impressed. "Do it again," Claflin demanded. They made the decision on the spot to use the Butterfly design. By this time, the Raleigh team working on the subnotebook design had shown their work to Claflin, and he got behind it, so it was now an official development project. The Butterfly keyboard would be tried out in the 701C notebook.

They had their breakthrough idea, but now they had to make it work mechanically and to manufacture it. Karidis didn't want the computer user to have to do anything to deploy the keyboard. When the user opened the lid, the thing would pop out automatically. Getting that approach to work would take a lot of tinkering. But rather than handling all of the details himself, Karidis passed the project over to Goldowsky and Gerard McVicker from IBM

Research, along with Larry Stone and Joe Lamoreux in Raleigh. Meanwhile, Karidis moved on to become technical assistant to the head of Research, McGroddy. In midsummer 1993, when the first mechanical prototypes of the keyboard design came back, there was trouble. The devices were too flexible and didn't work reliably. Formichelli, who was still in charge of manufacturing at the time, called Karidis to his office in Somers to discuss the problems. Karidis didn't savor the idea of being pulled back into the thick of things, but Formichelli insisted. He felt Karidis was happy to get the accolades for the invention, but didn't want to be bothered making it work. They argued, and when they left Formichelli's office to go talk to another executive about the issue, Formichelli shouted at Karidis all the way down the hallway. "He said, 'You got us into this and you're going to get us out!' " Karidis recalls.

Formichelli got his way. For the next six months, Karidis traveled from New York to Raleigh every week and stayed at a Holiday Inn near IBM's campus in Research Triangle Park. He was often accompanied by Lucente, who did the industrial design for the computer. Karidis and a small mechanical engineering team tweaked the cam that opened and closed the keyboard, and they refined the dimensions of the slots underneath the keys that guided the two pieces into place. The keyboard needed to fully deploy every time and handle many openings and closings, so they then tested their prototypes with motorized testing devices that would open and close them thousands of times to verify the durability of all of the mechanical parts. They gradually worked through most of the problems, but, with two days left before a crucial deadline, one glitch remained. To make an electrical connection between the two pieces of the keyboard, they had designed a flexible electrical cable that looked like a slim golden ribbon. It ran along the edges of the keyboard where it split. They discovered that the cable was rubbing in one spot. How to fix it? Karidis and his colleagues worked around the clock and finally came up with an answer: they'd hold the cable in place with a small metal clip, which would cost less than one cent. That way the cable wouldn't slip out of place and cause friction. "When we put in the clip, the problem totally went away," recalls Karidis. They made their deadline.

The main lesson that Karidis took away from the Butterfly experience was that engineers and designers had to learn to judge when a brilliant concept they had would actually be doable—and how much effort it would take to make it work. "This is the way you have to operate if you're on the leading edge of technology," he says. "But it's really scary."

The top brass in the PC division loved the Butterfly keyboard. Claflin would proudly take some of the later prototypes of the machine on airplane flights to see how people reacted when he opened his laptop on the tray table and the keyboard popped out. Once, he recalls, he was sitting on a plane in the middle seat between an elderly gentleman, on his left, and an attractive young woman, on his right. He wanted to impress the young woman. He saw her glance at his ThinkPad when he placed it on the tray table. He opened it with a dramatic flourish. Unfortunately, he had just been served a mixed drink, which the flight attendant had set down on the table to the right of his ThinkPad. So when he opened the machine the Butterfly keyboard popped out, struck his drink, and splashed it into the lap of the attractive young woman. "Well, I got her to talk, but not the way I had in mind," Claflin says. "She shouted at me."

The ThinkPad 701C was launched in March 1995 and caused a sensation in the tech industry and beyond. The model was expensive, at $3,800, and its Intel 486 microprocessor made it underpowered compared to other top-of-the-line laptops, but the machine's small size and Butterfly keyboard captured the imagination of tech mavens and was written up in design magazines. The Museum of Modern Art in New York even bought one and put it on display. Because it was so small and light, the model found a new audience for ThinkPad: women. Claflin recalled that around the time of the introduction, two female reporters approached one of his product managers and told her, "You've finally created a product for women." He overheard this snippet of conversation and decided on the spot to begin marketing the 701C to women. One of the print ads that had been developed for the computer showed a man holding one of the slim machines with just three fingers. Claflin ordered the ad people to airbrush out the hair and make other changes to transform it into a woman's hand.

The hoopla lasted about six months. Lots of technology mavens bought the Butterflys and showed them off to their friends. But, after a while, the limitations of the machine began to emerge. Shortly after the product was launched, Intel came out with its first Pentium microprocessor—a tremendous advance on earlier chips. But the chip consumed too much power to go into the 701C without significant modifications to the machine. Then there was the issue of the screen size. As Toshiba and other display manufacturers improved their technology and manufacturing processes, they were able to manufacture ever-larger screens at ever-lower prices. Displays were on the way that would be 11.5 inches wide, so there would be no need for a foldout keyboard. The reason to use the Butterfly design was rapidly going away. Like the Erie Canal when the railroads came along, this innovative laptop had an all-too-brief viable economic life. "That was the death of the Butterfly," says designer Sapper.

The Butterfly wasn't a failure, though. The computer sold reasonably well during the short period it was on the market. And, coming on the heels of the first generation of ThinkPads, the Butterfly demonstrated that IBM would be on the forefront of laptop design. Claflin, as head of the IBM PC division, pushed the product development teams to operate right on the cutting edge of possibilities. "Our philosophy was it was okay to fail if you tried to do innovative things, but don't fail with a lot of inventory stacked up," says Claflin.

Sometimes the willingness to fail resulted in products that didn't sell well. One of the notable slow sellers was the ThinkPad 755CDV, which came out in 1995, and was another of Selker's brainchildren. It had a built-in projection panel that allowed users to remove the display cover and use the display with a standard overhead projector to project a presentation onto a wall screen. Selker had dreamed of making a computer that doubled as a projector for years, and, to gain traction for the idea, he walked around the giant COMDEX computer trade show in Las Vegas with a prototype of the machine hung by a strap over his shoulder. He'd explain his invention to anybody who would listen. After he finally got it produced, and it didn't sell well, Selker blamed the marketing staff for the slow sales.

Some of the most interesting ideas to come from IBM designers, engineers, and researchers never even made it to market. Karidis dreamed up the idea of putting all of the core electronics of a ThinkPad into a personal digital assistant (PDA) that would slip into the side of the laptop machine to run it, but when you wanted to travel light, you could pull the PDA out of the side of the computer and slip it into your pocket. The bosses didn't go for it.

Another stuck project was code-named LeapFrog. Back in 1989, two years before the ThinkPad project started, Sapper showed Hardy his idea for a multipurpose portable computer. He envisioned an elegant, thin tablet that people could carry around like a legal pad. It would also have a docking station so it could double as a regular desktop computer. Hardy assigned Lucente to work with Sapper and develop the concept into a product design. Lucente was excited by the notion of building a computer that you could draw on or speak to—replacing the keyboard with more natural means of communication between human and machine. He found scientists in IBM Research with expertise in voice processing and handwriting recognition to develop software for the project. He and Sapper produced industrial design specifications, and the researchers built a functional prototype by 1992. They kept refining it and adding innovations. One was the ability for the image on the screen to automatically switch from horizontal to vertical as the user turned the machine sideways—which ultimately became one of the impressive features of Apple's iPhone when it was introduced 15 years later. By 1995, they had built 40 limited-edition prototypes and let company executives, engineers, and customers try them out. The goal was to get some people excited enough about the project that they would fund a final round of development. But the LeapFrog never made the grade. Claflin loved the idea, but Cannavino hated it. At a meeting in Somers in the end of 1992, Claflin showed one of the prototypes to his boss. "Cannavino looked and looked at it," Claflin recalls. "He said, 'I see the frog but where's the leap?' " Lucente admitted by 1995 that the technology just wasn't advanced enough to make LeapFrog viable as a commercial product.

The ThinkPad inventions that went nowhere were disappointments to the people who gave birth to them, but, to Claflin, it was all part of building a powerful brand image. "Quite a few of the innovative ideas failed, but we failed nicely. It promoted the idea of innovation," he says.

What most people remember are the successes. With one model after another, the ThinkPad development teams set the pace for the industry. David Hill was put in charge of PC design in 1995. He and his team overhauled the entire desktop and server product lines. His goal for the laptops was to maintain the essence of Sapper's core concept for ThinkPad but to constantly refine the design over time. "It was about making ThinkPad better, not different," he recalls. The ThinkPad 560, released in 1996, was an ultraslim device with a 12.4-inch display. The ThinkPad 770, in 1997, was the first notebook computer in the industry to include a DVD drive. The ThinkPad I Series machines, out in 2000, were the first laptops with wireless communications capabilities designed in. ThinkPad engineers were the first to use a mix of titanium and composite materials to provide lightweight and superior strength. The Active Protection System, which debuted in ThinkPads in 2003, had a motion sensor and would detect when a person dropped his or her laptop. Before the machine hit the ground, the protection system would lock down the hard drive to protect the data on it from being scrambled on impact.

Over the years, ThinkPad built up a fiercely loyal following among hard-core techies and businesspeople who traveled extensively. Steve Peltzman, the chief information officer of the Museum of Modern Art in New York, was one of the ThinkPad fans. During the 1990s, when he was in the Air Force and got an MBA at Columbia University, every laptop computer he'd owned had been too heavy or too easily broken. But when he joined a technology start-up called EarthWeb in 2000, he had a chance to pick whatever laptop he wanted, and he chose a ThinkPad. He liked the design, the sturdiness, and, especially, the TrackPoint. He liked the machines so much that he had selected them to put on the desks of all of the employees in the lobby of MOMA when its massive redesign was unveiled in 2006. "When people walk into the museum you want them to see well-designed computers on the desks," he says. "The aesthetics, the black color, the sleek shape; It was a perfect match for us."

Even though ThinkPads weren't marketed to consumers or sold by big-box retailers, they made their way into the popular consciousness. They were sometimes even seen as fashion items. Early on, the ThinkPad PR team toyed with the idea of introducing the entire array of models in a fake fashion show, with models walking down a runway carrying the laptops. They didn't get approval from the bosses. But, in 1996, they placed a loaner of the ThinkPad 760, which had a 12-inch display and a built-in CD ROM drive, with a Hollywood insider and landed a story in *Vogue* with the headline, "The New Little Black Book" and a photo of a ThinkPad spilling out of a Hermès bag.

As one year and one model followed another, a succession of leaders struggled to improve profits and compete with the likes of Toshiba, Compaq, and Hewlett-Packard. Formichelli, fed up with the difficulties of getting the Butterfly made, moved all product engineering to Yamato. After him came Steve Ward, who was later to be named Lenovo's first American chief executive after the company's acquisition of the IBM PC division was completed in 2005. He was succeeded at ThinkPad by Adalio Sanchez, who later was a top IBM executive; Fran O'Sullivan, head of Lenovo's product group; and Peter Hortensius, who ran the notebook business after the merger.

Throughout the mid-1990s, IBM gradually came back from the brink. Gerstner decided to remake the company as a services outfit—running computing systems and help desks for corporations. The PC division lost money and market share year after year, but ThinkPad made money. Many people, insiders and outsiders alike, credited ThinkPad, along with IBM's improved financials, for reviving the company's brand image. Ted Clark, general manager of Hewlett-Packard's notebook computing unit, was at Compaq when the first ThinkPads came out and has competed against them ever since. "There's no question but that this helped save IBM's brand and reputation," he says. "Their desktop business had pretty much been blown up by Compaq, but ThinkPad revitalized their entire perception. It was well respected. It was a cool image. It was a breakthrough product." Gerstner himself doesn't give ThinkPad that much credit. "David Ogilvy [the famous Madison Avenue ad man] said building a brand is like a bird building a nest. It takes hundreds of twigs to build a nest," Gerstner says. "ThinkPad was not the major reason, but neither was anything else."

The people who made ThinkPad the most durable franchise in portable computing history took many different paths since those early days. After 22 years at IBM, Claflin went on to run the PC division at Digital Equipment Corp., and then to be chief executive of networking gear maker 3Com—where, among other things, he oversaw the Palm Pilot personal digital assistant. Formichelli went to Toshiba and later was a top executive at PC maker Gateway. Hardy left IBM to start his own design consulting business, working for clients including Ford, Verizon, and Samsung. Lucente went to Netscape, the browser company, where he guided much of the company's software user interface design, and later ran corporate design at Hewlett Packard. He still dreams of making the LeapFrog. "I built the prototype and I was in a waiting game for the technology," Lucente says. "I'm still waiting, but I know in my lifetime I'll see people walking around with half-inch thick slates talking to them and writing on them." Others who figured in the ThinkPad drama are still playing similar roles to those they had in the early days. Sapper is the design consultant not just for IBM but also for Lenovo. Naitoh, the father of ThinkPad engineering, is a Lenovo Fellow and still the vice-president for product development in Yamato. Yamazaki, collaborator with Sapper on the original ThinkPad, is a consultant to IBM and professor at Chiba Institute of Technology. And John Karidis is a Distinguished Engineer at IBM Research in Yorktown Heights. He's still dreaming and tinkering.

5

YANG'S DREAM

On a bright September afternoon in 2006, a black Mercedes S320 pulled up to a curb in the middle of Beijing's bustling Zhongguancun, the consumer-electronics shopping district. Out stepped a man in a conservative gray suit, with ink-black hair, a round face, and wire-rim glasses. He still possessed some of the youthfulness he had 18 years earlier when, as a shy, bean-thin science student, he first arrived in this neighborhood to begin his career in the computer industry. Then called Swindler's Alley, the area had been a disreputable bazaar for knockoff consumer electronics and black-market software. By 2006 all of that had been replaced by neon, steel, and glass—the physical embodiment of China's aspirations as an economic powerhouse.

Yang Yuanqing, 42, chairman of Lenovo Group, the leading PC company in China, stepped into the Ding Hao Electronics Mall and a dizzying scene. Everywhere there were signs, lights, and swarms of shoppers. Strolling from one store to another to peruse the displays of his company's devices, Yang, spoke quietly with shopkeepers. But each time he stopped, he was immediately surrounded by a scrum of people giddily snapping his picture with tiny digital cameras and camera phones. Yang was a rock-star executive—a Chinese Bill Gates.

It was in this neighborhood in 1988 that Yang began working for Lenovo—then a tiny company called Legend Group—in a nondescript three-story building. Yang slipped back into the

Mercedes and was soon gliding past the spot where he once bunked with four roommates in a company dormitory. Looking around, he realized that the building had been demolished to make way for a parking lot. "Everything has been torn down," marveled Yang. "It's a total changeover."

Yang himself had undergone no less startling a transformation. He grew up poor in Heifei, a backwater city in eastern China, during the Cultural Revolution. But on that day in 2006, he headed up a PC company with $13 billion in revenues—thanks in part to his high-risk 2005 purchase of the IBM PC division. Once a bumpkin in a country that turned its back on the world, he had become a globe-trotting executive with a luxury apartment overlooking New York's Central Park, a home in suburban Beijing, and a condominium in Raleigh, North Carolina, near Lenovo's executive headquarters.

Yang's dream for the future was even more audacious: to turn Lenovo into a highly respected global brand. He wanted it to become the first Chinese company to make the transition from local champion to global powerhouse. Yang's strategy was ambitious. Over several years, he wanted to boost Lenovo's already dominant 35 percent market share in China while expanding to other emerging markets. In the West, he tapped IBM for help in selling to large corporations. Meanwhile, the company was retooling the old IBM PC manufacturing supply chain to make it as efficient as Lenovo's China operations. Yang didn't have to do it all himself. He was surrounded by a team of veteran PC executives from America, China, South Asia, and Europe. His right-hand man as CEO was the hard-driving William Amelio, a former Dell executive.

As China's first truly global capitalist, Yang had a chance to help his homeland shed its image as a cheap manufacturing hub. For Yang's dream to come true, Lenovo would have to replace that negative image of China with a positive one. "Innovation is how we're going to differentiate ourselves," Yang vowed that day in Beijing. To make Lenovo's PCs stand out, Yang needed a potent weapon. He believed he had found it in ThinkPad. The famed IBM portable computing group had been the IBM PC company's one bright spot within a business that lost money and market share year after year. Throughout the 1990s and early 2000s, ThinkPad laptops had won praise from tech industry analysts and product reviewers for their quality, technology, and industrial design. Now, for Lenovo, Yang hoped ThinkPad would become a major source not just of revenue growth but of brand equity. To help make that happen, he set aside 20 percent of his R&D budget for cutting-edge ideas. "We have told our ThinkPad people that we're very loyal to innovation," said Yang. During the last years under IBM, the ThinkPad unit had become focused largely on cost-cutting. "It used to be, 'Can we save a penny?' Now it's, 'What new ideas do you have?'" said David Hill, Lenovo's executive director for corporate identity and design.

Richard Sapper, IBM's long-time industrial design consultant, had been concerned when Lenovo bought the PC company that it might throw out the ThinkPad design. "There were many dangers and many unknown things," he says. But he quickly discovered that Yang was committed to innovative design. Lenovo hired Sapper as its design consultant, and Sapper felt reassured when he met Yang. "I was very impressed," he says. "I found him to be very bright. He's very interested in design."

In the year after the IBM deal was done, the pressure on Yang was intense, and not just from shareholders. In the summer of 2005, a few months after the IBM sale closed, Chinese Premier Wen Jiabao paid a visit to Lenovo's Beijing offices. Yang took him on a tour of the facilities and showed him the latest PCs and cell phones. According to someone who was there, as the short visit wrapped up, Wen told Yang: "You carry the hopes of China on your shoulders."

Meanwhile, other Chinese business kingpins were watching closely to see if Yang stumbled. With China's domestic economy growing at 10 percent per year and foreign reserves topping $1 trillion, they were hungrily eyeing attractive overseas takeover targets—everything from oil to consumer electronics. Yet many Chinese executives wanted to see how Yang fared before they, too, plunged into globalization. Edward Tian, a friend of Yang's and former vice chairman of telecommunications giant China Netcom Group, explained how others viewed him: "In China there's an old saying, 'don't be the first one to eat the crab. It's difficult to get the meat out, and you might be poisoned.' People see Yang as the guy eating the crab. They're waiting to see if he'll survive."

While Yang is more of a risk taker than one might expect of a person who grew up in a communist state, his style is also highly calculating. Colleagues who spend evenings with Yang playing Tuolaji, a Chinese card game, say he studies his cards for a long time before making a move. Even when dealt a bad hand, he tries to figure out a way to win. They see parallels in how Yang plays cards to how he runs the company. He's willing to take risks, but only if he has thoroughly studied a situation and figures he has a reasonable chance of prevailing.

It's no mystery where his character traits come from. Yang's parents were tough taskmasters who demanded that he study hard and rank at the top of his classes. Both were surgeons, yet in 1960s' China they were paid the same as manual laborers and repeatedly sent to the countryside for reeducation and community service. They did what was expected of them without complaint. "They both had a lot of integrity," says Guo Liping, a family friend in Heifei. "They treated all of their patients the same way. It didn't matter if they were rich or poor, or a government official or a regular person." Yang recalls that his father was very strict and disciplined: "If he set a target, no matter what happened, he wanted to reach it."

The demands on his parents forced Yang to grow up fast. Starting at age 8, he cooked meals over a smoky coal fire for himself and two younger siblings on the balcony of the brick housing project where the family lived in a cramped apartment. In the summer, when the temperature could top 40 degrees centigrade, the children sometimes slept on the floor where it was a little cooler. Yang's only toy was a bag of marbles. If he wanted to play ball, he'd scrunch up a cast-off cigarette package. His mother, Wang Biqin, gave him a tiny allowance each month, but he rarely spent it because he knew that she might have to take it back to buy food. Yang knew nothing of the outside world. "It was a tragedy, but it was also lucky," he says, looking back. "If you don't know what's going on outside, you don't know what you're missing."

Yang escaped from the crushing drudgery of the housing project by visiting his mother's parents, who lived in a small house with a backyard garden in another part of Heifei. This was his haven. They were a little better off than his parents. His grandmother had managed to save a collection of hundreds of books from the Red Guard, which she kept in a small room. The volumes included classics of Chinese literature such as *The Westward Journey*, *The Dream of the Red Chamber*, and *Three Kingdoms*. During those visits with his grandma, he would lose himself in her books.

When asked what Yang was like when he was growing up, his father, Yang Furong, launches into a long tale. Yang studied ferociously for the national university entrance exams. One evening, he accompanied the rest of the family on a rare outing to a movie theater, but when the house lights came up at the end, the family discovered that his seat was empty. In midmovie, he had raced back home to study. "From very early on, Yuanqing didn't like to be behind anybody. He was never satisfied being number two. He always wanted to be number one," says his father.

His parents didn't want Yang to follow in their footsteps and become a doctor. The working conditions were just too harsh. And, rather than pursuing literature in the university, Yang decided on computer science on the advice of a professor who was a family friend. For the first time in his life, he began to dream of bigger things—including the possibility of eventually going to the United States to study. He got a bachelor's degree in 1986 from Shanghai Jiao Tong University, and a master's degree in 1989 from the University of Science and Technology of China, in Heifei, one of the country's premier technical institutions. It was when he was studying in Beijing to finish up his master's degree that he spotted an ad for a job at Legend in a newspaper. At the time it was a 100-person company that sold Sun Microsystems and Hewlett-Packard computers at retail. Yang had planned on being a university professor, but Legend intrigued him. He took a big risk when he signed on as a salesman at one of the few truly market-driven companies in all of China. His pay: $30 a month.

It was a fortuitous choice. Legend's chief executive, Liu Chuanzhi, had been one of 11 scientists at the Chinese Academy of Sciences who left the organization in 1984 to form New Technology Developer, China's first technology start-up. The academy backed the group with a $25,000 investment. Liu was already 40 years old, but he had amazing energy and was determined to take advantage of the economic reforms brought in by the country's leader, Deng Xiaoping. The company's first product was a small circuit card that could be added to a standard PC to translate Chinese characters. A short time later, the company changed its name to Legend and set up two separate organizations in Beijing and Hong Kong. Legend had a rocky first few years, but, by the time Yang landed there, it seemed to be on solid footing. Shortly after his arrival, the company introduced its first homegrown PC. Yang excelled as a salesman, and Liu eventually put him in charge of small businesses and then the company's crucial engineering workstation unit. There, he got to know Americans who worked for Sun and HP, and he gathered up every bit of knowledge he could about how to run a successful business.

A pivotal moment came in 1994. Liu was laid up in a Beijing hospital suffering from exhaustion and stress. Legend had begun selling its own PCs in 1990, but, when China opened the market to direct imports by foreign PC giants, it was caught in a pincer. As a publicly held company, Legend did not receive government support like state-owned PC outfits. Also it didn't have the financial strength of foreign PC makers. Flat on his back for weeks, Liu used the time to consult with his employees. He came away impressed with the youthful Yang's knowledge of the PC business and his Boy Scout–style honesty—not a small consideration at a time when Chinese enterprises were rife with corruption. Upon leaving the hospital, Liu decided to stay in PCs and create a separate division with the 29-year-old Yang in charge.

What Yang accomplished far exceeded Liu's expectations. In just three years he transformed Legend from an also-ran into the leading PC player in China. He switched from using only a direct sales force to also selling through a vast network of retailers. He also introduced a new management culture to Legend. He decided that managers needed to connect with their staff. For one thing, there were too many had highfalutin' titles with the word *zong*, the equivalent of *president*, in them; Yang wanted everybody addressed by their given name. To make the point, he ordered all of the *zong*s to stand outside the building every morning and greet workers while holding signs with their names written on them. "After two weeks, the change finally stuck," recalls Wang Xiaoyan, who is currently Lenovo's senior vice president for information services.

Along the way, Yang learned management lessons that would later prove vital. As the new boss of the PC division, he supervised several of the company's founders. That was hard for them to swallow. To make matters worse, Yang didn't have a diplomatic sinew in his body. He fired half of the staff, forced managers to radically alter the way they did business, bawled out people when they screwed up, and ignored criticism. It was not very Chinese of him. Liu saw that he very nearly had a revolt on his hands, so he called a management meeting to deal with it. "I criticized Yang so severely he almost broke down in tears," recalls Liu. "But this had a good effect. He started to change his work style."

While Yang became more diplomatic, he remained a reformer. When the PC division switched buildings in 1997, he used the move to break with the past. He insisted on a more formal dress code and trained all employees in phone etiquette. It wasn't until later that Legend employees understood what Yang was up to. He wanted Legend managers and employees to think and act like techies in Silicon Valley, Boston, or Berlin. Yang knew that unless Legend expanded beyond the borders of China, it would not be able to match the clout of the foreign PC giants. Legend's people had to get ready for that huge step.

Yang's other major priority was turning Legend into an innovation machine. Until then, the technology in PCs sold in China had been a generation behind those sold in the West. Legend shipped PCs based on Intel's new Pentium processor at the same time they were shipped in North America. Yang also opened up the now-vast consumer market with low-cost, super-easy-to-use PCs. One Legend model let PC novices set up an Internet connection with a single push of a button. His interest in design really took off after he visited Samsung's design center in Korea in 1998 and came away deeply impressed. Back in Beijing, he decided that Legend should have the same kind of design facility, so he set one up in 2000. The design center later moved to another location in Beijing. The staff there expanded to include a wide range of skills—everybody from industrial designers, user-interface specialists, and mechanical engineers to anthropologists and user-centric designers. They had rooms with one-way mirrors on the sides so they could watch people using computers without bothering them. Employees sat in cubicles around the edges of a large room. In the middle was a space called the "green house," a room with glass walls but with curtains all around so the latest designs could be kept secret from the prying eyes of visitors.

As Yang rose rapidly through the ranks at Legend, he also made his share of mistakes. The company was hobbled by an ill-advised foray into Internet businesses, which he had backed. The PC market had grown at a rapid pace between 1996 and 2000, but, as the millennium turned, PC demand softened at the same time the dot-com bubble burst. Legend needed to find new sources of revenue growth. First, in his role as Legend's president, Yang proposed a diversification strategy. The company would get into providing tech services, PC peripherals, and mobile phone handsets. The board approved his plan, and, in 2001, Liu handed over the CEO job to him. But the diversification strategy didn't fare well. With the exception of mobile phones, sales of the new products and services were disappointing.

Yang needed to do something else to get Legend back on a rapid-growth trajectory. The company was being challenged on its home turf by HP, IBM, and Dell. To remain viable, he concluded, it would have go global. "I decided I wanted to become an international company." Yang says. His first big opportunity came in the summer of 2002, when IBM's chief financial officer, John R. Joyce, traveled to China in May in hopes of selling the company's struggling PC business. Yang saw this deal as a way for Legend, which was about to rebrand itself as Lenovo, to become global without having to grind it out country by country. But the woeful condition of the IBM PC business put him off. The business had lost nearly $300 million the previous year, and, over the previous five years, it had lost more than $1.5 billion. So the discussions didn't go anywhere. Yang asked Mary Ma, his chief financial officer, to explore other possibilities. She talked to a small American firm, eMachines, and felt out Japan's NEC about buying its PC business. Nothing came of either foray.

A year and a half later, IBM came back into the picture. Lenovo was even hungrier for global expansion, and IBM had whipped its PC business into better shape. The loss in 2002 had been just $68 million. They agreed to begin talks that could have ended in anything from a strategic alliance to a takeover of IBM's PC business by Lenovo. Ma took her first trip to New York in November 2003 to get things going with IBM negotiator Peter Lynt. Liu had cautioned her not to fall in love with the deal, but Ma saw that IBM had radically restructured the PC unit. Costs had been slashed. Manufacturing for everything but the ThinkPad laptop line had been outsourced. "We were astonished to see the better numbers," says Ma. She returned to China an advocate for the deal.

She was in a distinct minority, though. The entire board of directors lined up against Yang. Think about what he was asking the Lenovo elders to do: a $3 billion company based in China would be taking over a $10 billion global behemoth. IBM had practically invented the PC industry; if Big Blue couldn't make money selling these machines worldwide, how could little Lenovo hope to do any better? "We had all built this company, and nobody wanted to take such a big risk," explains Liu.

Yang and his team were insistent. During the winter of 2004, they made presentation after presentation to the board. Ultimately, Yang won his elders over. Beginning on April 20, 2004, in the Beijing offices of the parent company, Legend Holdings, the board of directors had gathered in a windowless conference room on the tenth floor to grill Lenovo's executives and others about potential pitfalls of the acquisition. The event was something akin to a courtroom trial. In addition to Yang and Ma, the lineup of people making the case for the deal included people from consultant McKinsey to investment bank Goldman Sachs. The directors' chief concern: were Lenovo's execs really capable of running a complex global business? The breakthrough came after three days. The directors concluded that if Lenovo could recruit some of IBM's top executives to help manage the company, this merger could succeed. "The board felt there were positive solutions," says Liu.

The next challenge for Yang was negotiating an actual deal. IBM was cagey. It sought out private equity giant Texas Pacific Group as a rival bidder to use as leverage against Lenovo. "Peter would use the other bidder against us," recalls Ma. "He said, 'If you don't do that price, you're out.'" One of the key goals for Yang was to gain control of IBM's PC-related patents. He saw that a lot of the value of the deal would come via intellectual property and innovation.

A major breakthrough came in the summer of 2004 during secret talks at the luxurious Siena Hotel in Chapel Hill, North Carolina. After a series of meetings, Yang and IBM CEO Samuel J.

"Sam" Palmisano agreed this would be more than just a simple sale of assets. Instead, the two companies would form a strategic alliance, as well.

While the general idea had been floating around for months, the two companies nailed down the details to make a long-term partnership compelling for both sides. IBM would sell Lenovo PCs through its sales force and distribution network. IBM also would provide services for Lenovo PCs—and allow Lenovo to use the vaunted IBM brand name for five years. In turn, Lenovo, leveraging its connections with the government's Chinese Academy of Sciences, would help IBM in the fast-growing China market.

IBM ended up with two options for its PC division. At a board meeting on October 26, 2004, Ward and IBM CFO Mark Loughridge laid out the offers from both Lenovo and Texas Pacific. They were attractive enough that directors OK'd a deal with either one. Ultimately, on the first weekend in December, Palmisano accepted Lenovo's bid. The offer was higher, at $1.25 billion, and the help in China was a substantial sweetener. Even Texas Pacific saw the logic behind Palmisano's decision. The company, along with private equity players General Atlantic Partners and Newbridge Capital, later invested $350 million in Lenovo.

But who would be the CEO of the new company? The Chinese chose Steve Ward, another veteran IBM executive who had also run the PC company. Ward was thrilled. Interviewed about it later, he recalled how he had listened to news of Nixon's historic visit to China on the radio when he was a 17-year-old pumping gas at his father's Exxon station in Santa Maria, California. "If you had told me then that I would lead the first-ever merger of a Chinese company and an American company, I would have been stunned," Ward says.

The deal, which was announced on December 7, 2004 in Beijing and Armonk, New York, was greeted with a mixture of reactions. Some tech analysts predicted that the merger would be very difficult to pull off and the new Lenovo would lose a substantial amount of market share while its new leadership team sorted things out. Others saw the new company as an important counter-weight globally to Dell, which was then seen as a dominating force in the PC industry. IBM's Palmisano believed this was an historic opportunity to change the dynamics of the industry. "The rest of the PC industry is now competing with a Chinese company, with its aggressiveness on price, backed with the quality and services of IBM," he said on the day the deal was announced.

A few years later, looking back on the transaction, it became clear what it had meant to IBM. While the company gave up some revenue growth by shedding the PC business, its profit margins had improved dramatically. PC companies made 3 to 4 percent in operating profits, about the same as a good supermarket chain. IBM's operating profit margin in 2007 was 15 percent. There were other benefits for IBM, too. By helping to turn Lenovo into a global PC player, IBM increased the pressure on its main rivals in the overall computer business, Hewlett-Packard and Dell. "We like to see a fragmented, competitive marketplace where these guys have to put money and research and focus into getting a few points of profit margin," explained a senior IBM executive who had been involved in the Lenovo deal. "Let them fight like crazy, and compete like crazy, and we stay off in our own space."

Back in late 2004, when Palmisano agreed to the merger, there were plenty of details to work out. When Ward and Yang met for lunch at IBM's Madison Avenue offices in New York City for a get-to-know-you session just before the deal was announced, Yang said that he favored setting up dual headquarters, in the United States and China. It was a point of national pride. Ward disagreed, saying there should be a single one, in New York. They couldn't resolve the issue over lunch. But a couple of days later, Yang came around. "Steve made a lot of sense," he says. "Putting the headquarters in New York tells our global customers that we're a global company."

After the deal was announced, Yang and Ward set out to meld two corporate cultures into one by selecting the best attributes from each side. Yang declared English to be Lenovo's official language. But they found that the culture gap was huge. For instance, the Chinese didn't tolerate being tardy for meetings, while IBMers were often late. Also, the Chinese stood on ceremony while the Americans did not. In late December 2004, when Yang, Ma, and eight other Lenovo execs landed at John F. Kennedy International Airport in New York for their first planning meetings, nobody met them. Not good; in China, visitors are greeted and taken to their hotels in limos. "We blew it," says Brad Hall, an IBM consultant working on the transition. "Yuanqing brought it up at a meeting, and Steve said, 'We'll fix that.' "

In the first few months after the deal was announced, executives from both sides worked feverishly to get off to a fast start. Initially, to avoid disruptions, they planned on operating three separate business units—China PCs, China cell phones, and international operations, which were formerly IBM's. But they planned to quickly integrate the supply chain. Lenovo executives moved into the fourth floor of a small office building five miles from IBM headquarters. Seventy people worked there, including Ward, Yang, and Ma. Meanwhile, back in Beijing, Liu prepared to give up command of the company he had led for 21 years. It was an unsettling big change for someone who started the company with $24,000 in a two-room cottage near Swindler's Alley and built it into one of China's most respected businesses. "I am quite satisfied with what I have accomplished so far," he says. "So now I'm stepping back and letting a younger generation lead."

After the acquisition closed in May 2005, Yang seemed to fade from view while Ward emerged as the new company's front man. Yet, behind the scenes, Yang was positioning Lenovo as a firm ally of Intel, the leading supplier of microprocessors for PCs, and Microsoft, the operating system giant. Both companies agreed to set up cooperative innovative centers in Raleigh and Beijing. Even more important, thanks to his influence in China, Yang was able to address Microsoft's concerns with software piracy there. Microsoft had been struggling for years to get Chinese computer users to pay for software, yet most of them still bought PCs that didn't include Windows and later loaded illegal copies on their machines. In July 2005, during a meeting at Microsoft headquarters in Redmond, Washington, Gates and Microsoft Chief Executive Steven A. Ballmer asked Yang for help with piracy, and, over the next few months, Yang worked out a deal with Microsoft China executives. They agreed to give him a rebate on Windows and marketing help in exchange for him agreeing to load it on most Lenovo PCs sold in China. Yang gambled that other Chinese makers would follow suit, and, thanks to pressure from the government, they did. Microsoft's sales of Windows shipped on PCs in China tripled in the following 12 months. Says Ballmer: "Yuanqing made a huge difference. He was willing to go out on a limb."

Yang also proved to be surprisingly adept at dealing with U.S. politics. In the spring of 2006, a hail of criticism greeted news that the U.S. State Department had bought 16,000 Lenovo PCs for use in offices worldwide. Critics, including CNN's Lou Dobbs, tarred Lenovo as a government-owned company that might help the Chinese government spy on the United States. In a surprising move, Yang spoke out publicly about the matter. "We are not a government-controlled company," he insisted, pointing out that Legend had been the pioneer of the Chinese transformation from the planned economy to the market economy. In the early 1990s, the Chinese PC market was dominated by four government-backed organizations that got special treatment. "We beat them," Yang said. As a result, Legend became the dominant PC maker in China. In the end, the State Department transaction went through, though some of the Lenovo PCs, which had been manufactured in the United States and Mexico, were shifted to less sensitive roles in the sprawling organization.

Concerned that the issue of Lenovo's relationship with the Chinese government would continue to be an issue in Washington, D.C., Yang made his case directly to Congress on a sweep through Capitol Hill. In June 2006, at a business conference in San Francisco, he switched name tags at a table so that he could sit next to C. Richard D'Amato, a member of the congressional advisory committee that had raised the security concerns. D'Amato later said he was impressed with Yang's earnestness, but "nothing really changed my thinking." Still, the issue quickly died down.

In the meantime, Lenovo's board had made a switch at the top. Although Ward and Yang denied there was ever any major tension between them, in December 2005, Yang and the board pushed out Ward, in part because he was too slow to cut costs. Ward's replacement as CEO was Amelio, who had been running Asian operations for Dell. Amelio thought the combination of Lenovo's strength in Asia and efficiency combined with the global reach of the former IBM operations gave him something to work with. So he said he was interested.

The initial encounters between Yang and Amelio were tense. No wonder, they had been head-to-head competitors in the China market. Amelio recalled their first awkward meeting at a Hong Kong hotel: "Here we were, two guys who have been trying to slit each other's throats talking about doing something together."

At their second meeting, Yang surprised Amelio by pulling out a single sheet of paper listing the roles for Lenovo's chairman and CEO. His job included setting corporate and technology strategy and communicating with investors. Amelio's main task was running the PC business day to day. This is not the typical split between chairman and CEO—Yang would be much more hands-on, like a co-CEO. Still, Amelio went along without complaint. "I was surprised that he agreed so quickly," says Yang. "He looked at it for three minutes and said, 'OK.' "

Amelio had grown up in a blue-collar family in the south end of Pittsburgh, the son of a shoe repairman. After getting a degree in chemical engineering at Lehigh University, he went to work for IBM in 1979 and rose rapidly through the ranks until he ran the ThinkPad business and then was general manager for operations at the IBM PC division. He had executive positions at Honeywell and NCR before going to Dell in 2001. Amelio, whose appearance reminded some of his new Chinese colleagues of Russia's Vladimir Lenin, was energetic, blunt spoken, and impatient. He explained why he took the job: "This is probably one of the most challenging assignments on the planet, but you have a chance to do something unique. You feel like a pioneer."

Yang as chairman and Amelio as CEO made for an unusual management setup. Yang ran the company, and Amelio reported to him. But they shared a lot of responsibilities for overseeing the sprawling organization on a near-equal basis. "Bill often calls me boss, but I don't want to put myself only in the boss position," explains Yang. "I want to contribute more to the company at all levels." Amelio's attitude was, "We divide and conquer."

If Lenovo stumbled, it wouldn't be for lack of intensity. Former IBMers say the pace of business and decision making picked up after Ward left. That relentless style was visible in the summer of 2006 in the massive third-floor atrium of the Lenovo Building in Beijing's sprawling Shangdi Information Industry Base, where a huge billboard with a map of China was divided into 18 sales regions. Across the bottom were columns showing the sales and ranking of each region. Every day at 7:30 p.m., totals were tallied and messages went out to all of the managers' mobile phones. If a region came in with less then 100 percent of its quota, its manager immediately was required to produce a plan for turning things around.

Yang's stature grew gradually after the IBM deal was consummated. Shortly after the takeover, the board created a powerful strategy committee headed by Yang but packed with other strong voices, including IBM's Bob Moffat and Lenovo cofounder Liu. At first, the committee met monthly. By mid-2006, it was meeting just once a quarter. Bill Grabe of General Atlantic Partners, one of Lenovo's private equity investors, explained: "Today, Yang is the guy who runs the strategy and sets the agenda."

That September, at the time of Yang's triumphant tour of Beijing's gleaming electronics shopping district, he seemed to be on top of things. Yet he was anything but complacent. At the end of a long workday, he sat at a table in the Bai Family Courtyard Restaurant in Beijing—a setting as far from the smoky balcony in Heifei as you could imagine. The restaurant was decorated in the style of Beijing's Imperial Palace, and the waitresses dressed like Qing Dynasty princesses in elaborate headdresses and lavishly embroidered silk clothing. They brought dish after exquisite dish, an overabundance that seemed designed to make up for the privations of China's past.

For a moment, Yang appeared relaxed—China's modern-day prince in repose. But that was only temporary. When asked what kept him up at night, Yang quickly answered: almost everything. "I have a lot of anxiety dreams," he said. "It's the normal emergencies of running a company every day. A customer complains. We're not able to meet demand. There's a shortage of parts. I often wake up, and sometimes I'm up all night." One of his worries was whether Lenovo would be able to come up with a steady stream of innovative products—including ThinkPads—that would help it establish a global brand.

6

KODACHI

David Hill, who headed up corporate identity and design for Lenovo, acted like a museum tour guide as he ushered me through the design center at what was then Lenovo's headquarters building in Raleigh's Research Triangle Park. The large room, perhaps 30 feet by 50 feet, was jokingly called the "fancy eating room" by the Raleigh designers—a reference to the 1960's TV show *The Beverly Hillbillies*. It seemed like every object there held a story. Dozens of design award plaques lined the walls, and trophies were displayed prominently on glass shelves. In one corner were two rows of gray airplane seats that had been pulled from a worn-out craft on its way to the salvage yard. They were used by human-factors design engineers to test out the usability of notebook computer designs. Perhaps three dozen PCs of different vintages were scattered around the room on top of a flotilla of three-foot-tall white cubes. The dark blue fabric-covered chairs, scattered around a long black table at one end of the room, had been fashioned by the legendary designer Charles Eames in 1957. In an embarrassing miscalculation, Eames gave the aluminum-frame chairs four casters instead of five—which made them devilishly unstable. Once, years before, when IBM design consultant Richard Sapper was sitting in one of the chairs during a meeting, he leaned over to pick up something he had dropped and the chair flipped over—depositing him unceremoniously on the floor. "I seem to have fallen out of my chair," Sapper said drolly. It was a case of design getting the best of a designer.

Hill, who was 49 years old at the time, gave this tour in late June 2006, just over a year after Lenovo had bought the IBM PC division. This was a turning point. During the final few years, IBM had lost interest in being in the PC business. The company was getting rid of commodity and low-margin businesses like PCs and focusing on services, software, chips, and high-end computers. That had been a dismal time for the ThinkPad crew. Their orders from headquarters were to make improvements, sure, but to mainly focus on changes that would cut costs. There was trepidation in Raleigh when Lenovo took over. Would their new Chinese masters be any more interested in innovation than their old American masters had been? But, quickly, Chairman Yang Yuanqing sent a clear message to the product development teams: breakthrough innovation was back in style. To signal how much he cared about design and engineering, he flew to the ThinkPad lab in Yamato, Japan, within a few days of the merger closing and spent an evening of beer drinking and karaoke singing with a group of employees. Hill understood that if ever there was a time for the ThinkPad designers to push forward with new ideas, June 2006 was it. During breaks in the executive strategy sessions he had collared Yang and William Amelio, the company's new chief executive, and walked them through a little show aimed at getting them excited about new design concepts.

He gave me the same tour. First stop: the first prototype for the original ThinkPad notebook computer, produced by Sapper in 1992. It was a simple rectangular box about an inch and a half (38 millimeters) thick, flat black, with nothing marring the external surfaces. Sapper's concept had been to make something simple, elegant, and timeless. Next, Hill showed me the most famous of the early ThinkPads, the 701C, also known as the "Butterfly," which was released in 1995. This was the slim nine-inch (228.6-millimeter)-wide subnotebook model that opened up and a full-size keyboard popped out—extending over the right and left sides by an inch (25.4 millimeters). Hill opened and closed the Butterfly a few times so I could appreciate its precision. I was impressed.

"Hmmmmm," I said. "Why don't you combine these two concepts and come up with a new machine?"

"Funny that you should suggest that," Hill said.

With a showman's flourish, he pointed to yet another small black object sitting on a nearby tabletop. This one was just as simple as the original ThinkPad prototype. It looked like a perfect piece of black granite about half an inch (12.7 millimeters) thick. There were no connector plugs or ventilation grills or on/off switches marring its smooth shell. He explained that it was inspired by the simple and elegant Japanese black lacquered "bento" lunch boxes. Hill slowly lifted the lid of the box, which was about ten inches (254 millimeters) wide, and he pointed to a series of connector plugs that were positioned along the side of a case that rose up out of the outer shell as he opened the lid. They were hidden when the lid was closed. Hill explained that he thought it just might be possible to eliminate all of those plugs altogether—even the power cord. What if this new computer connected to the world totally wirelessly? And what if it was powered and charged by placing it in a docking station where the electrical current would be received through a flat piece of metal on the bottom of the machine? No plug. The only mark on the external shell of this machine would be a tiny hole on the bottom—the drain for the keyboard in case somebody spilled coffee on the computer.

Next, Hill showed me another black plastic model. When he opened this one, a keyboard that had been folded inside popped out and into place as a full-size keyboard very similar to the original Butterfly design. It was called Butterfly II.

His idea was to revive and bring together two of the design concepts that had made the ThinkPad brand famous. He would update those concepts for modern times with the very latest in computing technology. It would be the epitome of design and engineering excellence—what a Mercedes CLK-Class Cabriolet convertible is in the automobile world. "We took the two ideas and combined them. I call it the Bento-Fly," Hill said, smiling at the quirkiness of the name.

Craig Merrigan, then the vice president of strategy and market intelligence for Lenovo, who had accompanied me on the design tour, wanted to make sure I understood just how big Hill's idea was. "This will be the best ThinkPad ever. In fact, it will be the best computer ever built," he declared.

Chairman Yang had urged his designers to think big, and they were taking him up on it. Hill, Merrigan, and the design teams in Raleigh and Yamato had this crazy idea that they should fashion a new computer that would be the ultimate expression of excellence in the notebook form. This machine would demonstrate to the world that the ThinkPad brand was as strong as ever—no—*stronger*. They'd deliver this new machine in the months leading up to the Olympics, where Lenovo was to be one of the top sponsors, and they'd show people, prove to the doubters and the naysayers, that Lenovo, this melding of cultures and countries, could design and manufacture the best computer. Better than Apple, Hewlett-Packard, Dell, or Toshiba. Better than IBM had ever done.

Hill got positive reactions when he showed his design concepts to the company's top executives. Yang asked: "When will people be able to buy this?" Hill explained to him that it was still just a concept computer.

This conversation happened the day before I took the tour of the fancy eating room. To me, as my tour ended, Hill explained that the journey between a compelling design concept like Bento-Fly and a finished notebook PC would take more than a year and involve dozens of designers, engineers, marketers, and procurement experts. This is where the journey started—with a design concept and a spark of excitement. Hill left me with this thought: "Design is viewed in Lenovo as being a cornerstone of our strategy. It's the cornerstone of innovation. It's innovation you can see and use."

Over the following months, during what Lenovo calls the "concept phase" of a potential product development project, some of Hill's concepts would come in for a real drubbing. One by one, the most radical elements would fall away—victims of the realities of designing and building a thin and light computer for sale in a fast-changing and intensely competitive market. But the core idea would remain: an ultralight, ultraslim, ultrasimple design packed with all of the cutting-edge technologies that would put ThinkPad back on the map and help establish Lenovo's brand globally as an innovative company. The goal was still to produce the best portable computer ever.

Hill had long played an important role in keeping the ThinkPad design concept alive and current even as technology and times changed. He was designing big machines at IBM's minicomputer division in Rochester, Minnesota, when Richard Sapper defined ThinkPad's design language back in 1992. And the most radical ThinkPad designs had already been done when Hill arrived at the IBM PC division in 1995. But from then on he managed the design of one ThinkPad after another. Over the years, the notebooks became ever thinner and lighter. Designers chamfered the lower half on the front of the machines to make them easier to pick up. They installed a "ThinkLight" on the inside of the lid so people could see the keyboard when they were flying in a darkened jet liner. And they improved the latch so people could open their ThinkPads one-handed. Hill was an apostle for Sapper's concepts. His Bento-Fly idea was an attempt to take ThinkPad back to its roots and to extend what he saw as a great design tradition into the future. Here's how he explained his thinking: "I asked myself, 'What if we could make it perfect?' This is the perfect expression of the original ThinkPad idea."

Indeed, one of Hill's main missions in life was protecting the ThinkPad brand and design essence. Shortly after he arrived at the PC division in 1995, one of the top executives had called him into his office and told him it was time to come up with a new design for the ThinkPads. Hill was stunned. He sought counsel from his own boss, who advised him to do nothing and see if the idea blew over. It did. A few years later, after Apple came out with a candy-colored laptop, another executive called him up and shouted at him—telling him he was out of touch with the latest design ideas.

"David has faced a lot of challenges over the years," said Aaron Stewart, a human-factors design specialist who worked for Hill. "When something doesn't change much, you get the question, 'Doesn't that look too much like what we've done before?' Other companies change design all the time. David has to defend the idea of keeping the essence."

Hill grew up in the cultural backwater of Bartlesville, Oklahoma, where his father was a research chemist at Phillips Petroleum. As a youngster, he made elaborate machines out of Tinker Toys, and, as he grew up, he took a considerable interest in motorcycles. He bought one as soon as he was permitted—which was age 14 in Oklahoma. Even in his late forties, he was still interested in cycles. He restored a 1979 Husqvarana, made in Sweden, which he rides in vintage motorcycle races. "It's an important piece of my life, this combination of art and design and motorcycles and how things work," he told me.

It was at Kansas University that Hill discovered design. He had the good fortune of studying with Downer Dykes, a professor of design who reveled in the role of devil's advocate. Dykes would assign his charges what seemed on the surface like simple projects, like, say, a hot plate. He'd give them very little information to go on, and when they brought in their first sketches, he'd ask endless questions—most of which seemed designed to reveal that they hadn't thought very deeply or practically about the uses of the object they were designing. How would the hot plate be stored, or cleaned, for instance? "I found out there was a lot to learn about designing something so simple," says Hill.

Hill remembers clearly the first time he saw Sapper. In 1981, he won a scholarship to the International Design Conference in Aspen, Colorado, where Sapper was one of the speakers. The theme of the conference was the Italian Idea, and, though Sapper was German, he had long before established his aesthetic residency in his adopted country of Italy. In the Aspen presentation, Sapper described how he had gone about designing the Tizio lamp in 1972. Hill was impressed by how down to earth Sapper was. He didn't act like a design god. He was dressed in jeans and a blue work shirt.

They first met years later when Hill worked for IBM and Sapper was the company's industrial design consultant. The encounter took place in 1990 in Poughkeepsie, New York, where IBM manufactured mainframe computers. Hill showed a computer display he had designed—essentially an electronic clipboard that attached to a large server computer so technicians could do diagnostic work on the machine. Sapper liked it so much that he approached Hill after the meeting and told him so.

Later, they worked together closely on designing a product—the IBM NetVista X40, which went on sale in 2000. It was an all-in-one PC that could fit compactly on an office desk. To save space, they put all of the electronics in the back of a 15-inch (381-millimeter) flat-panel display. Like every other product at IBM, it was flat black. The NetVista won all sorts of awards and accolades. It debuted the same year as Apple's all-in-one iMac computers—which came in a variety of candy colors. Hill took great satisfaction in one review that said the NetVista X40 looked like it could steal the iMac's lunch money and beat it up after school. He gives Sapper a lot of the credit for the design. Says Hill: "Richard has an uncanny ability to turn the ordinary into the extraordinary with almost everything he does."

With a shared history like that, it was no surprise that Hill took his Bento-Fly concept to Sapper to get his advice. Sapper was ready to help. After Lenovo bought the IBM PC division, it hired Sapper on as a design consultant, in the same role he had played—and continued to play—at IBM. "He's helping us to envision the future and continuously evolve the ThinkPad," said Hill. "It's very collaborative. He's like our friend. He helps us stay on course, and makes suggestions on how to improve things."

While Sapper most often met with the Lenovo crew in Raleigh and Yamato, this time Hill decided to meet the master on his home turf. He took with him Tomoyuki Takahashi, manager of technical operations and design for the Yamato lab, who had designed the much-praised ThinkPad X41 convertible tablet PC—which functioned either as a conventional laptop or a pen-based tablet. Takahashi, called "Tom" by the Americans, was a 25-year IBM veteran with lanky, shoulder-length hair and a quiet, Zen-like manner. This was to be his first visit with Sapper in Italy, and he got upset with himself when he realized he had forgotten his camera.

They were to meet Sapper at his studio in Milan, but at the last minute he invited them to visit him at his house on Lake Como. He even volunteered to pick them up at their hotel and chauffeur them to the meeting. This was on a Sunday in mid-June. Sapper fancied himself as something of a Formula 1 race car driver and it was a hair-raising trip on curvy roads in his BMW 5 Series station wagon. The house, which had been designed by Sapper's friend and former business partner, the famous designer and architect Marco Zanuso, was set on the edge of the lake, in a V shape facing the water. The three sat around a table on a deck in the middle of the V with the lake and the Alps spread before them. They discussed several designs, including Bento-Fly—examining models that had been made by craftsmen in the Yamato lab.

Sapper liked the Bento-Fly concept. He had been deeply involved in the original Butterfly design, working with John Karidis, the mechanical engineer and inventor from IBM Research. Hill wanted to make the keyboard on Bento-Fly deploy manually. The computer user would snap it into place. The point was to avoid some of the complexity of the original design—which had caused some hard-to-overcome manufacturing problems. Sapper disagreed. He thought the keyboard should still deploy automatically. "It has to have an element of magic," he told Hill and Takahashi. They talked about the possibility of using a tiny motor to lift and spread the keyboard. At the end of the day, Sapper dropped his two colleagues off at the railroad station at the north end of Lake Como so they could catch a train back to Milan.

Two weeks later, they were back together again in Morrisville. At the same time that Lenovo's top executives were meeting there to map out strategy, the designers had come in from all over the world to review their projects and get Sapper's feedback and advice. This gathering included Hill and his Raleigh design colleagues; Yao Yingjia, the head of Lenovo's design innovation center in Beijing, and some of his key designers; and Takahashi, and some of the other designers from Yamato. Two companies with three predominant national cultures had merged into Lenovo when it bought the IBM PC division. The goal was to create a single corporate culture, and this meeting was aimed partly at settling on a unified design strategy. "We talked about the idea of having some design attributes or functional aspects carry across the entire product line," Hill recalls. "When you take two companies and put them together, you have two worlds. We want to create a more seamless world with two slightly different views to it. This was an opening discussion, not a conclusion."

It was an intense discussion, though. One dozen people met around the table in the design center for four days straight. One of the Beijingers, Johnson Lee, said later that he had initially been intimidated by the prospect of meeting Sapper. Lee was the head designer for what was then called "Old Lenovo" to distinguish it from the part of the company that was "Old IBM." He had studied Sapper's work in school and thought the German, then 73, looked severe and unapproachable in photos that were published on the Internet. In person, though, Sapper was "warm and easy to communicate with," said Lee.

Still, there was a rift between Lenovo's American and Chinese designers. Hill wanted to stick to the ThinkPad design tradition as it had been laid out by Sapper. Yao and his people were interested in breaking new ground. Hill was in charge of commercial product design globally, and Yao was in charge of design for consumers. So their customers were very different. But could their design philosophies be very different, too? It was one company now. There was no need to answer this question immediately, but, still, the unresolved issue stuck like a thorn.

Wary of cultural differences getting in the way of effective collaboration, Hill had been trying to build bridges between the three design and engineering teams. A couple of months earlier, when Yamato and Beijing colleagues had been in Raleigh for a series of meetings, he had arranged for a one-day off-site meeting at Ray Price Harley-Davidson in Raleigh, one of the biggest Harley motorcycle dealerships in the country. The sprawling multistory building had showrooms for motorcycles, a museum, an accessories shop, and a room set aside for meetings of the Harley Owners Group, called the HOG Room. Hill thought the dealership would be an inspiring setting, since Harley's powerful brand, quality engineering, and design traditions had kept the company successful decade after decade. ThinkPad had the same kind of tradition, and he wanted to make the similarities between the Harley and ThinkPad brands crystal clear. "If you changed the design of the Harley-Davidson Motorcycle, game over. Nobody would buy one," says Hill.

There was plenty to learn from Harley-Davidson. The company had two brands, Harley-Davidson and Buell. Harley-Davidson kept the old-time religion for the company's die-hard customers, and Buell was a sporting modern bike whose stylings would change with the shifting tastes of young motorcyclists. During the Lenovo brainstorming session, which took place in the HOG Room, Hill, Takahashi, Yao, and a dozen other designers talked about creating a ThinkPad subbrand that would be aimed at consumers. It was just an idea. Nothing came of it. But within a few months the Beijing team had launched a new development project that ultimately resulted, in early 2008, in a new line of notebooks for the global consumer markers, called Idea-Pad.

Yao was a slightly built man with a round face and a lawn of short-cropped black hair. He dressed like an elegant bohemian, often in black and white, and sometimes in clothing of his own design. In September 2006, Yao and I were having lunch in an executive dining room at Lenovo's headquarters in the northern suburbs of Beijing. We sat by a glass wall, with a beautiful artificial waterfall just outside. Yao was anything but calm. He barely picked at his food and explained that if he ate a big lunch he'd feel sluggish later in the day.

The challenges before him were huge. In fact, they were so great that he had decided to expand his knowledge of business by getting an MBA even while he ran design operations in Beijing. At that point, Lenovo sold consumer products only in China, but it was planning on expanding its consumer business all over the world over the next few years. It would be risky. Consumers are fickle. They would have different tastes in different countries. And profit margins are ultrathin. So Yao had a heavy load on his shoulders as he marched into the future. Even more than with commercial products, consumer PCs depend a lot on design for their appeal. "Design should be like flowing water," he told me, pointing to the waterfall. "You need to keep going. Don't stop your thinking. Always get new ideas."

Yao had met Sapper a handful of times since the two companies merged. Some of Sapper's feedback had been useful, but Yao didn't think the new Lenovo needed an external design consultant. "There are some differences within the company over what his role should be," Yao confided. "Richard is a good designer, but if we want to define the design strategy for our future, we should do it for ourselves, not let somebody else control it."

For his part, Sapper was high on the potential for industrial design coming from Yao and his Chinese designers. Earlier, Sapper had taught courses at the Academy of Fine Arts in Beijing, and was familiar with the design scene in China. He was encouraged by his first encounters with Yao and other Lenovo designers from Beijing, and he felt that it was just the beginning of what he hoped would be a long and fruitful relationship. "When I first worked with the [IBM's] Japanese designers, it took me about 5 or 10 years to gain their faith. They were very much afraid," he told me when I visited him at his Milan studio in October 2007. "Now everything is wonderful in Japan."

Yao's strong views on PC design came out of the economic explosion he had witnessed in China over the previous decade. He had grown up in northern China and studied graphic design and industrial design in the university—then got the job as Legend's first industrial designer right after graduating. Legend was already the number-one PC seller in China, and Yang, who ran the company's PC business, meant to keep it that way. He wanted to use design to differentiate Legend's products from those of its Chinese and foreign competitors. He handed the task to Yao and told him to set up a real design department. "He wanted people-oriented design, not just technology," says Yao. At first, Yao concentrated on designs that would make it easy for China's PC beginners to learn to use the machines. One of his most important designs, the Tianxi, included a button that would take them instantly to the Internet. It also had a small handwriting tablet for users to enter Chinese characters. The Tianxi was the most successful PC ever in China up to that point, with more than one million machines selling in the year 2000 alone. Yang was so pleased with the work of the designers that, during a party to celebrate Tianxi's success, he praised Yao and two other designers and then did something that was very much out of character for a Chinese executive at the time: he hugged them.

Yao constantly refreshed the look and feel of Legend's computers. And, as time went on, he increased the pace of new product development. Often, the PCs he introduced would have only a six-month life cycle, and, in some cases, they'd only last three months in the marketplace before they needed to be updated or replaced. "The customers are getting lots of new stuff. They're quick to accept new concepts, so market trends change fast," he explained during that interview in Beijing. "You have to introduce a lot of new products and change them rapidly."

Over time, Yao's designs became more and more sophisticated, and he was more than willing to try new and potentially controversial things. In mid-2006, wherever he traveled, he took with him a consumer notebook PC, the Tianyi F20, designed for the

Chinese market, which was red and black molded plastic and had a textured grip that invited people to pick it up and carry it. His industrial design crew, led by Johnson Lee, had created another consumer notebook for the China market, called the Mountain PC, which had a drawing of craggy mountaintops on the lid. These designs were about as far from ThinkPad orthodoxy as you could get.

Lee had a style of working that drew deeply from Chinese traditions. Around the office, he carried with him a 2,500-year-old collection of Chinese sayings, and, if he got stuck on a design problem, he'd read the book to get inspiration. He had underlined many of his favorite passages in yellow marker. He considered his collection of aphorisms to be like the unseen roots of a tree. Taken together, the tree and its roots represent to him the design process itself. "The physical elements, the surface, need a soul and a spirit beneath them," he told me when we met in Beijing.

Like Lee, Yao sometimes sounded more like a Confucian monk than a twenty-first-century design trailblazer. During a tour of his design center shortly after our lunch by the waterfall, he told me: "You can think of product development like a peach. R&D is the pit. Design is the fruit and peel."

In the year and a half since Lenovo bought the IBM PC business, many of the operations of the suddenly global company has been integrated and consolidated—often with work being moved to China, India, or another low-cost country. Yet the product designers and engineers for the two companies continued to operate in different orbits. ThinkPads were still conceived, designed, and engineered in Raleigh and Yamato, just as they had been for more than a decade. The shallow interactions between the company's designers frustrated Yao. Sure, the designers from the different countries met occasionally, reviewed designs, and talked about design concepts. Hill had set up a group blog called Design Matters, and invited Yao and Takahashi to coauthor it with him. But, so far, designers from the three countries hadn't actually worked together directly day in and day out on development projects. "I think we should work together, not just discuss together," Yao told me. "If you want to have a good team, you have to have them face challenges together."

What did Yao think of David Hill's Bento-Fly concept? He replied cautiously during a telephone interview in October 2006. "We all want to combine good ideas together, but we should think deeply and make sure this is what the customer wants," he said. Yang was just as noncommittal. During a ride through traffic-jammed Beijing that September, he told me he welcomed the ThinkPad design team adding new twists to old ideas. But he said he and Amelio wouldn't predetermine whether Bento-Fly would get the go-ahead. "It's not the management who will decide and approve these projects," he said. "It's up to the marketing people. If they look at it and say it has a good chance of selling, we'll go ahead with it."

Several risky product design ideas were flying around Lenovo's Raleigh headquarters during the summer and autumn of 2006. Like other PC companies, Lenovo has an annual planning process. At the beginning of a year, product development and marketing leaders survey the competitive and technology landscapes and lay out a roadmap of PCs they plan on introducing during the next year or two. These projects pass through a well-defined process of design, engineering, parts procurement, manufacturing, launch, and distribution. Usually, the new-product plans are driven by advances in technology from suppliers like microprocessor maker Intel. But, in mid-2006, the design teams had caught a fever. Yang signaled that he wanted innovations, and the staff responded. Bento-Fly and a couple of other projects had a chance of being added to the product road map as special add-ons. It was exciting, but also a bit chaotic. The designers and engineers couldn't tell from one day to the next which projects would catch on and which ones would fall by the wayside.

One of the other notable concepts was code-named Scout. That was the name of the horse ridden by Tonto, the sidekick in the 1950's TV show *The Lone Ranger*. Scout was the brainchild of

Sapper, Hill, and Merrigan. They envisioned producing a very high end ThinkPad that would have some of the attributes of a luxury automobile. The machines would be covered with fine leather and embossed with the owners' initials. The idea had gotten its start back when IBM still owned the PC division. The company's marketers had done a study to determine how consumers responded, psychologically, to different physical forms. The feedback they got was that people didn't want designs that accentuated the technology contained in products; instead, they liked forms that suggested warmth, nature, and human relations. "I thought that sounded a lot like Ralph Lauren, so out of it came the leather computer," recalls Sapper.

The leather-covered ThinkPad, ultimately called ThinkPad Reserve Edition, would come with a package of premium services, too—sort of a virtual concierge. If the owner ran into a problem anywhere in the world at any time of day or night, he or she could call a special number and get help immediately. There would be none of that endless waiting on the phone for a help-desk person to answer. This limited-edition product, clad in tan French leather, was released in September 2007 and priced at a hefty $5,000. "People feel this is an icon. You may not touch it," says Sapper. "So I said, 'If we want to make something different, it must be radically different, and it must be in a completely different price range so it doesn't interfere with the image of ThinkPad.' So that's how we came to do this."

Another product idea was code-named Razor, after the then-popular, ultraslim mobile phone from Motorola called Razr. Sam Dusi, vice president for marketing for all non-China laptops, had noticed that three technologies would be converging within the coming year or so that would make it possible to produce a very thin, light, and advanced-technology ThinkPad. The first of them was solid-state storage, a small package of memory chips attached to a computer's main circuit board, which would eventually replace the mechanical disk drives that had been a mainstay of all computers since 1984. Disk drives are complicated and have been vulnerable to breaking—especially when they are installed in a mobile computer. That isn't a problem with solid-state storage. The second key technology was another brand-new technology, light-emitting diode (LED) backlighting on flat-panel computer displays, which would improve viewing of movies on long airplane flights. The third technology was a new ultrathin optical drive for playing DVDs that was just 7 millimeters thick—compared to 9.5 millimeters and 12.7 millimeters on other ThinkPads.

The Razor concept would eventually merge with some of the Bento-Fly ideas to become the Kodachi project, but, in the summer and early autumn of 2006, they were still separate. "You start with wide nets. You gather a bunch of ideas. And you finally settle on the elements that are most promising," Hill says.

At that time, Hill was still most excited about the prospects for Bento-Fly, but his ideas were being put to the test by designers and engineers in Yamato. Could they fit all of the components, including the folding keyboard, into an ultrathin box? Could they design a very small motor to automatically deploy the keyboard? Arimasa Naitoh, the head of product development at the Yamato lab, operated under the principle that there should be creative tension between the designers, who are supposed to be thinking out a year or two ahead and not worrying so much about feasibility, and the engineers, who have to make the designs work. "We encourage them to design something that's not too real," he says. "If they stick to super-reality, nothing will be fun, nothing will be new." Once the early design concepts were handed over to the Yamato engineers, Naitoh wanted them to put a tremendous amount of effort into trying to make them work. Every day or so, Hill would receive design drawings from Yamato showing how the components and electrical parts might fit together. And every couple of weeks, he'd receive a model showing the exterior of the machine, the early ones made of high-density foam and the later ones, with more detail, made of wood and plastic.

The ThinkPad product marketing team had done a bit of research and concluded that there would be demand for such a compact and capable device. The question was: How much? Subnotebook computers with 10-inch (254-millimeter) screens had not sold well in the United States, typically. But was the hang-up the relatively small size of the screen or the fact that they didn't have full-size keyboards? Hill was betting that the keyboards were the problem—and the new Bento-Fly design would take care of that. He pointed out that when Sony first contemplated producing the Walkman in the late 1970s, market research showed scant demand for such a device. In spite of those results, Sony chairman Akio Morita decided to go ahead with it. He was right. The Walkman was a huge hit and defined a product type that has remained a hot seller for decades—and flourished again with the advent of Apple's iPod. "Sometimes it takes a leap of faith and somebody who's willing to take the risk," Hill says.

But risk was one thing; impossibility another. By the end of September, Bento-Fly ran into what's called a "showstopper" in tech engineering parlance. Actually, it was two showstoppers. The first one had to do with the Butterfly concept. A new generation of flat-panel displays that were wider than usual—13.3 inches (337.8 millimeters) measured on the diagonal—had become popular on consumer notebook PCs because they were the perfect shape for movie watching. Now it looked like they might become a must-have item for businesspeople, as well. Microsoft had designed a new element called Sidebar in the version of Windows that was due out before the end of the year. Sidebar was a pane on the side of the Windows interface where people could position little items called Gadgets containing updates on everything from stock prices to weather. So now there was a use for a wider screen even if you weren't watching a movie. With these new screens, designers could fashion compact and light notebook PCs that were 12½ inches (317.5 millimeters) wide—with no need for a foldout keyboard.

The second showstopper concerned the Bento part of the Bento-Fly. The idea of designing a notebook PC with no connectors or wires visible when it was closed wasn't going to work either. Using an extra shell to cover the connectors added too much weight and expense. And wireless communications technologies weren't so widely used yet that the engineers could eliminate all those wires and connectors altogether. Also, there was no technology yet available to enable Lenovo's engineers to eliminate the power cord. "Today we can't make it," Naitoh said at the time. "In two years, it might be possible. We have more time and the technology guys on the development side can start thinking about how to do this."

This situation was not unusual in the mobile computing world. Designers and engineers would dream up ideas to solve a problem or give their customers a thrill. Then, suddenly, another piece of technology would come along that obviated the need for the solution they had in mind. Or something that seemed at first like a brilliant design concept just couldn't be done yet because the technology didn't exist to make it possible. Still, it's sometimes difficult to let go of a dream. Hill had invested a lot of time and energy in Bento-Fly, and it took him a few weeks to accept the fact that two of the big concepts were dead—for the time being, anyway. "Butterfly II is back in the cocoon," Hill acknowledged. But he hoped that it might return someday. "Sometimes ideas sit on the shelf for a decade, and things change and they come out again. We might come back with this later—maybe in a handheld computer."

What he was left with was the idea of producing a new ThinkPad that would be ultraslim and packed with the latest in cutting-edge technology. It could still, potentially, be the best portable computer ever made. That was Razor.

Only Razor wasn't called Razor anymore. The product development team didn't want to name something after another company's product—not even a code name. This naming of electronics works in progress is something of an art. The name has to be new, cool, and, if possible, symbolic. In October 2006, just about the time that Bento-Fly was vaporizing, the ThinkPad crew dropped the name Razor and renamed the project Katana. The code name refers to a samurai warrior's sword that's extremely thin and sharp, which was popularized among Americans in Quentin Tarantino's *Kill Bill* movie epic. But, almost immediately, the Japanese engineers wanted the name changed again. Suzuki had a motorcycle named Katana. In the end, they settled on Kodachi. It's like the katana sword, only shorter—so a warrior can draw it quicker. In every way, the Kodachi is optimized for speed.

Fortunately, it was easier to get people behind the Razr/Katana/Kodachi concept than it was to get agreement on a name. Among its major fans was Canadian Peter Hortensius, the company's senior vice president for portable products. Hortensius, a 17-year IBM veteran with a doctorate in electrical engineering, had a gruff, no-bullshit style, but he endeared himself with designers and engineers by backing some of their more out-there ideas. Mark Cohen, vice president of engineering operations, showed Hortensius a mock-up of Kodachi in his office during a product planning meeting in November 2006. Hortensius turned the model over on his desk to see if it had Naitoh's signature on a sticker on the bottom—the Yamato engineering seal of approval. Sure enough, it did. "What excited me about it was it had all the small and light features, but it would also be very reliable and durable," Hortensius recalls. "It was an opportunity to redefine what the PC industry could do with ultralight machines."

Within a matter of days, Hortensius showed the mock-up to his boss, Fran O'Sullivan, and to everybody's boss, Chief Executive William Amelio. O'Sullivan saw it at one of a series of meetings she was holding to review the entire array of products in the company's pipeline. Kodachi wasn't in the queue yet, but she had heard about it, and Hortensius wanted her to start thinking about finding money to fund the project. Hill, ever the showman, brought the mock-up into the review meeting in a paper bag. When called upon by Hortensius, Hill pulled the model out with a flourish. O'Sullivan was impressed. She urged Hortensius and Hill to press forward with the project.

Amelio was impressed, too, when he saw the model a couple of days later. This was his second time around with ThinkPad. He had run IBM's PC operations in the late 1990s, and brought to it an enthusiasm for basic, get-the-job-done aggression and efficiency that had later landed him the job as Lenovo's CEO in early 2006. Amelio gave *no-nonsense* new meaning. "You have to have your costs in line or else people won't pay for your innovations," he told me a couple of months after he got the job and just weeks after he fired 1,000 people to get costs in line with revenues. But he also knew that it would take outstanding design and engineering for Lenovo to build a global brand. He wanted a notebook that was thin, yet packed with all the latest cutting-edge technologies. He urged Hortensius to see what he could make of the Kodachi concept. "I challenged the team to come up with something that would knock people's socks off," Amelio later recalled.

For people down in the middle ranks, Kodachi represented an escape from the stifling last years under IBM rule. "If this was still IBM, we'd never make this," Takahashi said at the time. "We've always made the next generation of laptops to be relatively thin, relatively light, relatively compact, and at relatively reasonable prices. This time it will be very, very thin—and it won't be the cheapest."

Kodachi wasn't just going to be thin, though. Lenovo's product developers had a host of design, engineering, and technology ideas that they hoped would make it stand out from the pack. Everything that had happened with Bento-Fly and Kodachi so far was part of the preconcept phase. The designers could potentially have the biggest impact in that time period because there were no inhibitors. A bunch of ideas were tossed around and tested. But in early 2007 Kodachi was entering the first formal part of the product development process, called the "plan phase." It was to be launched at a meeting scheduled for January 22, the so-called concept kickoff, when Kodachi would officially became a development project.

They had a long list of features they planned on, including when Kanehide Ibayashi, the acting team leader for the project in Raleigh, would present the proposal to the portable division's leadership team at the concept kickoff meeting. This was ambitious stuff. The plan at that point was to make Kodachi the first in a new ThinkPad product family, the S series. The machine would be ¾-inch (19-millimeter) thick on the front end and slightly thicker on the back and would weigh just 3.4 pounds (1.54 kilograms). It would have the 13.3-inch (337.8-millimeter)-wide screen with LED backlighting. And it would be powered with an Intel Centrino chip package, including a microprocessor with tiny circuits spaced just 65 nanometers apart—the width of a few atoms. The Centrino package would include chips for Wi-Fi wireless communications, the kind used in home networks and airports. In fact, there would be nine different wireless radio antennas embedded in the lid. Kodachi would also have solid-state storage and the ultrathin DVD drive. It was to be high end all the way. Yet the goal was to have the machine cost less than $3,000 at retail—quite a feat given all of the new technology that was to be shoehorned in.

Kodachi was also to be remarkable in part for what it *didn't* include. That was a modem. These devices, which transmit e-mails and Web pages across telephone lines, had been standard equipment in all PCs for more than a decade. Yet, by early 2006, PC developers could anticipate a time when few purchasers of commercial laptop computers would have any use for a modem. Between wireless radios and wired broadband connections, they were covered. Some of Lenovo's salespeople were shocked when the Kodachi team suggested they might drop the modem. But they gradually came around after the Kodachi people promised to persuade the company's peripherals division to offer an optional external modem that could be attached to the computer via plugs on its side and back.

Hill and his colleagues planned a handful of fancy design touches for Kodachi. They anticipated producing two versions, one with a conventional top cover and the other with a glossy black surface—a rare departure from their traditional black matte finish. In both cases, they wanted the hinges to be invisible when the clamshell was closed. This was to be one of the first ThinkPads to drop the IBM logo from the top. Instead it would just have the ThinkPad logo, with the red dot in the *i* illuminated when the computer was turned on. ThinkPads had long had a small white LED at the top of the screen to illuminate the keys when people typed in the dark on airplane flights. Kodachi would have an ultra-violet LED and the keys would have special ink that would make them glow in the dark.

The concept kickoff meeting went smoothly. Hortensius and his lieutenants gave the project a quick okay. But that didn't mean they expected it would be easy going from then on. Their approval was simply the go-ahead for the Kodachi crew—then the equivalent of a pickup basketball team—to put together a more formal proposal in the next 25 days. Their deadline was February 16.

During that time, the Lenovo designers in Raleigh moved from their old digs in a former IBM building to a new building that had been constructed for Lenovo nearby. It wasn't as simple as shifting from one office to another. They had to move their design and usability labs. "It's like taking your life in a box, shaking it, and dumping the contents on the floor," says Hill. While designers worked on the Kodachi plans, they had hundreds of boxes stacked in the room where they built and stored models.

Tim Gitchell, a product development lead who had put in 28 years at IBM, had been assigned to run development for Kodachi at the last minute. It was an add-on to his normal load of projects. So now it was his job to assemble what was called an Offering De-velopment Team made up of about 12 people from a variety of functions, including design, engineering, marketing, and procure-ment. They had to come up with a plan that determined the ex-act thickness of the computer, the components that would go in it, the cost of the components, the price, and a sales estimate. "This is the most complex project I have ever worked on," Gitchell said at the time. "You have all those new technologies, the technical risk, the supply risk, and the sales risk."

Things didn't go so smoothly at the February 16 meeting. This session was held in Hortensius's conference room on the new Lenovo campus in Morrisville. It included Cohen, Mark Godin, the vice president of marketing, and a handful of product managers. They worried that all the new components coming from suppliers might not be ready in time. Would they be able to bring the product in at a cost where they could sell it for between $2,500 and $3,000? Some of the executives weren't satisfied with the Kodachi mock-up they were shown. It didn't have all the exterior design details, and, inside, none of the design had been fleshed out. The session had been scheduled to last one hour. It went on for two.

In spite of all the concerns, Hortensius gave Gitchell clearance to begin designing and engineering Kodachi in earnest. And he gave him a "plan exit" date of April 6—meaning all of the basic engineering and industrial design had to be finished before then. The goal was to be able to launch the product in February 2008, during the run-up to the Beijing Olympics. Hortensius's parting shot as the team left the meeting was an exhortation to make Kodachi look beautiful. "Let's make sure that when somebody looks at this thing that they immediately realize why they're paying more for it," he told them.

A lot had to get done in a very short time. Hill called up Takahashi in Japan and asked him for a couple of more detailed mockups. He figured it would take about three weeks to get them done. Meanwhile, Hill went to work with Aaron Stewart, his human-factors engineering specialist in Morrisville, who was also the design department's representative on the Kodachi Offering Development Team, to work out the details of their keyboard lighting scheme. They had been designing white LEDs into ThinkPads for years. When blacklight LEDs first became available, in 2003, Stewart and Hill duct-taped one of them to the top of a ThinkPad. When they turned off the overhead lights in the lab they noticed that the yellow highlighting on a document that was lying nearby reacted to the blacklight and glowed in the dark. So now, about three years later, they saw an opportunity to use their chance discovery in Kodachi. The trick was to find the right chemical to mix with the paint that would form the letters and numbers on the keyboard keys. They searched the Internet and asked Lenovo's procurement specialists to check with their suppliers.

Another major challenge for the designers was the top cover of Kodachi, They wanted it to have the glossy black surface of a fine grand piano. And they didn't want the hinge to show. "We want to have a completely clean, unbroken surface," Stewart explained. "We call it the 'magic hinge,' because we don't know yet if it's achievable." Responsibility for the glossy surface and the hinge design were now in the hands of Naitoh's team in Yamato. But things weren't looking good. The Japanese had designed a ThinkPad with a glossy top that they released only in Asia in 2001, and it had proved to be very hard to manufacture without visible flaws. "The manufacturing people remember how hard it was, and they don't want to do it again," said Takahashi, who was frustrated by his colleague's can't-do attitude. "We're always considering cost, costs, costs, costs," he said. "I think that's stupid. If we eliminate features, some people think we can still sell the same number of machines. I think we'll sell less."

With all the unresolved issues, it became clear that it would be impossible for the Kodachi team to meet the April 6 deadline, so Hortensius pushed it back to April 20. Takahashi flew to the United States with two detailed models—one called the "wish" model that contained every feature the designers had dreamed up, and another one, the "feasible" model, which included just the features that were clearly affordable and technically possible. He and Hill photographed the models from every angle and sent them to Sapper via e-mail. Then they scheduled a 7 a.m. conference call with him on April 7. Sapper was in his studio in Milan, where he had just returned from judging the annual Industrial Design Society of America contest in Washington, D.C. On the phone, Hill explained that it didn't look like the invisible hinge would be possible. The hinges had to be thick enough so assemblers could thread through them the wires for the nine radio antennas. It was clear now that they wouldn't be able to make the hinges thin enough to be invisible from the top of the machine. Sapper critiqued a few of the design elements—including a honeycomb-shaped grill on the bottom that was supposed to help with cooling. "You must get rid of that," he said. But, overall, he gave the "feasible" model his stamp of approval—and he urged them to show the "wish" model to the bosses as well.

Hill, Takahashi, and Stewart assembled a large spreadsheet on which they listed every single design element proposed for Kodachi. The master list totaled more than fifty items. They priced each feature, added the costs up, and saw that they were over budget—though not substantially. So they began slicing away a penny here and a penny there. This process went on for two days, April 10 and 11, at the Morrisville design center. Paint was a major issue. You wouldn't think that it would add a lot of cost, but they planned on using an expensive rubberized paint that would feel silky to the touch. They figured they could save two cents per computer by not putting the special paint around the display screen—a sliver that people would not touch much anyway.

They also conducted an exhaustive review of the possibilities for painting the top cover. They lay down a variety of shades and textures of black paint on three-millimeter-thick panels the length and width of the cover. One was the mirrored black surface they favored. Another was metallic black. Curious about this one, they walked over to the windows and held the panel in direct sunlight. Rays reflected off particles of metal danced around the room like lights on a disco ball, which would be very un-ThinkPad like. They made a note to themselves: always look at things in the full sun. "Peter is saying, 'Bring me the new black that people will pay a premium for,' but that's a challenge," Hill said during an interview the next day.

The phone lines between Raleigh and Yamato were getting a workout. Normally, Hill conducted regular Wednesday night calls with Takahashi and the design team in Yamato, starting at 8 p.m. Eastern Time, and, once every two weeks, he'd get on the phone with Naitoh and Takahashi together. Now he was in near-daily touch with the Japanese via phone and e-mail.

People were getting tense. The plan exit meeting was scheduled for April 20, and there was still a lot to do. Hill kept pressing some of his most adventurous design ideas right up to the deadline. He still wanted the bottom of Kodachi to be as plain as possible—the Bento idea. At every design review meeting, he'd show the executives the bottoms of models. The latest ones had two drain holes on them—nothing else. "This is the way this process works," he explained to me a few days later. "It's like when you make a concept car in Detroit. You know from the start that it's not going to look just like that. But you plant the flag anyway. If we started out by taking shortcuts, we'd never know what is actually possible. Design stretches the organization to try new things."

As the April 20 meeting loomed, Hortensius got reports about Kodachi that troubled him. The marketers had surveyed Lenovo's regional sales leaders around the world—asking them to estimate how many Kodachi units they thought they could sell. The answer that came back was stunningly disappointing. Gitchell and his crew had estimated sales of 130,000 over 12 months—an amount befitting a successful niche product. The tally from the sales leaders came in at just 60,000. Another issue was bothering Hortensius. The estimated weight of Kodachi had crept up slightly over the past few weeks as more detailed engineering work was done. He wanted the folks in Yamato to see if they could squeeze out a few ounces of weight. Also, the issue of whether or not to use the glossy finish on the cover was still being hotly debated among designers, engineers, and manufacturing specialists. "I'm not known for being warm and cuddly," Hortensius told me. "I told them the product looks incredible and will be incredible. The team has fixed a lot of boinks, but not every one. I said we're getting close but we have to make it more ready before I'll authorize this."

Up until that point, only about 10 percent of the money it would take to bring Kodachi to market had actually been spent. Hortensius didn't want to commit to spending the rest until he was sure the product was on exactly the right track. The new deadline for plan exit was April 27.

Before then, Hortensius wanted another review from the sales force. Sam Dusi, the vice president for notebook marketing, asked his marketers to contact the salespeople in far-flung capitals and make sure they understood all the qualities of the product—including the advanced technologies and classy design. He'd also have them help the salespeople understand where Kodachi fit within the current Lenovo product families. It was larger than the ultralight X-series notebooks, yet smaller and lighter than the T-series machines. The salespeople were accustomed to being able to predict demand in those two well-defined segments—but Kodachi was an outlier. Its supporters believed it would expand the market for ThinkPads, rather than rob sales from either of the established families. Dusi saw it as a must-have item for corporate executives. "I believe Kodachi will be a very profitable product. People will pay a premium for it. It's the iPhone of the ThinkPad line," Dusi told me. He also felt the sales bosses would change their minds about prospects for Kodachi when they actually saw it. He said: "I could talk until I'm blue in the face about solid-state drives, but when you can see it and touch it, sex sells, and this thing is sexy looking."

Though the Kodachi plan exit meeting on April 20 had been canceled to give the planners more time, something of note happened on that day that raised doubts about Lenovo's future. Amelio announced a restructuring of the company aimed at reducing costs and streamlining operations. He eliminated 1,400 jobs in the United States and Europe, and moved 750 of them—mostly sales support and procurement jobs—to lower-cost Asia. These moves were supposed to produce $100 million in annual savings. No jobs were lost from the Kodachi design or engineering teams, and there was no hint that belt-tightening would kill the product while it was still in its infancy. Still, these were unsettling times in Morrisville and Yamato. Since the merger, Lenovo's market share had declined. The company continued to thrive in its home market of China, but, in the United States and Europe, where it competed most directly against juggernaut Dell in corporate markets, it was getting hammered. Even ThinkPad sales were slipping.

Meanwhile, the design team was running into glitch after glitch with Kodachi. The cover was to be built out of a combination of ABS plastic, which was inexpensive and good for conducting radio waves, and either magnesium or carbon fiber reinforced plastic, which would give it extra strength. There were to be seams where the materials met, and, after much experimentation, they decided it would be too costly to use enough of the glossy paint to hide the seams. In its place, they now planned on a premium rubberized paint, which would hide the seams plus any imperfections on the surface. It would have a nice sheen to it—not glossy—but a satiny finish. "It will have the feel of leather," Stewart said. "We'll get an acceptable level of yield at an acceptable cost, and yet we'll still create a story." While the glossy paint was now out for the mainstream version of Kodachi, Stewart and Hill still hoped to make a limited-edition version that would have the grand-piano-style patina. But, within a few weeks, they abandoned that idea. It was just too complex for manufacturing. The ultraviolet light for illuminating the keyboard was also out. Stewart couldn't find a chemical that would make the letters glow bright enough. When I asked Hill how he felt about so many of the design flourishes that he and Stewart and Takahashi had come up with falling by the wayside, he was philosophical. "This is all part of going through the game of going from concept to reality," he said.

While Kodachi would be thin, it would not be the thinnest notebook computer ever. That's partly because so much technology was packed into it. But, also, the engineers wouldn't compromise on some attributes that were fundamental to the ThinkPad brand. They had spent years perfecting the tactile feel of the keyboard, and it was something that added thickness to the machine. But the superior feel of the keyboard was worth it, they thought. Typing on some notebook PCs wasn't much different than using a microwave oven control pad. The other thing that ThinkPad had going for it, and which added thickness, was the structural reinforcement that the engineers had designed into it. They put magnesium pieces in the shell, and they attached all of the electronics to a magnesium frame—something they called a "roll-cage"— which protected them from damage if the computer was dropped. "Some of the thin laptops from other companies don't have this kind of engineering, and some of them bend like a fruit roll-up," Stewart told me.

Finally, D-Day had arrived for Kodachi. The plan exit meeting was held in a large conference room on the fifth floor of Building 2 on the new Morrisville campus. About thirty people packed the room, which had a dramatic view out floor-to-ceiling windows onto an outdoor courtyard below. David Critchley, one of Dusi's marketers, started things off by giving an update on the expected demand for Kodachi. The bad news was that the sales team had not significantly increased their estimates—in spite of entreaties from not only Dusi's staff but from Mark Godin, the vice president of marketing. But Critchley said he wasn't alarmed by the sales forecasts. He felt they were overly conservative. Kodachi would define a new category. The sales guys simply didn't know how to forecast for it. Justin Comisky, the financial controller for the notebook division, also gave Kodachi his okay. "Even at these volumes, we think it can be a good business," he told the group.

Hortensius made no comment on sales forecasts. (He told me later: "This is always the fun of releasing real products. You're now at the commitment stage. It's not a penalty-free discussion anymore. On a new technology thing like this, people will be gun-shy. They'd rather overachieve their commitment than over-promise.") Instead, his focus was on Kodachi's weight and on the fit and finish of the product. Use of the rubberized paint would add 40 grams to the overall weight. He wanted those grams shaved off elsewhere. He also had high expectations for the latch that would hold the two sides of the clamshell together. It would make a statement about quality. "I want the click of the latch to sound like the sound of a Mercedes door closing," he told the Kodachi crew.

One by one, the executives sitting around the table made their final comments. And, one by one, they gave Kodachi a thumbs-up. Stewart was elated when the meeting ended. He and the rest of the Kodachi team had been up very late the night before settling the final details of their presentation. And he had forgotten to eat lunch, so he was famished. He made a beeline for the coffee shop and bought a turkey sandwich that he carried on his ThinkPad as he strode back to his desk. As he sat in his cubicle munching on his sandwich he was both relieved and excited. "This fundamentally says it's committed," he told me a few days later. "The plan exit was the summit we were all climbing towards, and we're there. Now we have to execute. That's a whole other project. But it's in plan. We're doing it."

Hill didn't attend the big meeting. But, later in the afternoon, Stewart popped into his office to give him the good news. "I wasn't surprised," says Hill. "I knew the thing was too impressive to be stopped or slowed down."

The machine that emerged out of the plan exit meeting was very different from the concepts Hill had shown me in the "fancy eating room" nearly a year earlier. The pure Bento idea was gone. So was the Butterfly II concept. Yet Hill was proud of Kodachi's design. He was confident it would be a great computer. "The search for something new takes many paths," he says. "This is the nature of creativity and innovation. Design starts with many ideas and then funnels them based on many filters, like cost, technical feasibility, and timing."

Yet, Kodachi, in the spring of 2007, was really still just an idea. It had finally entered the "development phase." Over the coming months, Lenovo's designers, engineers, software programmers, procurement specialists, and the factory crew in China would do the hard work to produce the machine itself. Only then, when Kodachi was released to the world, would its creators know for sure whether it was truly something new and wonderful or would be seen as just another commodity PC in a world awash in copy-cat computers.

7

THE RACE

From the moment the Kodachi development team got the okay to go ahead, a new worry set in: would a rival company produce something similar before they did? The competition was intense between Hewlett-Packard, Apple, Sony, Dell, Toshiba, and Lenovo to come out with ever-thinner, ever-lighter and ever-more-capable notebook computers. Within days of the Kodachi plan exit meeting, Sam Dusi, head of notebook marketing at Lenovo, admitted that, "From the day I charter a product, I worry somebody will beat us to market." In the race to be first with new technologies and gain marketing advantages, PC companies would sometimes put a single advanced feature in a laptop that was otherwise ordinary. Kodachi was a no-compromise product, but marketing-wise, it was vulnerable to ploys like that by other companies that would make it seem less remarkable than it was. Already, in just a few days, Fran O'Sullivan, Lenovo's head of operations, and William Amelio, the CEO, had sent out e-mails when they spotted new product announcements from Toshiba and Apple. Every time Dusi got an e-mail like that he'd quickly send a note to his staff asking them to investigate and report back. "Sometimes you have to kill a project. It just won't be competitive," said Dusi. With Kodachi, so far, so good. But it would be ten months before it arrived in the marketplace.

Another concern: industrial design was becoming more important to the entire top tier of PC makers. At one time IBM's

ThinkPads and Apple's notebook PCs had stood out from the rest of the pack. But, now, HP, Sony, Dell, and others were putting a lot of money and effort into design. In a clear signal of this shift, Dell on June 26, 2007, introduced notebook PCs that came in eight colors at a high-profile launch event at Macy's flagship department store in midtown Manhattan. In addition to black and white, the PCs were available in candy-colored pink, yellow, green, and red. Analyst J.P. Gownder of Forrester Research said this signaled that the PC industry had entered the "Age of Style." A few weeks after Dell's Macy's event, at a New York press briefing, CEO Michael Dell said the company was investing in building up its own internal design team. "We're in the fashion business. The products we sell increasingly make a statement about who you are," he said. "This is especially true in mobile computing. A notebook computer is a personal extension. You take it with you."

Lenovo's chief designer, David Hill, dismissed Dell's efforts at distinguishing itself through design. "I think the idea of offering color options is a bit weak in a world where people are looking for design that provides them with true advantages," he said. "Color is an emotional statement, but little else. We strive to create innovation that is more meaningful. Great design combines style with substance." Still, Dell's design moves would pose additional challenges to Lenovo at a time when it was trying to build a global brand on a reputation for strong engineering and design.

Like any other PC company, Lenovo had a lingo all of its own for describing the product development process. The path from "plan exit" to "general availability" of Kodachi was paved with jargon. Kodachi was now in the "development phase." Tim Gitchell, head of the Kodachi Offering Development Team, was the keeper of the "plan of record" and the schedule for completing it. He tracked everything on a giant software spreadsheet on his computer. Over the coming weeks and months, the bulk of the work would be done in Yamato. A product development team there, headed by Hiroyuki Kinoshita and made up of about a dozen mechanical and electrical engineers, would take the requirements laid out in the plan and try to fulfill them. They would finalize the engineering of the display, the chassis, the hinges, and how all the electrical and mechanical parts fit together. Their most challenging task was bringing in the machine at the specified weight (3.4 pounds, or 1.54 kilograms) and thinness (¾-inch—19 millimeters—on the front end). No ThinkPad team had ever packed so much new technology into such a thin package before. Meanwhile, a small industrial design group headed by Tom Takahashi would complete detailed designs of things like the covers and logos.

Everything was tightly scheduled, with a steady drumbeat of deadlines and reviews—all aiming for crucial dates many months in the future. The schedule looked like this: early September, Kodachi prototype; September through October, testing of prototype and components; November, final prototype; early December, preproduction preparation and testing. On December 6, 2007, according to the plan of record, a review board made up of half a dozen quality managers was scheduled to meet in Yamato to decide if Kodachi was ready to go into production at a factory in Shenzhen, China, just outside of Hong Kong. If so, a few hundred machines would be produced and distributed to the development team, company executives, and salespeople. If they cleared it, high-volume manufacturing would start in late January and the product would be announced in February. That was the plan, but there was no telling if it could be met. "There are some particular challenges here," said Gitchell, just as Kinoshita and his crew were getting started. "We want to get it as thin and light as possible. Smaller is more expensive. Also, we not only want to make it thinner and lighter, but also stronger."

To make the process even riskier, like other PC companies, Lenovo didn't control its own fate. It depended on dozens of suppliers for the components that would go into Kodachi, everything from the solid-state storage device to the set of chips that controlled the machine and to the fan that would cool it. In several cases—the storage device and ultrathin DVD drive among them—the technologies Kodachi's planners had chosen were new to the suppliers as well. This was the first time the ThinkPad team was using the thin DVD drive, and it had only one supplier. Gitchell was concerned about the durability of the drive. He had two suppliers for the solid-state storage, but this technology was so new that there were not yet industry standards for specifying the size and capabilities of the devices. To make matters even more complex, because the technologies were new, the suppliers would be completing development of their pieces of the puzzle even while Kinoshita's team in Yamato was piecing the whole puzzle together. In a sense, the Yamato engineers were helping the suppliers develop their own products. Gitchell and Kinoshita had laid out a "qualification schedule" for the main components, which they hoped the suppliers would be able to meet. If a supplier fell behind schedule, Lenovo would have to consider alternative components. But, at this point, everything was still on schedule. "The suppliers want to get into this product," Gitchell said.

Throughout the development process, Aaron Stewart, the human-factors designer in Morrisville, would review and test every new prototype that came out of Yamato. He'd look for usability problems and think of modifications that would make the machine easier to use. Of particular concern to him was the keyboard. IBM had spent years engineering and refining a keyboard for laptops that had just the right feel and clickity-click sounds. The keys had a satisfying give and spring, and they depressed just the right distance. In Kodachi, however, to save a sliver of space, the developers had decided to make the keyboard slightly thinner under the top two rows. Those were the number and function keys. They would "travel" slightly less when they were touched. The difference would be a fraction of a millimeter. Would customers notice? Would it matter to them? Stewart had to make sure the slimming had no negative impact on customers' perceptions of the keyboard. Another issue was the touchpad. The screen would be different dimensions—wider than usual. Computer users liked to have touchpads that were the same shape as the screens. So Stewart was working with Yamato engineers to make a wider touchpad without adding to the thickness of the laptop. He and Hill spoke via conference call with the design team in Yamato every week, Wednesday evening for the Americans, Thursday morning for the Japanese.

Meanwhile, the product marketing team had plenty of work to do, too. Kodachi still didn't have an official name. At the time, there were two ThinkPad product series that it could conceivably fit into, the X Series, which had 12-inch (30.5-centimeter) displays, and the T Series, which had 14-inch (35.5-centimeter) and 15-inch (38-centimeter) displays. At 13.3 inches (33.78 centimeters), Kodachi fell between them. Some marketers and designers favored giving Kodachi a brand-new designation, perhaps calling it the S Series, to set it apart. But others felt there were already enough product segments and that adding another would sow confusion among the sales force and customers. While those discussions went on, the marketers talked to sales team leaders in various countries where the laptops would be sold to get their input into naming and positioning. They also checked with the salespeople to see what standard configurations they should create. One version would have a traditional disk drive rather than solid-state storage, so it could be cheaper. How many of those would sell? After getting estimates from the salespeople, the marketers decided how much of each component should be ordered. All of this information went into the plan of record so the company's purchasers, stationed in China, could place orders with suppliers and the components would be on hand in Shenzhen when manufacturing started at the end of the year.

Since plan exit, the Kodachi team had been busy focusing on its engineering, marketing, and purchasing challenges. Everybody knew their job. Gitchell, who was also running several other projects, would check regularly with the people on the Kodachi Offering Development Team representing each functional group, including Stewart. In June, six weeks after the plan exit, Stewart reported: "No news is good news. We have found no show-stoppers."

Lenovo's Yamato lab was in a suburb of Tokyo, about a 45-minute subway ride from the center of the city. The engineers and designers, under the command of Naitoh, occupied a single floor in what was otherwise an IBM building. The space was packed tightly, with people working at desks lined up against each other. A lot of the human interactions happened in the beige-colored hallways or in a conference room with one glass side that faced onto the main office. There was a different rhythm in Yamato than in Morrisville. The designers and marketers in Morrisville communicated with each other via instant messaging software on their computers—sometimes even if they were sitting very close to one another. In Yamato, people still tended to communicate the old fashioned way—face to face.

Kinoshita, the Kodachi project technical lead, had been a ThinkPad engineer for 15 years. He got his start designing PC motherboards—the large circuit boards in PCs where most of the important microchips are placed. In the summer of 2007, at age 48, he had been a project manager for seven years, so he was somebody the bosses could count on to deliver high-quality work on a strict deadline. For years, Kinoshita had been a serious sailor in his free time. He was the forward deck crewman on a 24-foot sailboat that competed in international competitions and had qualified for World Cup events in 1990 and 2002. But as the Kodachi project ramped up, he had less and less time for sailing. He typically worked from 9 a.m. to 10 or 11 at night.

Even before Kodachi went through plan exit, he had ordered some of the components from suppliers. This process is called request for quotation—or RFQ. He wanted to get as much done as early as possible because, normally, his team would have 12 months to develop a product, but, with Kodachi, the work had to be done in 10 months to hit the launch deadline the top executives had set out. After plan exit, Kinoshita put his engineers to work on two challenges: how to make the touchpad bigger and where to put the battery. During the concept phase, the developers had decided to place the main battery within the chassis underneath the touchpad. (It would also be possible to attach a second battery by plugging it into a bay in the side of the machine that normally held the DVD drive.) The main battery had to be small enough to fit there and still keep Kodachi very thin. But if the touchpad was going to be larger, there would be less room for the battery. They decided to come up with a brand-new battery design to make room for the larger touchpad. At the same time, they needed to make sure that the battery had a long-enough life to satisfy customers. Often, PC makers offered customers the option of buying a longer-life battery. Typically, longer life meant bigger. Engineers would offer a special battery that stuck out of the back or front of the notebook chassis. But the Kodachi designers didn't want an ugly bulge on their beautiful machine, so they searched for another way to get longer battery life. In this case they decided to offer a larger battery as an option, but position it on the bottom of the computer. It would bulge out a little bit, but nobody would see it unless they turned the machine over. One factor they had in their favor with Kodachi was that they were using light-emitting-diode (LED) backlighting for the display. LED technology consumed less electricity, which would prolong battery life.

The Kodachi team faced one of those classic portable computer design dilemmas: one goal fought against another. They couldn't make any major changes in the interior layout of the components, because that would set back the product development schedule. So Kinoshita's engineers worked with touchpad and battery suppliers to come up with components that would fit together under the Kodachi keyboard and allow it to remain as thin as planned. Once they accomplished that, because the parts had to be slightly different dimensions, they had to revise some of their RFQs with suppliers.

After Kodachi plan exit, the major project was to make the first working prototype. It was supposed to be ready by September. Some of Kinoshita's mechanical engineers had started to make a mold for the outer shells of the computer in advance, but, when they learned that they might have to make adjustments for the battery and touchpad, they stopped and waited for the changes to be made. Meanwhile, they worked on finding the right balance between weight and strength. How thin could they make the parts of the shells and chassis without making them too thin? They ran computer-aided-design (CAD) simulations to test different combinations of part size and materials and see how they would react later to all of the stress tests the machine would be put through—including being dropped, twisted, and squeezed.

One of the problems that arises when you set out to design a thin and light computer is that it's difficult to be thin and light and also strong. People abuse their computers. Machines get knocked off desks or dropped out of overhead bins on airplanes. People hold their laptops in ways that put an incredible amount of stress on them. For instance, they'll hold an open laptop with one hand clamped on a corner. Since mechanical disk drives are often positioned in the front corners, holding a computer that way puts a lot of pressure on the drives, sometimes breaking the moving parts. While the ThinkPad division was still part of IBM, a handful of the Yamato engineers came up with a novel idea for strengthening laptops. They designed a metal frame that nestled in the bottom of the computer, which they called a "roll cage." It worked like a roll cage in a race car—only, in this case, the "passengers" in the car were the motherboard, the hard drive, and other critical components. With Kodachi, they invented a new generation of the roll cage that was just as strong, but thinner and lighter. The magnesium bottom shell of the laptop formed the base of the roll cage, and, running horizontally along the length and width of the bottom half of the laptop, they placed a magnesium frame that served both as the top of the roll cage and the bezel that supported the keyboard. Each of the structural pieces served those two purposes.

While the mechanical engineers worked on refining the shape, size, and materials, Kinoshita's electrical engineers began to put together a prototype of the motherboard, where the important chips in the computer were arrayed. Most of the electrical parts would be available in September, and they knew their dimensions and capabilities. But some would lag, so there was some uncertainty about how they would fit on the board. A major challenge would be verifying that all of the components worked together when some of them would not be available until later.

One of the tardy parts was the liquid crystal display. For the first time in a ThinkPad, they would be using an LED-based display. The technology was so new that display and PC makers had not yet come up with standard ways of building them. Kinoshita's engineers couldn't simply order displays that were already sitting on a shelf somewhere. They had to collaborate with the LED and display producers to come up with a panel that would be custom-designed and custom-built for Kodachi. This meant that they'd receive several rounds of prototypes from the suppliers and it would take months to get the displays working and fitting right.

By August, the Yamato team had some of the Kodachi components in hand and was testing them. Almost miraculously, they had been able to make adjustments in the battery and touchpad without adding to the size or weight of the machine. "We've succeeded in not getting worse," said Offering Development Team leader Gitchell. "That's a challenge you can't underestimate. When you work on a design on paper you don't know if you'll be able to actually do it." He was worried about the solid-state storage device. It was just 1.8-inches (45.72 millimeters) across and 0.31 inch (8 millimeters) thick, but the technology was new and he wasn't sure the suppliers would be able to send prototype parts on schedule. "If there's even a little glitch, we'll have trouble meeting our launch date," he said.

Another concern for him was a group of chips provided by Intel under the brand name Centrino. The package included a microprocessor, chips for wireless communications, and chips for handling the graphics that appear on the display screen and for managing the memory chips, where programs and data were temporarily stored when they were in use. All of these chips were designed to be plugged into the computer's motherboard, where most of the key electronics in a PC are arrayed. About once a year, Intel would issue new versions of the chips that contained the latest technologies. The versions that Gitchell had selected for Kodachi included a new processor, called an Intel Core 2 Duo, designed especially for mobile computing, which sipped electricity efficiently and helped make the battery last longer. The processor and two other chips had been repackaged so they took up less space on the motherboard—making it possible for the board to be shrunk by about 10 percent.

Gitchell's concerns focused on the other element—the wireless communications chips, which handled e-mailing and Web browsing. These chips were packaged on a small card, the size of two postage stamps, which was designed to plug into the top of the motherboard. The state of the art in short-range wireless communications at the time was a technology called Wi-Fi. It was used to set up wireless networks in offices, homes, and public spaces such as airports. But Intel was also preparing a newer technology, called WiMAX, which made it possible for mobile computer users to receive radiowaves from transmitters several miles away. Gitchell wanted to get this technology into Kodachi, if possible. But it didn't look like it would be ready in time. "We're not sure we'll make it. We're slightly misaligned," Gitchell said.

Misalignment with Intel was a big deal for any PC maker. Since the earliest days of the info tech industry, Intel had been a force to reckon with. The company, started in Silicon Valley in 1968, had been one of America's pioneering semiconductor companies. It initially built a huge business in designing and manufacturing memory chips, vital to the workings of any computer, and then, when low-cost Japanese memory chips swept the marketplace in the mid-1980s, it shifted to make microprocessors its main business. A key break had come in 1981 when IBM chose the Intel microprocessor design for its first personal computer. When IBM's computer technology emerged as the standard for the PC industry, Intel's microprocessor business took off.

By 2000, Intel thoroughly dominated the PC microprocessor business, with more than an 80 percent market share, but the dot-com crash forced the company's executives to take a hard look at how they were doing business. In addition to the decline in demand that came with the crash, Intel took note of the fact that sales of desktop computers were leveling off and notebook sales seemed poised for acceleration. In fact, some analysts predicted that within a decade, notebook sales would overtake desktop sales. Up until that time, Intel was an engineering-centered company. The chip designers would come up with improvements, the manufacturing people would make the chips, and the sales and marketing people would sell them. But Paul Otellini, then the company's executive vice president, who had a product marketing background, thought it was time for a change. Intel needed first to map out where its markets were going and then design chips suited for those new demands. In response to his urging, CEO Craig Barrett divided the company up into business units targeting different market segments. One of the units was for mobile computing.

Two men were put in charge of mobile computing: Anand Chandrasekher and Dadi Perlmutter. Chandrasekher was a 13-year Intel veteran who had earlier been technical assistant to Barrett and had run marketing for Intel processor products. Perlmutter was one of Intel's top technical managers. Up to that point, Intel had never designed a processor specifically for portable computing, but Chandrasekher decided it was time to do so, first by modifying existing chip designs and later by designing a new processor from the ground up for mobility. A watershed moment came at a meeting conducted by Chairman Andy Grove, Barrett, and Otellini in May 2001 at Intel's headquarters building in Santa Clara, California. Chandrasekher led a discussion of what Intel could do to "jazz the PC." His major proposal was increasing the focus on notebooks.

But how would a chip designed for mobile computing be different than one designed with desktop computing in mind? Two months later, Alex Peleg, a strategic planner, presented an analysis of the mobile computing market and laid out the issues that Intel would have to address, what he called the "four vectors of mobility." They were battery life, wireless connections, weight, and processor performance. He believed that the processors designed for portable computers should perform just as well as those in desktop machines.

One of the company's design teams had already started working on technology that would ultimately address the battery life and performance issues. Back in the late 1990s, Perlmutter, who was then the general manager of the company's Haifa, Israel, development center, had an encounter with an engineer that ultimately changed the way the company designed processors. The engineer, Simcha Gochman, stopped Perlmutter in a hallway and told him that if Intel lowered the so-called clock speed of its processors, it could still produce the same amount of processing power while consuming less electricity. At that time, Intel, like the rest of the microprocessor industry, operated under the belief that the faster the speed with which electrons cycled through the chip, the better. So this was a radical thought. With permission from the top executives, however, Perlmutter launched a development project, code-named Banias, to find out if Gochman's ideas would pan out. By the middle of 2001, Banias had progressed to the point where Perlmutter felt it should become a mainstream development project for the company. Some other executives who favored the clock-speed strategy tried to kill the Banias project, but Otellini sided with Perlmutter. Banias, soon to be officially named Pentium M, the first Intel processor designed for mobile computing, was on the way to the market.

Another Intel team was taking on the wireless connectivity issue. In 2000, more than 26 million laptop computers were produced worldwide, but only one percent of them were capable of receiving or sending wireless messages, according to market research firm ABI Research. That meant that while the owners of these machines could take them anywhere, they couldn't use them everywhere. People would lug their laptops from office to home and on trips, but they couldn't see their latest e-mail or access the Web unless they plunked the machines down and plugged them into a computer network. A few people bought special add-on cards that connected to cellular data networks. But it was becoming clear to leaders at Intel that if laptop PCs had wireless technologies built into them, they'd be much more useful, and people would buy more of them, which would mean more sales of Intel processors.

In late 2001, Intel's leaders decided it was time to make wireless connectivity widespread in laptops by including the technology on the PC motherboard. They chose Wi-Fi as the technology they would put on the boards they produced for PC makers. But there was a drawback to including wireless capability in a notebook computer: it would constantly draw electricity, shortening battery life.

It was at that point that Chandrasekher had a big idea that would reshape not only Intel's strategy but the direction of the entire PC industry. He thought: why not create a package of chips that included a low-power processor, wireless technology, and other chips that help reduce energy consumption on the laptop? He also thought Intel would have more success selling this package if it branded it and marketed wireless computing directly to corporations and consumers. His reasoning: if people demanded wireless communications in their laptops, PC makers would provide it—and Intel would be standing ready to supply all the technologies they would need in a convenient package. That was the beginning of Centrino.

It took more than a year to bring all of the pieces together. Intel's Wi-Fi technology lagged, and, in late 2002, its leaders held what Chandrasekher called a "gut check" meeting to decide whether to launch Pentium M without it. Some sales executives favored going ahead. They said the PC makers weren't demanding Wi-Fi. According to Chandrasekher, the tide of the meeting turned when Jeff Hoogenboom, an Intel sales manager for a large

PC maker, said, "My customer is going to hate what I'm going to tell you, but, for Intel's long-term benefit, you should wait and launch with Wi-Fi." After much discussion, Barrett and Otellini agreed that the company shouldn't sacrifice long-term gain for short-term advantage.

It was a smart decision. Launched in March 2003 with Wi-Fi included, Centrino became one of the most successful products in Intel's history. Chandrasekher and Perlmutter roused the sales team by vowing to shave their heads if sales exceeded the official targets by 25 percent in the first year on the market. It happened, and they made good on their promise. The two caused an uproar when they walked on stage at Intel's 2004 sales meeting in Anaheim, California, with their heads shaved bald. But, as important as Centrino was for Intel, it had an even greater impact on the PC industry. Intel helped generate demand by promoting Wi-Fi hotspots in airports, hotels, and public spaces. In fairly short order, wireless computing became widespread. By 2006, of 70.4 million laptop computers sold, 67 million had Wi-Fi built in, according to ABI Research.

From 2003 on, with each new version of Centrino, the wireless technologies in the package improved rapidly. Transmission range lengthened, and data transmission speeds got faster. PC makers wanted the latest capabilities. Otherwise, their notebooks wouldn't be competitive. That explains why Lenovo was so intent on getting the WiMAX version of Centrino into Kodachi. It wanted the computer to possess all of the cutting-edge technologies that were available.

While Intel and Lenovo engineers worked on that project, a change came in the leadership of the Kodachi development team. Gitchell was replaced by another veteran ThinkPad manager, Andy Kozak. The reason for the switch was simple: Kodachi hadn't been part of the normal product development plan for 2007. Neither had the ThinkPad Reserve Edition. But Gitchell had volunteered to take charge of both projects on top of his normal workload. It was just too much. "My eyes were bigger than my stomach. My managers recognized that and did some rebalancing of the workload," Gitchell explained. He stuck with the Reserve Edition, which was further along, and gave up Kodachi.

Kozak was a 25-year computer industry veteran. He grew up in the dreary mill town of Fall River, Massachusetts, but an appointment to the U.S. Naval Academy was his ticket out. In the computer industry, he had worked at Digital Equipment for many years, then at Compaq, and then at IBM. So he had been involved with nearly every kind of computer from the largest mainframes to the smallest portables. For almost his entire career he had been a program manager—like he would be for Kodachi. He got the Kodachi assignment because two of his projects happened to be winding down just then. He was excited to get the job. In Lenovo's Morrisville offices, people were spread around at desks in open floor plans, with low cubicle walls, so they overheard a lot of what their colleagues were doing. Even before he got the Kodachi assignment, Kozak knew plenty about it.

When Kozak's boss, Ned Brady, called him into his office in late July 2007 to ask him to take on the job, he made it clear just how important Kodachi was to the corporation. He also handed him some aggressive deadlines. At this point, the plan was to introduce the product on January 22, 2008, and have it available for shipping worldwide on February 12, just after the Chinese New Year celebration. The manufacturing plant would shut down for a week for the celebration, and that meant the manufacturing actually had to get started earlier than it normally would have been the case. While a lot of the most intense work on Kodachi in Morrisville had already been done, Kozak had to shepherd the follow-up product, Kodachi II, through concept phase and plan exit. The second version would have updated components and a few changes to the industrial design, including a privacy filter that would prevent passengers on an airliner from seeing what the Kodachi II owner had on his or her screen, by distorting the view from the side. Kodachi II was supposed to hit the market in late August 2008, just after the Olympics.

Meanwhile, most of the action on the first version of Kodachi was happening in Yamato. In July, the engineering team put together its first functional prototype, called a System Integration Verification (SIV) unit. Only a few of the major components were available, so Kinoshita and his colleagues concentrated on the motherboard and its parts. They also handmade a model of the exterior shell of the computer. In late August, Tom Takahashi, the Yamato design lead, shipped that model to Stewart and Hill in Morrisville. Hill was pleased. "It's every bit as thin as we had imagined," he said. "It's like one of the circus acts where they have a tiny car and all of the clowns come piling out of it. You look at Kodachi and you don't know how they get all the parts to fit inside."

One of the components that the Yamato engineers had packed in was a set of stereo speakers. At the time of plan exit, the official blueprint called for a single mono speaker. But Hortensius had urged them to try to squeeze stereo speakers in. The engineers had placed them in the bottom left- and right-hand corners of the palm rest.

Another item had been dropped, however. The designers had hoped to put backlighting behind the ThinkPad logo on the top cover of Kodachi. The challenge to the Yamato engineers was to add the backlight without making the machine thicker. But they found that between the display and the cabling for wireless radios, there simply wasn't room in the top shell for any more electronics. It would have added a millimeter of thickness, which was a millimeter too much.

Kozak had a very different reaction than Hill on October 1 when he opened a cardboard box containing a prototype that had been hand-built by engineers in Yamato. Inside was a crude hinged aluminum box containing Kodachi's electronics that had little resemblance to a finished notebook computer. He lifted the machine out and placed it on his desk. This was an anticlimax. A keyboard was held on with two pieces of white masking tape. And two big components were missing: the display and the solid-state

Alan Kay's drawing of
his original portable
computing concept:
empowering devices for
children, 1968.
Source: Courtesy of Alan Kay

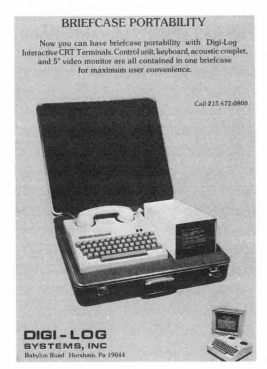

BRIEFCASE PORTABILITY

Now you can have briefcase portability with Digi-Log
Interactive CRT Terminals. Control unit, keyboard, acoustic coupler,
and 5″ video monitor are all contained in one briefcase
for maximum user convenience.

Call 215 672-0800

DIGI - LOG
SYSTEMS, INC
Babylon Road Horsham, Pa 19044

Digi-Log's "portable" computer
from the 1970s.
Source: Digi-Log

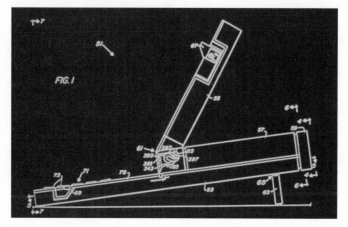

Patent drawing for America's first truly portable computer, GRiD Compass, 1982.
Source: Courtesy of John Ellenby

The Doonesbury cartoon that mocked Apple's Newton PDA in 1993.
Source: Doonesbury © 1993 G.B. Trudeau. Reprinted with permission of Universal Press Syndicate. All rights reserved.

Design consultant and ThinkPad creator Richard Sapper in his Milan studio, 2007.
Source: Courtesy Lisa Hamm

Design consistency: The original ThinkPad prototype, left, compared to a modern ThinkPad, 2007.
Source: Courtesy Lisa Hamm

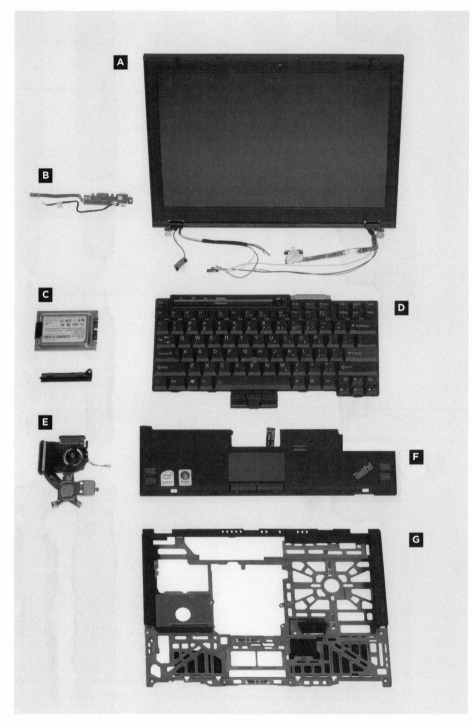

A. Top cover and display, 447 grams. B. Display connector, 13.6 grams. C. 64–gigabyte solid-state drive, 41.3 grams. D. Keyboard, 129 grams. E. Cooling fan, 34.3 grams. F. Palm rest and touchpad, 50 grams. G. Magnesium chassis, 82.7 grams. H. System board with Intel Core 2 Duo processor, 119.3 grams. I. Internal battery, 2.4 grams.

Source: Davies and Starr

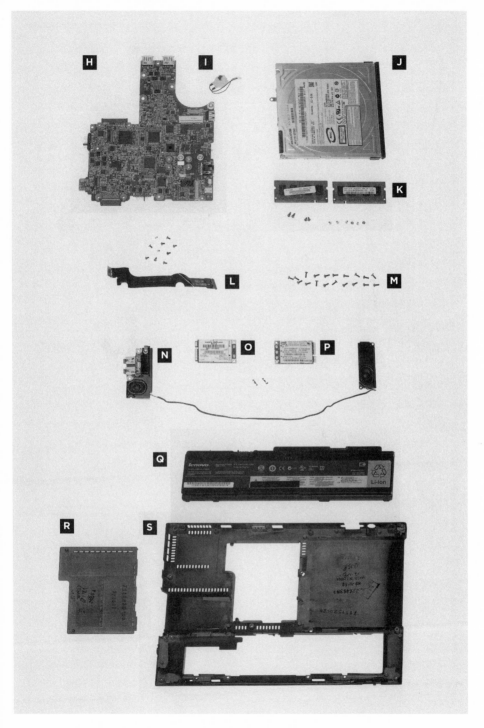

J. DVD drive, 99.3 grams. K. Memory chips, 15.4 grams. L. Audio cable, 3.5 grams. M. Screws, 6.16 grams. N. Stereo Audio System, 17.5 grams. O. Wireless wide network, 10.7 grams. P. Wireless local network, 7.1 grams. Q. Replaceable battery, 210 grams. R. Expansion cover, 0.316 gram. S. Bottom cover, 130 grams.

Source: Davies and Starr

Tomoyuki "Tom" Takahashi (left) and David Hill with the Lenovo X300.
Source: Courtesy of David Hill

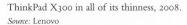

ThinkPad X300 in all of its thinness, 2008.
Source: Lenovo

drive. He had expected the display to be absent. That was supposed to come in later. But not having the solid-state drive was a major disappointment. "I explored with my fingers to see if it was there, and I realized there was no drive. I said, 'Oh shit!' " The problem, he discovered, was that both models of the solid-state drives they had ordered, from two Asian suppliers, were having "data integrity issues." That meant data would unexpectedly go missing during tests. In some cases, when the testers plugged in a drive to a test computer, it registered the drive as having a lower capacity than it was supposed to have. The drive problems were a worry, but not yet a disaster. Kozak still expected that the devices would be ready in time.

Mark Cohen, the head of ThinkPad operations, had asked Kozak to keep him apprised of every bit of news related to Kodachi. He typically didn't look at prototype units later in the process. So he was shocked when he saw the SIV unit, which Kozak had left on his desk. "I walked in and saw this thing that looked like an Erector Set version of a computer. It wasn't something I could do anything with. I think Andy gave it to me more as a joke," Cohen said.

At around the same time, they got some mildly bad news on the Intel front. It turned out, they weren't going to be able to get the WiMAX wireless technology into Kodachi. They had pushed Intel to get it ready on their deadline, but that proved impossible. "It became clear in October that no matter how hard we pushed, it wasn't going to happen," says Cohen. Instead, with Intel's help, they arranged things so when the WiMAX technology was ready, it could be loaded onto the small wireless card along with Wi-Fi and plugged into the motherboard.

While Kozak and Cohen sweated the details, Lenovo's executives and marketers debated how to announce Kodachi. They wanted to make a splash. But, unlike in the early days of PCs and notebooks, companies could no longer hope to hold a press conference and have a lot of journalists show up. (Apple, with its hyperloyal fan base, was the only exception.) Kodachi would be a cool machine. It would create buzz. But it would be expensive. So it wouldn't be a huge seller. The last thing they wanted was to call a press conference and have only a handful of reporters respond. At one point, they considered announcing Kodachi at the International Consumer Electronics Show (CES) in Las Vegas in early January. Thousands of journalists would be there, and a good turnout was practically assured. But Kodachi wasn't a consumer product. So it wasn't a great fit. And also they planned on announcing their strategy for selling consumer products worldwide at CES. That's where they'd get the big publicity lift. They decided Kodachi should be kept separate from that announcement to avoid confusion. The Kodachi marketing plan as of October 2007 was to distribute loaner models of Kodachi to product reviewers in mid-February and issue a press release announcing Kodachi's availability on February 26. This was a few weeks later than they had originally planned, but they wanted to play it safe since some of the components were delayed. Hopefully, the reviewers would love the machine and all of the gadget Web sites on the Internet would spread the word. Maybe Lenovo would hold a launch lunch in New York City for a small group of handpicked business and technology journalists.

One more thing on the marketing front: Kodachi finally had an official name. There would be no brand-new S Series. They'd include Kodachi in the X Series. It would be called the ThinkPad X300. The 3 stood for 13 inches (33 centimeters) wide. A working prototype of Kodachi, called the System Verification Test unit, had been sent by the Yamato team to people throughout the company, including product development, marketing, and top executives.

Throughout the development process, Kinoshita's team had subjected each Kodachi prototype to a series of stress tests. This is the machine equivalent of torture. In the basement of the IBM building in Yamato was a lab where all of the testing for laptops took place. There were a series of rooms, each with its set of devices. The most extreme test in Room 1 was the "Free-Drop, Torture Drop Test." For this test, the laptop was open and turned on, and it was held in a contraption that looked like a guillotine—only with no blade. The laptop was lifted to about five feet off a stone slab. A beep sounded. The laptop was released and hit the floor with a loud smacking sound. If all went well, it stayed on and continued to be usable. Other tests included those for electromagnetic interference, noise levels, cold down to zero degrees Celsius, heat, humidity, and reaction to pressure on the enclosure. It takes a month or two to run every test required for a new laptop model. Different tests are run at different stages of development.

In October, when Yamato engineers were testing the so-called System Integration Test prototype—which had all of the components inside the enclosure—they discovered a vibration problem. The electrical components in a laptop give off a lot of heat, especially the processor. So when mechanical engineers design the enclosure, they create paths for the heat to escape. With Kodachi, they had originally put a small vented bump on the bottom of the computer to allow hot air to get out. Later, they thought they could manage without the bump. But in stress testing, when they pressed the enclosure in certain ways, they'd get a small vibration from the tiny exhaust fan being too close to the plastic sheathing. So they put the bump back in—only smaller this time. In fact, they made a bump that measured only 0.4 millimeters, so it was barely visible.

Another problem that came up in that round of testing was a smear on the display screen. It looked like a small cloud. Kozak learned of the problem in early October and kept track of it through weekly engineering reports that were sent out via e-mail to about eighty people by the team in Yamato. He kept asking about the smear during the weekly telephone conferences with Yamato. These meetings would start at 6:30 a.m. in Morrisville, which was 7:30 p.m. in Japan. Finally, good news: by shifting components within the top cover, they had relieved the pressure, and the smear on the display screen went away.

Kozak still had work to do on the external appearance of Kodachi. The outside shell of the machines was to be coated with a special matte black rubberized paint that wouldn't look shiny but would feel like satin. To save money—approximately 87 cents per machine—they had decided to put one coat rather than two on the bottom shell. They had been concerned about scratching, but, after tests in Yamato, they decided that a single coat of paint would be enough. Kozak looked at the final paint samples in early November. They were fine. That was something Kozak could check off his list of unresolved items.

Another issue was the appearance of the bottom of the machine. Back at the very beginning, when the designers and marketers were dreaming up Kodachi, Hill set the goal of making a machine that would look elegant and uncluttered on the outside—a perfect simple black box. Yet, by rules and practice, the bottoms of laptops were covered with labels and markings recording the safety checks done on the machines and attesting to the authenticity of various components. The result was that the bottoms of the machines looked like those well-traveled suitcases from the early twentieth century whose proud owners slapped stickers on them from various cities and countries to show where they had been. Hill's goal was to remove every single label from Kodachi. The solution that Lenovo's designers had come up with was to transfer the labels to the inside surface of the battery bay. That way, people who bought the machines could see all of the serial numbers and certifications before they installed the battery. Kozak checked with each organization, government agency, or company that was behind each label. He got permission to move them inside the bay from some outfits, but not from others. Microsoft was the big hang-up. Its label had the Windows serial number on it and the four-color Windows logo. After several rounds of discussions between Kozak and Microsoft officials, they were at an impasse. Microsoft simply wouldn't budge. It wanted its brand featured prominently all over the machine. In the end, there would be a handful of labels on the bottom. Not the clutter of the past, but, still, the bottom would not have the elegant simplicity that Hill had been hoping for.

In Yamato, Kinoshita was getting frustrated with his suppliers. The final working prototype of Kodachi, called the System Verification Test unit, was supposed to be ready for final review by the end of October. After final modifications, it was to be test-manufactured in December. But, on October 29 Kinoshita said the project was two weeks behind schedule. The core mechanical parts and electrical components were set—the metal and plastic parts, the outer casing, and the motherboard. But the display panel, the solid-state drive, and the optional hard disk drive weren't ready. As a result, the Yamato engineers had not yet completed "qualification testing" on them. The display was delayed by a design mistake in the circuitry pattern on the glass. When Kinoshita's engineers got the first sample in the end of September and turned it on, all they saw was a blank screen. The solid-state drives had "many bugs." One problem, Kinoshita said, was a mismatch between the latest version of Microsoft's Windows operating system, called Vista, and the way data was stored on the early solid-state drives. A few PC companies had already included the drives in a handful of laptops, but, said Kinoshita, "We have found many problems with the technology, even those that were supposedly production-ready." Another glitch, Intel had sent the wrong version of Centrino for testing.

Back in Morrisville, Kozak was fretting, but not yet in panic mode. "Every computer development project is fraught with bad things in the beginning," he said. "It's very common that we have problems. And we are." In addition to those weekly conference calls between Morrisville and Yamato, engineers and developers on both sides of the Pacific kept in touch via a constant flow of e-mails and instant messages. But they also used collaboration software to track progress—or the lack thereof. Kozak had set up what's called a "team room" on the computer network, where anybody with permission could see status reports or type in the latest information. At this point, Cohen was getting updates every Tuesday morning from Kozak and other members of the Kodachi team. "Based on the pressures he's under on Kodachi, Mark wants everything to be just perfect," said Kozak. "He told me—and I quote: 'I will accept no delays on this product.' And it's my job to ensure he won't have delays."

On the morning of November 6 they had met and talked about all of the hang-ups. The most serious glitch right then was the delay in getting the Centrino chips. Cohen himself was going to escalate the matter and speak directly to Intel. They needed the components in Shenzhen on December 3 if they were to begin manufacturing the final test versions of Kodachi on schedule on the new target date of December 17. Cohen told Ned Brady, Kozak's boss, to pull together a Kodachi task force and hold meetings every morning until everything was back on schedule. On his own, Kozak was at his desk some mornings at 5:30 a.m. and still there as late as 10 p.m. A crucial meeting was coming up: the manufacturing design readiness review. It was to take place in Yamato starting December 6. Kozak would fly in a couple of days earlier. "God forbid it's not ready," he said.

The review was held on the fifth floor of the IBM building in Yamato. The first day's session was conducted in a conference room with a glass wall on one side that looked out onto the Lenovo engineering offices. The other three walls were covered from top to bottom with whiteboards. A panel of five reviewers sat on one side of the conference room table. It was headed by Noboru Kodama, the quality assurance manager in Yamato. In his early forties, Kodama had the gravitas of a judge. He spoke nearly perfect English and had a serious demeanor that set the tone for the meeting. About two dozen people sat at chairs around the table or back against the walls, and another dozen were on the phone. Kozak kicked things off with a high-level summary of the project—everything from how much money was being invested to how many sales were forecast and when manufacturing was supposed to begin. Then, one by one, members of the Kodachi Offering Development Team and the Yamato engineering team made presentations about electrical and mechanical engineering, quality, marketing, and readiness for manufacturing. There were about twenty presentations in all. This meeting dragged on from 9 a.m. to 3 p.m.

There was no covering up Kodachi's problems. The 64-gigabyte solid-state drives from the primary solid-state drive supplier still weren't ready. Kozak had hoped to have enough of them on hand on December 14 to begin building 620 test machines in Shenzhen. Instead, he told the reviewers, the drives would trickle in: 30 on December 14, 190 on December 18, 100 on December 27, and 300 on January 7. The goal was to build all of the machines between December 17 and January 18. Earlier, he had planned on finishing the manufacturing in the first week of January, but now the batch wouldn't be done until two weeks later. Because of the delays in getting the solid-state drives, Kozak told the reviewers, the program's status had shifted from medium risk to extremely high risk.

There were also problems with the Centrino package. After Cohen interceded, Intel had come through. Intel managers had promised that PC motherboards with Centrino cards soldered to them would be in Shenzhen by December 8. But there was still a technology glitch. Some test computers had seized up. They simply stopped working all of a sudden. The engineers had determined that the Centrino chips were at fault. Intel and Lenovo engineers were working together to fix the problem. The plan was that they would write a software patch that would be loaded on the chips later, after they were already in Shenzhen.

As the first session came to an end, Kozak was nervous. Usually, in meetings like this, there was plenty of lighthearted banter back and forth between the product developers and the quality reviewers. This time: none of that.

The review panel's decision was supposed to come down the next day. Starting again at 9 a.m., the group assembled in the Yamato board room. Kozak summarized the presentations from the previous day; then the panelists asked questions. At noon, Kodama dismissed everybody but the reviewers from the room. It was the panel's responsibility to give the project a rating. The possibilities were: ready, ready with risk, and not ready. Kozak had lunch and then waited outside the boardroom to be called back in. The summons came at 2 p.m. Kodama didn't waste words. The verdict was "not ready." He and his colleagues would not approve this project. They told Kozak what had to be done before they'd okay Kodachi.

Kozak was beside himself with worry. A few hours later, back in his hotel room in Tokyo, he sent an instant message via his laptop to Cohen, who was in Morrisville. Kodachi had been deemed "not ready." Cohen wrote back that he had been expecting this outcome, and he had a plan for dealing with it. Even though the development team still had some issues to work through, Cohen was going to instruct the factory managers to begin manufacturing the test machines. In fact, he ordered several of the Yamato product developers to fly immediately to Shenzhen. The plan had been to start manufacturing on December 17, but Cohen decided not to wait that long. Instead, they'd start on December 10—three days after the quality review ended. The first machines off the assembly line would not all have solid-state drives in them. The drives would have to be installed later. Kodachi would keep moving forward.

The ThinkPad factory in Shenzhen had been an IBM plant for several years, but Lenovo inherited it when it bought the IBM PC Co. The plant occupied a six-story concrete building in a Shenzhen free-trade zone. Outside, there was a small parking lot with a few dozen cars but hundreds of bicycles—evidence of the modest salaries Chinese factory workers still drew, in spite of the country's economic boom. As the shifts changed, the streets filled with bikes and company-owned buses that ferry workers to and from the zone's factories. On December 10, a Monday, which was normally a slow day on the fifth floor, a skeleton crew of young people—mostly women dressed in blue Lenovo smocks with lighter blue caps—began assembling the first 25 Kodachi test machines. There was no haste. Working under banners exhorting them to "Eliminate Idle Time," and "Meet Customer Requirements," their job was to spot any problems and to develop step-by-step instruction sheets for the assembly line crews that would handle high-volume production, starting on January 25. If they discovered that a part didn't fit quite right, they'd order up changes in the design by Yamato engineers that would quickly result in slight adjustments in how the components fit in the chassis. Lenovo called its technique of gradually ramping up production of test units "smart launch." The idea was to move slowly, find flaws in the design or assembly process, and fix them immediately.

On that day, the process started with employees picking parts from bins that came from suppliers the likes of Samsung, TDK, Foxconn, LG, and Chi Mei Optronics and placing all of the parts needed for each machine in its own black plastic crate called a "kit." The kits traveled along a conveyor belt to assembly lines where each of about a dozen employees did their small part to put Kodachi together. It was like a choreographed dance, with each move planned out in advance. After about 10 minutes and 25 steps—including installing the storage device, attaching a display screen, and so on—the finished machines rolled off the line. The workers plugged each sleek new laptop into one of a bank of PCs to run a battery of tests to ensure that the electronics were hooked up correctly. Then the machines were left to run for 24 hours to make sure they didn't overheat or encounter other problems. Finally, they were shipped off to a lab where technicians placed them in shipping boxes and dropped them from a height of 90 centimeters (about three feet) to simulate the kind of stress they might undergo in shipping. A couple of Yamato engineers were in the factory overseeing manufacturing and testing. And a procurement engineer wrote up reports for suppliers.

The man in charge of this process was John Egan, a burly, silver-haired, veteran of Dell's manufacturing operations in Austin, Texas. He had joined Lenovo four months earlier to oversee its worldwide manufacturing. "I'm trying to treat Kodachi as just another notebook," he said. "We build lots of different notebooks. This one's a little more delicate, but it's just another product going through the lines. It won't have its own line because I want to design the factory for maximum flexibility."

Lenovo was in the middle of ramping up its worldwide production capabilities. It had four factories in China, and some of its machines were made by contract manufacturers in Europe, the United States, and Mexico. But the company planned on growing rapidly once it launched its new consumer products in early 2008. So Egan was building plants in Poland, Mexico, and India. The idea was to build PCs the same, no matter where the job was being done—and to do it with maximum efficiency. The ThinkPad plant in Shenzhen was serving as a laboratory for new manufacturing ideas. Even in a low-wage country like China, there could be no slack in the process. Right then, he was studying ways to shorten the trip of the kits from the inventory section to the assembly lines. He was also studying and fine-tuning the assembly process so each stop along the way would take exactly the same amount of time and there would be no bottlenecks. "We need a pipe that has exactly the same capacity throughout," he said. "Then we can keep expanding the pipe and get more units per person or per square foot of factory space." His factory managers from Poland, Mexico, and India had visited the Shenzhen plants to learn the manufacturing process. Almost every day, Egan was on the phone with colleagues from the United States, Europe, and Asia to go over sales figures, production snafus, order backlogs, and the like. If they spotted a problem at one site, they'd check to see if the same problem was popping up elsewhere. If they saw a pattern, they'd investigate until they understood the cause—then they'd fix it once for everywhere.

Kodachi was slowly making its way through the final phases of the development process. As of early January, crews in the plant in Shenzhen had built 425 of the prototypes. But, still, the product had not cleared System Integration Test approval. There were still two technical hang-ups. The most serious one concerned the solid-state drives—the devices that replaced the traditional disk drive with one where information was stored on microchips instead of a disk. In tests of the drives, anomalies showed up that indicated problems. The primary supplier's engineers had been working to fix them for weeks, and had made 27 revisions of the software that served as the intermediary between the drive and the rest of the computer. If they didn't get this right, people who bought Kodachi would experience so-called blue-screen crashes, meaning their computers would stop working all of a sudden and all they would see on the displays would be an empty blue screen. Kozak was concerned that the glitch wouldn't be fixed in time for the launch of volume production, scheduled for January 25, so he had asked Samsung, which also was producing a 64-gigabyte solid-state drive, to speed up and get its device ready to go into Kodachi if the other supplier couldn't sort things out in time. "Unfortunately, this isn't an unusual thing," explained Naitoh. "But we need every product to be perfect. We have to be perfect."

The other technical problem was with Intel's Centrino. In tests, some of the prototypes would still suspend operations temporarily. Kozak had asked the engineers to come up with an estimate of the ratio of machines that would have this problem. If it was high enough, meaning if the problem rarely came up in normal use, he was prepared to give the Centrino package the go-ahead. Any customer who ran into problems could get his or her machine repaired or replaced. One other problem had come up during testing of the new prototypes: When you set them on a table, they rocked slightly if you pressed on the front right corner. So the bottom shell of the machine had to be retooled to eliminate the rocking. In Japan, Kinoshita, the Kodachi project leader, had pulled engineers from other projects and assigned them to help out with Kodachi. "It's all hands on deck now," said Kozak. He estimated that more than one hundred Lenovo people were working on the last fixes to Kodachi in Yamato, Morrisville, and Shenzhen. Plus, more than one hundred people from suppliers, including Samsung and Intel, were helping out.

While there were still technical problems to work through, the Kodachi development team was starting to feel more comfortable that everything would work out in the end. They had gotten some very encouraging feedback about the machine from an advisory council made up of about a dozen leading PC industry analysts and product reviewers. IBM had set up this council in the early ThinkPad days, and Lenovo had kept it going. The idea was to give these experts early looks at strategies and individual prototypes and get their input. The council met once or twice a year, and, at the most recent meeting, at the Adolphus Hotel in Dallas in December, Sam Dusi, the head of marketing for the portable division and one of the fathers of Kodachi, had passed a prototype around the conference room table so his advisors could get a sense of its look and feel. There was no big introductory speech. He simply said, "Here's this new one we've got coming." Then he waited to see what the reaction would be. Steve Kleynhans, an analyst for the tech market research firm Gartner, at first thought it was a nonfunctioning mock-up because it was so thin. But when one of the other analysts opened the notebook up, he saw it was a working model. Everybody wanted to touch it. Kleynhans was impressed by Kodachi's shape, lightness, and bright screen. "It was the highlight of the event," he said.

The top executives in Lenovo's portable division in Morrisville had similar reactions when they got their first looks at the prototypes that were coming off the assembly line in China. On January 7, a Monday, Kozak was sitting at his desk in his cubicle eating his customary egg salad sandwich for lunch when Mark Cohen walked over from his office 30 feet away, and said he and Hortensius wanted to see the prototype. Only a few were in the building, and they were in the hands of testers who were racing to complete their tasks so the machine could go into volume production on schedule. Kozak called around until he found somebody who had one. But he was told that he could only borrow it for 10 minutes. So he dashed down to the lab and fetched the precious machine. He took it to Hortensius's conference room and laid it before his bosses. Their reaction was extremely positive. "I love this," Hortensius said as he hefted the machine in his hands. He had told the

Yamato engineers he wanted it made lighter, and they had found ways to do so. Kodachi was specified at 3.4 pounds (1.5 kilograms) at "plan exit" back in the previous April. It came in at 3.1 pounds (1.4 kilograms). And the version that didn't include the DVD drive weighed just 2.9 pounds (1.3 kilograms). It was thin, too: 0.73 inches (1.85 millimeters) at the thinnest point and 0.92 inches (2.34 millimeters) at the thickest.

Still, Hortensius and Cohen had their quibbles. Kozak made a list of small items they wanted fixed. For example, Cohen didn't like the color of a button on the keyboard that launched software to help people solve problems that arose with their computers. He wanted it painted a darker blue. The session in Hortensius's conference room lasted nearly half an hour, while testers waited impatiently to have the machine returned to them. Then Kozak rushed the machine back downstairs. By the end of that week, Hortensius, Cohen, and Kozak had their own Kodachis to play with.

Kodachi's next big hurdle was a review in Morrisville on January 15. About forty executives and managers would hear Kozak's progress report at 10 a.m. He had started his day at 7 a.m. on a two-hour conference call with sales leaders—something called a "sales and marketing readiness review." These were the people who had shown so little confidence in the prospects for Kodachi the previous April that their sales estimates had come in at just half of what the product marketing team had forecast. Now the mood was entirely different. The salespeople had their test machines, and they loved Kodachi. "They said they thought the machine was just a killer—with the lightness, the bright screen, the battery life. To a person, they said they thought they could do well with it," said Kozak. Two hours later, he was on another conference call. This one was about manufacturing planning. According to the master schedule, Kodachi was supposed to be available for ordering online by a handful of resellers and major customers on February 5. But, since the weeklong Chinese New Year celebration was going to begin February 7, Lenovo wouldn't be able to fulfill the initial orders. The factory would be shut, and so would customs. So they decided to move the "order window" to February 1. That way, at least a few orders could be dealt with before the whole country shut down for holidays.

Kozak was in a buoyant mood when he was called into the project review meeting. This took place in a conference room of Building Number 2 in Morrisville. About forty people were there, including Cohen. Hortensius couldn't make it. Kozak gave them the full status report on X300. Most of the problems were fixed. The rocking had been taken care of. The issues with the Intel chips had been resolved. The only remaining glitch was the solid-state drives. There were still anomalies showing up in tests, and Lenovo and engineers from both suppliers were working on fixing them. But Kozak was confident everything would be ready on time. The schedule was set: January 22 was "release to manufacturing." January 25 was "start of volume manufacturing." February 1 was "early order window." February 26 was "general availability." Cohen was pleased with the report. His only caution: make sure the programmers in Slovakia who were setting up the online configuration and ordering system for X300 would have it ready in time for ordering by customers on February 1.

So, happy days, right? Maybe not. Within a few hours of this meeting something would happen in San Francisco that would raise doubts about X300. Like I described briefly in Chapter 1, it was Steve Jobs's keynote at the annual MacWorld conference. Every year, just after the Consumer Electronics Show, Jobs would introduce Apple's latest products. In recent years, thanks to a series of hits, he had upstaged everything that came out of CES. This year, there had been rumors that he would introduce a very thin notebook PC. And, indeed, he did. Standing on the stage in San Francisco's Moscone Center, dressed in his customary blue jeans and black turtleneck, Jobs had first recapped what had been an excellent year for Apple. iPod sales were still going gangbusters. Ditto iPhone sales. Apple's new operating system update, Leopard, had been a hit—overshadowing Microsoft's Vista. He saved news of the new laptop until last. "Today we're introducing a third kind of notebook, and it's called the MacBook Air. In a sentence, it's the world's thinnest notebook," he told the crowd of Mac faithful. A huge, high-resolution photo of the Air appeared on a screen behind him as he ticked through its dimensions: 0.76 inches (19.3 millimeters) at its thickest point and tapering off to just 0.16 inches (4.06 millimeters) around the edges. To demonstrate just how thin this machine was, he held up an interoffice envelope and pulled an Air out of it. The crowd went wild.

Back in Morrisville, some Lenovo-ites were just about flipping out. This looked like the disaster that Dusi had dreaded starting back in April when X300 had emerged from plan exit. He worried that another company would come out with a notebook that was just as thin and light; or, worse, thinner and lighter. Hortensius heard whisperings about the Air announcement during a lunchtime meeting, and, afterward, he rushed back to his office and sat down in front of his PC. He quickly navigated to a Web site where photos from the launch were posted. There was Jobs. The envelope. The Air! He shouted to Phyllis Arrington-McGee, his executive assistant, who sat in a cubicle 10 feet outside his office, to bring him one of those envelopes.

Arrington-McGee quickly rifled through the drawers of her desk, but couldn't find the right envelope, so she rushed around the office asking other people for one. Finally, she found what she was looking for in a filing cabinet and took it to Hortensius, who was waiting nervously in his office with Dusi. She had no idea what Hortensius wanted the envelope for, and, after handing it to him, she returned to her desk. A moment later, though, she heard Hortensius shout, "It fits! It fits!" So she poked her head back into his office. Hortensius was beaming. He was holding his X300 in his hands, halfway pulled out of the envelope. It was tight, but it fit. Disaster had been averted.

Later that day, after things calmed down, Dusi made a close comparison of X300 and Air. X300 was slightly thicker at its thickest point, but the version without a DVD drive—which Air didn't have, either—was slightly lighter. Air had some nice features, including backlit keys on the keyboard and the ability to use iPhone-like finger gestures on the touchpad. But, he was greatly relieved to see that, overall, the Lenovo laptop was clearly superior when it came to basic capabilities. X300 had three different battery options, and the batteries were easily removable; Air's battery was built in. If you were on a long plane flight, you couldn't replace it with a backup. X300 had three USB ports, plugs where you could attach in a printer, a mouse, a small memory stick, or other peripherals; Air had just one. X300 had all of those wireless radios plus a plug for a network cable; Air offered fewer wireless options and no network plug. Air had a faster processor, but there were other matchups where X300 won, too.

Would corporate laptop buyers agree? Amelio would find out soon enough. A week later, on February 1, the early ordering system on Lenovo's Web site went live for select customers. Kozak didn't expect a flood of orders. The idea was to allow customers to buy a few X300s and test them out. Orders for 57 machines came in on the first day. It was a trickle, but, at least, it was a start.

After more than a year and a half of effort, Kodachi was finally finished. There was no celebration. Kozak was already immersed in his other projects. But he and other Lenovo people, from engineers all the way up to the top executives, felt that they had accomplished something momentous. When Yang saw the last test version, he decided he had to have one for himself. His assistant, Tony Lo, had been urging him to order a new laptop for weeks, but Yang said he'd wait until he could get one of the first X300s off of the manufacturing line. He said the project had accomplished exactly what he wanted: proving that Lenovo could be just as innovative as IBM. There could be no doubt about that now. He was so impressed with the work that had come out of Yamato that he had decided to transfer some of the top Yamato engineers to Beijing to serve as mentors. Kinoshita, the technical lead in Yamato for the X300, looked exhausted during a final interview, but his satisfaction shined through. "Kodachi was a completely new concept. We were designing a new platform from scratch," he said. "No one had a clear idea how it was going to be possible." Hortensius confidently predicted that the X300 would sell better than a lot of people in the company had expected. Looking back on the difficult journey, he said, "This tells people we can do better. It tells me we haven't reached the end of innovation in notebooks."

One day in late January 2008, Hill, Lenovo's chief designer, put one of the test versions in his bag at the office and drove to his home in nearby Cary, North Carolina. He had been talking obsessively about the project to his wife, Jena, for months, and he had taken home design models and prototypes to show her. Now he had the finished product. She was in the kitchen when he arrived. "I want to show you Kodachi," he told her. Standing at the work island in the middle of the kitchen, he slipped the machine out of his bag and handed it to her. "Wow, that's light," she said. She looked the machine over for a few minutes before passing it back to him. She asked how much it would cost. When Hill told her, she said, "Oh, my." It seemed a bit pricey. Then she asked to hold it again.

Hill was thrilled with X300. The designers and engineers had accomplished most of what he had dreamed of back in June 2006. His only real disappointment was that the bottom was still more cluttered with labels and vents than he would have liked. But that gave him new challenges to overcome. "I want to make something even more perfect than this," he said. "It's a continuous search for perfection." It had to be. The way the PC business operates, it was likely a competitor would leapfrog X300 before the end of the year—if not sooner.

8

HYPE, FUD, AND E-MARKETING

The scene was Las Vegas. It was early January 2008, and the oasis was teaming with more than one hundred forty thousand people attending the International Consumer Electronics Show. More than twenty-seven hundred exhibitors had set up booths in 1.8 million square feet of space—showing off everything from $30 wireless nunchucks for playing games on Nintendo's superpopular Wii video game console to $1,399, 42-inch (1,067-millimeter), flat-panel LCD TVs. The floor of the Las Vegas Convention Center was packed elbow to elbow with people, blaring with sound, and vibrating with color. But Lenovo was not there.

Instead, the company had rented space off the show floor in a back corridor of the convention center. The reason was cost. Lenovo wanted to play in the big leagues, but it didn't have the cash of bigger players Dell, Hewlett-Packard, or Apple. It budgeted between just 1 percent and 2 percent of its annual revenues for marketing and advertising. While Apple, for instance, advertised aggressively on television and in glossy magazines, Lenovo was focusing more on the Internet and on billboard campaigns in airports and train stations. "We don't have the muscle in the marketing budget," says Glen Gilbert, vice-president of brand management. "We need to be much more surgically precise, and to be where our competition isn't."

Being at the Consumer Electronics Show at all was an exception to that rule, but it paid off in a major way. Lenovo had announced its entry into the global consumer markets just before the show began, and one of its new consumer laptop models, the compact and stylish red-clad IdeaPad U110, won a handful of best-in-show awards from tech-industry publications. Meanwhile, in private, one-on-one sessions, the company's marketers stealthily revealed the X300 to a select group of 23 product reviewers— whetting their appetites to get their hands on the laptops a few weeks later. That move paid off in late February with a series of very positive reviews. Chalk up a marketing victory for the underdog.

Lenovo's underdog status was firmly established on the day that it announced the IBM acquisition in late 2004. A Chinese company virtually unknown outside its home country had bought an iconic but subpar business from one of the giants of American industry. The corporate strategy made sense. Lenovo could use the IBM PC division's global operations, the ThinkPad brand, and, through the partnership, IBM's vaunted sales force, to turn itself into a global PC industry player practically overnight. But the marketing challenge was huge. In its effort to create a strong global brand, Lenovo had to overcome powerful negative perceptions: (1) China is a scary nation that has suspect global ambitions, and it's taking American manufacturing jobs; (2) the Chinese make cheap, low-quality knock-offs, so they won't do justice to the ThinkPad brand; (3) ThinkPad has been on the decline, anyway.

So, while X300 was expected to help establish Lenovo as a brand that meant engineering quality and outstanding design, the little laptop had to battle against a current of negativity and skepticism. Think of a small, well-crafted canoe in a big, turbulent river full of huge boulders.

Immediately after the IBM PC division deal was announced, Lenovo's competitors had cranked up their FUD machines. *FUD*, which stands for *fear*, *uncertainty*, and *doubt*, is a marketing technique invented in the early days of the computer industry. After IBM established itself as the industry leader with its mainframes in the 1970s, its sales force proved expert at locking in customers by assuring corporate computer buyers that nobody ever lost his or her job by buying IBM. It was the safe bet. Microsoft used FUD very effectively by preannouncing products that were still on the drawing boards months or years before they were ready—thus inducing customers to delay purchases of competitors' products that beat Microsoft to market. In the case of Lenovo, sales and marketing people from Dell and Hewlett-Packard cast doubt on the future of the ThinkPad product line. It was a large target for them since ThinkPad had been adopted by many corporations as their laptops of choice. In response, IBM PC executives raced around to long-time customers to reassure them. But, early on, they were losing the battle. General Electric and others switched to Dell. "The new Lenovo will be good for us," said Dell's then CEO, Kevin Rollins, "We think a lot of the IBM customers will want to come to us." He was right. The combined global PC market share of IBM and Lenovo dropped from 7.9 percent to 7.4 percent in the year after the deal was announced, according to market researcher IDC.

Then the real trouble started. It was that big U.S. State Department deal. After the State Department announced it was buying 16,000 Lenovo PCs for $13 million in March 2006, CNN TV anchorman Lou Dobbs ran a segment about the sale—warning that the United States was opening itself up to a security breach by buying PCs from "Communist China." He interviewed Michael R. Wessel, a member of the U.S.-China Economic and Security Review Commission, an advisory body to Congress. In the ensuing days, other members of the commission criticized the deal and congressmen vowed to investigate. The chairman of the commission, Larry M. Wortzel, told me, "It's possible the Chinese government inserted somebody into the company." It was the Red Scare all over again. Never mind that the PCs were made in Raleigh, North Carolina, and that although some of the important internal electronics had been assembled in China that was also true for every other PC company in the world. Lenovo launched an aggressive defense, with Chairman Yang Yuanqing speaking out publicly and meeting with government officials privately. In the end, the deal went through with minor modifications. But the marketing damage had been done. FUD had been spread. Some at Lenovo suspected that Dell had tipped off the commissioners and planted fears in their minds, but it couldn't be proven.

While Lenovo was the victim of FUD, it was unable to use another marketing tool that had worked magnificently for many tech companies over the decades: *hype*. Making exaggerated claims about an upcoming product had long been on page 1 of the PC-Industry Marketers' Playbook. It had started when the industry was in diapers—with Adam Osborne whipping up excitement about the Osborne 1 luggable in 1981. Hype worked for the original Apple Macintosh, for Microsoft's Windows, for Netscape's Navigator Internet browser, and for Apple's iPhone. At the peak of its effectiveness, in the 1990s, hype was refined into a high art, and it encompassed not just individual products but also whole waves of technology. Here's how it worked: venture capitalists invested like lemmings in companies that were working on technologies that looked like they could become the next big thing in computing—be it pen-based gizmos or so-called push technologies for distributing Internet information to people's computer screens. The venture capitalists talked up their portfolio companies and their products to journalists, who also operated in a pack, and were starving for the next great thing. Meanwhile, large tech companies, determined to get in on the act, started developing similar technologies and products and touting them—often using FUD to try to delay adoption of the start-ups' products. When the hype machine worked perfectly, the media and consuming public would be whipped into a frenzy of software or gadget lust. But the hype machine could be risky, too, as the rise and collapse of pen computing in the 1990s showed.

By the time Lenovo was preparing to introduce X300 and its new consumer products in the winter of 2008, hype was only working selectively in the tech industry. The media and customers had been burned so many times by empty promises, especially in portable computing, that they were inclined to skepticism. The exceptions were few: any product coming out of Apple or Google and any new Web service from scruffy guys in a San Francisco loft—such as Twitter, the service that allowed people to share what they were doing at any given moment with their pals. There was no way Lenovo would be able to hype X300 the way Steve Jobs had amped up the excitement around the MacBook Air at MacWorld in San Francisco in January 2008.

There were plenty of opportunities for marketing that could pay off big, though. Lenovo's marketing team had to be creative about it, to use the Internet smartly, and to get the fundamentals right. Another consideration: X300 marketing wasn't happening in isolation. It would play an important role in a global branding strategy that was being based largely on the engineering and design of portable computers. "It's the strongest brand-building tool we have. It's much more valuable than a big glossy ad campaign," said Lenovo chief marketing officer Deepak Advani of X300.

The company's biggest brand-building opportunity was the Olympics. Even before Yang made the deal to buy IBM's PC division, he had already committed to being one of the main sponsors of the Olympic Games, in Torino, Italy, in 2006, and Beijing in 2008. This meant spending upwards of $100 million in cash and equipment, according to analysts' estimates. But Yang believed the payoff would be well worth the expense. More than one billion people worldwide would watch TV coverage of the games and see Lenovo's brand featured prominently. As soon as Beijing won the right to host the 2008 games, in early 2004, Yang had approached the International Olympic Committee about the sponsorship. And, after he bought the IBM PC division, he saw the Olympics as a powerful vehicle for establishing Lenovo's brand internationally. The Beijing Olympics would be nothing less than a worldwide coming-out party for Lenovo. But it was a risky gamble. Would it work? Most observers said the Olympics sponsorships would help Lenovo, but didn't see it as a cure-all. "They can't afford not to do it, but I don't think it will be magic for them," said

Wang Shuo, managing editor of China's *Caijing* Magazine, a few months before the Beijing games were to begin.

When Lenovo was just a Chinese company, it had carved out a big space for itself as the home-country champion. But, clearly, the new Lenovo had to start from scratch to build a global brand. As part of the IBM deal, Lenovo had secured the rights to use the IBM logo on its computers and in its advertising for five years. The trick was to get the most out of the IBM brand in concert with the ThinkPad subbrand while gradually transferring the brand equity over to Lenovo. Some corporate customers had urged them to make the shift quickly rather than dragging it out for five years, and they soon discovered that most customers seemed to be more attached to the ThinkPad name than to IBM. So, gradually, they began downplaying the IBM logo on products and advertising. A key element of shifting over was establishing Lenovo as being as good or better than IBM at laptop engineering and design. Unlike most other PC companies, Lenovo really could take credit for the engineering and design of its machines. It developed its laptops in-house, rather than farming the work out to design and manufacturing specialists in Taiwan and China.

The process of defining Lenovo with outstanding engineering and design started in earnest in the summer of 2006. It was at that time when design chief David Hill gave guided tours of the ThinkPad design center in North Carolina to Yang and CEO William Amelio. Remember, Hill showed them his Bento-Fly concept, which later morphed into the Kodachi project and X300. Shortly after his tour, Amelio met with Advani and said design and engineering would be vital to the company's future. "This is how we'll define ourselves as different and remarkable," he told Advani. In response, Advani set up the CEO's Design Office, made up of himself, Amelio, Hill, chief operating officer Fran O'Sullivan, product development chief George He, and Chinese design boss Yao Yingjia. They'd meet regularly to percolate ideas and make sure that design and engineering remained the company's top values. Advani believed that design could be a major plus for Lenovo, not just in making its products more attractive and in helping to build the brand, but also strengthening its hand when it came to setting prices. "I think people will pay $50 more for something that's really clever," he said. "They'll pay a premium, not a huge one, but a premium."

Advani was a good pick to run marketing at a company for which engineering was the linchpin of the brand. He was born in India, but, when he was 16, his business executive father had decided he wanted his children to go to school in the United States, so he moved the entire family to East Lansing, Michigan—even though it meant taking a lesser job. The young Advani had always been good at math and science, and he chose the computer science program at Michigan State and later got a master's degree in computer engineering from Wright State. He started his own engineering consulting business, but was soon hired by IBM to help design its Deep Blue supercomputer—the one that beat world champion chess player Garry Kasparov in a demonstration match in 1997. After getting an MBA from the Wharton School at the University of Pennsylvania, Advani started running IBM business units, including one of its server computer businesses. Then, two years before the PC unit was sold, he moved over there to run strategy and marketing. Industrial design had always been an interest of his, but it wasn't until he worked in the PC division that he got a chance to work with designers. He made his reputation with a series of advertising programs that accented the durability and security of ThinkPads, including TV ads that touted the new "air bag" technology for protecting hard drives from damage when the laptops were dropped. At Lenovo, it was clear from the start that ThinkPad would be the company's strongest marketing tool. "There's a cultlike following behind ThinkPad. We need to keep it up and strengthen it," Advani said shortly after the merger was completed. At that point, he was just beginning to think about the new Lenovo brand, but, already, he believed it would be built around the value of "thoughtfully designed products," he said. Meanwhile, Yang and then CEO Steve Ward set up a small business unit whose goal was to come up with a strategy for selling consumer products globally—with Yang temporarily in charge.

The next task was coming up with an *über*-brand strategy. Advani's team interviewed 4,000 customers, business partners, and employees to get their input. An important element would be the brand tag line that would accompany all communications and advertising, something like GE's "We Bring Good Things to Life." They wanted language that would set Lenovo apart as a different sort of PC company, neither Chinese nor American. Also, they wanted to signal that the company would be innovative. They chose: "New Company, New Thinking." Next, Advani and his team worked on the messaging language for the products. In August 2006, two months after Hill showed Yang and Amelio his Bento-Fly concepts, Advani convened the most important marketing meeting since the merger. He invited 20 marketing leaders from the company's four regions and ten of the top countries to Raleigh for a briefing on the global strategy. He revealed the company's primary marketing message, which many of them had helped develop. It was: "Lenovo produces the best-engineered PCs." The message had to be simple. It had to explain in a few words why customers should buy a Lenovo product rather than one from Acer or Dell. Lenovo spent more on R&D as a ratio of revenues than either of those two companies. Engineering and design excellence had been important for both sides of the company before the merger. Now those attributes would define the company. "Branding is not something you invent. It's something you uncover," Advani told me at that time. He also came up with the new messaging for the company's subbrands. For ThinkPad it was "Rock solid, thoughtful design, with the lowest total cost of ownership." For Lenovo 3000, a new subbrand aimed at small businesses that the company had launched in early 2006, the message was "Worry-free computing, great value, stylish design." The idea was that these messages wouldn't change for at least five years. To create a lasting impression on his marketing team, he conducted a little ceremony. He had workers pour cement to create three tablets, one for each of the branding messages. Then he and his people pressed their hands into the wet concrete to leave prints.

As word spread throughout the company that design and engineering would be of paramount importance, morale among engineers and designers soared. Fueled by hope, Hill had pushed ahead with Bento-Fly. "This is the biggest thing I have ever done in my career," he said. "We're working on the purest form of the ThinkPad and aligning it with a whole new company." Yao and the team at the innovation center in China were just as excited. They looked for ways they could demonstrate Lenovo's design expertise in China, and, quickly, focused on the Olympics. The Beijing Organizing Committee conducted a design contest for the Beijing Olympics logo, and Lenovo designers submitted a proposal. They didn't win, but when the committee launched yet another design contest, this time for the Olympic torch, Yao was determined to win the competition—which typically goes to a traditional design company.

To get the creative juices flowing, Yao conducted a brainstorming session on November 25, 2005, at the Jiu Hua Hot Spring Resort outside Beijing. He pulled together about eighty Lenovo designers, electrical engineers, and mechanical engineers, divided them into four teams, and challenged them to come up with design ideas. He wanted the torch to be light and easy to hold and hand off. But he also wanted striking imagery that would wow the people who viewed it—and he wanted it to reflect both the Olympic tradition and Chinese culture. The scene at the hotel was chaotic. The team members, including designers from China, Germany, Singapore, and New Zealand, were talking over each other in Chinese and English. "It was like vendors shouting in a crowded market," Yao recalls.

A major breakthrough came when Angela Qiu, a design strategy director, urged the group to make the torch look like a scroll. She pointed out that the Chinese had invented paper, and she demonstrated her idea by rolling a large sheet of paper from both ends until it became a compact, torchlike shape that could easily be held in a runner's hand. The next issue was imagery. Some of the designers wanted to use a dragon, the Great Wall, or the phoenix—all common Chinese motifs. But Yao pressed for a design that would meld the Olympics with China. They settled on clouds, a motif that captured both the essence of ancient Chinese design and the overlapping circles of the Olympic logo.

The brainstorming session proved to be the easy part. Over the ensuing months, a team of ten Lenovo designers and engineers led by Yao worked out the details. The torch had to be light, so they used an aluminum magnesium alloy with which they were familiar from their experience in building laptops. They also used a rubberized paint common in portable computing to make the handle easy to grip. They settled on red as a primary color in the design, but it took weeks to find the right red. They finally chose a bold red that's very close to the color of the doors on Beijing's Forbidden City. All the attention to detail paid off. Their design, called "Cloud of Promise," was chosen by the Beijing Olympic Committee from more than three hundred submissions. "Winning the design contest was important for Lenovo. It's about establishing your best-of-breed design on a world stage," says Lee Green, the corporate design and brand chief executive at IBM.

In the middle of the torch design process, some of Lenovo's Beijing marketers came up with the idea of designing a laptop computer using the design motifs from the torch. Yao and his team thought it was a great idea. They used the same red color and the swirling cloud design on the top cover. Yao wanted to capture the feeling of Han Dynasty lacquered boxes, which have bold designs and colors on the outside and simpler designs inside. The Olympic Torch PC, a version of Lenovo's Tianxi notebook line for consumers, was black and red, with a decorative cloud motif on the top cover. The company made a couple of thousand of them for promotional purposes, and it auctioned a few dozen of them online in the winter and spring of 2008 as part of its buildup to the Olympics.

With the Olympic Torch PC, Yao and the rest of the Chinese design and engineering team were just warming up. It was their task to create a new line of consumer products that the company would market globally. Yao had begun his research in 2006. He visited the United States, Europe, India, and a handful of other countries. In some places he even visited families in their homes to see how they used computers and consumer electronics. Before the IBM PC division deal he had rarely been outside of China, so Yao used this market research project as an excuse to soak up world culture wherever he could find it. During a trip to Australia in October 2006 he heard aboriginal music and liked it so much that he bought a CD, called *Tribal Offerings*, which was a mix of didgeridoo and music from other tribal cultures from around the world. Back in Beijing he played the music during meetings with his design team—for inspiration. The way he saw things, portable computing was at a crossroads. For 25 years, laptops had primarily been tools for business. Now they represented the convergence of computing, communications, and entertainment. The laptop would play an important role in an ordinary person's mobile life. "In the past, laptops were like a single instrument, playing a single melody," Yao said in mid-2007. "Today, it's like an orchestra resonating with other elements of our life."

Yao's chance to resonate with global consumers came on the eve of the International Consumer Electronics Show in January 2008. Finally, after 2½ years of planning and preparation, Lenovo entered the global consumer markets and introduced its consumer brand name—Idea. The laptops were called IdeaPad, and the desktop PCs were called IdeaCentre, echoing the ThinkPad and ThinkCentre subbrands Lenovo had inherited from IBM. The choice of *Idea* was even more fitting than anybody outside of China would realize. The word for *thought* in Chinese, *xiang*, is part of Lenovo's Chinese name, Lian Xiang. "This move is very important in the long run for us to meet our global aspirations," Advani told me a couple of days ahead of the consumer products launch event. "The ThinkPad is the gold standard in business notebooks, and it does help build the global brand, but with the consumer strategy we can turbocharge it."

Lenovo announced six products, three laptops and three desktop models. The star among them was the IdeaPad U110, a 2.3-pound (1.04 kilogram) laptop with a bold red top and a high-sheen, 11-inch (279.4-millimeter) screen that ran right to the edge of the lid. The laptop featured a vinelike texture on the surface of its metal cover. All six machines also offered facial recognition-based security: When you boot up, photographic software studies your face through a built-in camera above the screen, confirming your identity before it lets you start using the machine.

These products hadn't sailed smoothly from the drawing boards to market, though. The previous June, when Yao revealed his design ideas to the company's industry advisory panel at a briefing in Morrisville, some of the analysts hated them. The colors were too bright, they thought, and the textures on the outside shells of the computers were turnoffs. "There's some weird design stuff in China—with the bright colors and textures," one of the advisory board members, J.P. Gownder of Forrester Research, told me later. "They have a lot of work to do when it comes to design for the U.S. market." Another person who attended the meeting recalled that Yao didn't take the criticism well. Frustrated, he told the advisors: "You don't understand design!" Still, Yao knew he had to respond. Over the coming months, he made several compromises. They included changing the color on the outside of the U110 from a bright cherry red to a deeper red, and altering the texture on the outer shell. Still, when the laptop was released, it made a bold design statement. "You have to take some risks," Yao told me.

Lenovo, as a corporation, had recently taken a step off a cliff into the unknown. Although it had secured rights to the IBM name and logo for up to five years, in the fall of 2007 Yang and Amelio decided that they were ready to make the switch. It was like a parent taking the training wheels off their kid's bike. Gradually, with each new product released, they dropped the IBM logo, and, in November 2007, they announced that they would forsake it altogether—two years before the deadline. That was the official end of the transition. The symbolic end came on December 7 on what the executives had named Lenovo Pride Day. It was Amelio and Advani's idea to hold ceremonies during which employees in former IBM offices around the world would celebrate their emancipation. Amelio, O'Sullivan, and Advani were in Morrisville, where four hundred people jammed into a cafeteria at noon, and another three thousand or so dialed in on a conference line. The employees had been asked to bring their ThinkPads. Amelio gave a little speech about how proud he was of the staff's accomplishments and how he expected Lenovo to become one of the most widely admired companies in the world. Then he used a pin to peel the IBM logo off of the outside of his ThinkPad and replaced it with a Lenovo sticker. The crowd roared with approval. Amelio and the rest of the executives mingled with the employees and helped them replace their IBM logos. It was the end of a remarkable era in computing, and, potentially, the beginning of another.

There was no time for wallowing in sentimentality, though. The ThinkPad team was faced with a major marketing challenge. How would it introduce X300? Lenovo rarely held press conferences in the United States. Most tech product news was published online, and reporters wanted the information fast and early. They weren't inclined to travel to a press conference and sit through a long presentation. They wanted their information delivered by e-mail. Still, the public relations team figured that, in the right setting and with the right timing, they could get good turnouts for X300 press conferences and make a big splash. Ultimately, the plan for X300 was to issue a press release on February 26, a Tuesday. There would be no press conference in the United States, but they'd hold them in Paris, for all of the European press, and in Hong Kong, Singapore, and Sydney. In addition, Lenovo had shipped test models of X300 to dozens of influential product reviewers, such as the *Wall Street Journal's* Walt Mossberg and *Business Week's* Steve Wildstrom. The idea was for stories and reviews to begin pouring out starting on February 26 and continuing for weeks as reviewers put X300 through tests and came out with their detailed assessments.

A key piece of Lenovo's media strategy was a *Business Week* story I had been working on since that day back in 2006 when Hill had shown me his Bento-Fly concepts. I had decided on the spot that the tale of how the Bento-Fly proceeded from idea to finished product would make a great narrative for *Business Week*. Within days of my meeting with Hill, I had pitched the idea to Lenovo's PR people, asking them for unprecedented access to the company's designers, engineers, marketers, and executives from the beginning of the process to the end. I promised not to publish the story until they gave me the all clear. They quickly granted my request, and, in the months afterward I interviewed dozens of Lenovo employees, some of them many times over. Director of corporate public relations Ray Gorman told all of the people I interviewed to be frank, and they were. In the end, there were plenty of challenges and compromises, but nothing embarrassing happened. In early January 2008, it was almost certain that X300 would be launched on schedule. Gorman told me I could get a head start and publish the week before the official announcement.

All of the publicity pieces seemed to be in place, but in the Internet era it's almost impossible to control information. On January 8, a Tuesday, a Chinese gadget Web site published a grainy photo of X300 that looked like it had been taken with a mobile phone camera, plus details of its capabilities and features. Someone had leaked the information. Lenovo's marketers suspected it was one of the company's suppliers. Lenovo had planned on posting hints about X300 on the Web in advance of its launch to pique the public's curiosity—hoping that the tidbits would spread virally on the Net via a host of weblogs that focused obsessively on electronic gadgets. The gadget blogs, led by Gizmodo and Engadget, raced each other to post the first photos and descriptions of each new computer or nifty consumer electronics device. Usually, the bloggers made comments, yea or nay, and, typically, hundreds of readers would post their own comments on the blogs. The Lenovo marketers hoped that bits of information they put out would be picked up that way and curiosity about X300 would spread like wildfire. But this unsanctioned leak threatened to blow up the company's carefully orchestrated publicity strategy. When Peter Hortensius, head of Lenovo's laptop business, heard about the leak, he was furious at first. "I was on a march to tear somebody apart," he said. "If somebody's going to do something viral with it, I want to control it. Not some yahoo." But then he calmed down. The Chinese Web posting didn't get much pickup elsewhere in the world. It seemed a crisis had been averted.

A few days later came Apple's MacBook Air announcement. People loved Air's shape but found fault with the rest of the package. One acerbic commenter quipped that it was a smart purchase only for somebody who already had three computers. Three days after the Air announcement, Gizmodo posted a photo of X300 and official specification sheets detailing its weight, thickness, and components. Somebody, most probably one of Lenovo's suppliers, had leaked the information to Gizmodo. Suddenly, chatter about X300 was racing all over the Web, and many of the top blogs compared X300 favorably to Air. Some even called it the "Air killer." Though Hortensius and Dusi had worried about losing control of marketing, they now realized that losing control could be a very good thing. Lenovo was winning the online information war. The pot was stirred again on February 8, when retailer Best Buy accidently posted a preorder page on its Web site for X300. Lenovo contacted Best Buy and asked them to take the page down, which they did. Typically, when news of an upcoming product appears on the Net, it's quickly swept aside by news on some other upcoming product. But in this case, interest in X300 was persistent. Lenovo could not have bought better marketing.

As the launch date drew closer, there were even bigger online appearances for X300. The *Wall Street Journal*'s Mossberg, arguably the most influential tech product reviewer in the world, dedicated Mossblog on February 13 to a preview of X300. He ran a photo of the machine, open, from the side, sitting on top of an interoffice mail envelope. It showed just how thin the laptop was. Mossberg wrote: "Unlike the Apple, Lenovo's new skinny ThinkPad comes with a hefty complement of features—some of the very things critics complain Apple left out." His blog item was picked up by hundreds of other blogs. On February 14, *BusinessWeek* published my narrative about X300 online. The story, entitled "Building the Perfect Laptop," was read by one-quarter million people on BusinessWeek.com in the first four days, and 130 blogs linked to it. David Hill linked to the story on his Design Matters blog. In print, the story went on the cover of the magazine. *BusinessWeek* circulates to more than one million homes and offices worldwide, and is displayed on thousands of newsstands. So, potentially, a couple of million people saw the story.

At 6 a.m. on February 26, the long-awaited moment arrived for Hill and his colleagues. After more than twenty months of gestation, their mechanical creation was born. The Lenovo PR team sent out a press release announcing X300 on Business Wire, the principle online distribution vehicle for tech industry press releases, and marketing pages went up on the Lenovo Web site. The tagline on the site was: "The no-compromise ultraportable that goes beyond thin and light." Alongside X300, Lenovo also marketed some of its less expensive laptops. Within one day of the press release being sent out, more than one hundred news stories about X300 had been posted online in English—and countless more in other languages. Rob Enderle, one of the best-known PC industry market researchers, posted a note on his Enderle Group blog with the headline, "Has Lenovo created the perfect laptop?" His bottom line: "From a personal standpoint, this is the first ThinkPad I've lusted after since the great Butterfly of the mid-'90s." For the folks at Lenovo, it was Christmas, Japan's Shogatsu, and Chinese New Year all wrapped up into one.

Seemingly out of nowhere, the blogosphere had become one of the most important marketing venues for PCs and personal electronics. At first, Lenovo had tried to discourage speculation about its upcoming products on the blogs. Then it went with the flow, deciding on a case-by-case basis whether to confirm or no-comment a posting. It turned out that what was being said about a company and its products on the Net was some of the most important marketing intelligence the company could get. So, in mid-2006, Lenovo had set up a formal Net monitoring program. A team of five people, in Morrisville and Kuala Lumpur, tracked online mentions of the company. In some cases, if somebody complained about a Lenovo product, they'd have the customer service team try to contact that person. Lenovo's marketing people also developed relationships with the most influential gadget sites and bloggers. They'd send loaner machines to important bloggers just like they had for so many years to official media reviewers. Typically, Lenovo didn't leak information about upcoming products to the bloggers. But the one time it did paid off. It passed along information about the leather-clad ThinkPad Reserve Edition to Dan Lyons, keeper of the Fake Steve Jobs blog. Lyons chided Apple for not having its own leather-covered laptop. "We declared victory on that one," says David Churbuck, head of online marketing for Lenovo. With X300, Churbuck had mainly sat back and watched. When interest in the product broke out on the Net, he posted photos on the photo-sharing Web site Flickr. That way, anybody who typed X300 into the image-search box on the Google search engine would see the machine, and could link to it from his or her blog or Web site. Advani was thrilled with the reaction to X300 on the Net. "This is a very special product for us—one that comes along maybe once in a decade," he said. "We're getting so much buzz. People have gone crazy over it. They're doing our marketing for us."

As the Olympics approached, the plan was to incorporate X300 into online, print, and TV advertising. In the winter of 2008, the company launched its major advertising campaign for the year, called "Ideas Everywhere." The ads featured small yellow helium balloons in the shape of lightbulbs. Each ad highlighted a different product. At first, Lenovo advertised mostly in print and in airports and train stations. Just before the Olympics started, they began advertising heavily on TV.

The challenge with X300 was to figure out how best to express its thinness and lightness. That task fell to Rod Vallis, an Australian who headed up the Ogilvy & Mather (O&M) advertising creative team that worked hand in hand with Lenovo's marketing office in Bangalore, India. In 2007, Advani had decided to make Bangalore the hub for Lenovo's global marketing. The reason: the company had tested its consumer product strategy in India starting in 2006, and enjoyed remarkable success; much of that, Advani felt, could be credited to the marketers in Bangalore. For the Lenovo and O&M people in Bangalore, who worked together in one office, expressing thinness wouldn't be a problem. They could show X300 from the side and contrast it to other thin things, the way Apple had compared its MacBook Air to an envelope. But lightness was another matter. It couldn't be seen. During a brainstorming session, members of the team threw out metaphors for thinness and lightness—things to which X300 could be compared. One person suggested sticking X300 on a wall, like it was a Post-it note. But there were some real duds, too. Another person suggested a "flounder." They sent a long list of possibilities up Lenovo's chain of command. In the end, they picked half a dozen visual metaphors that seemed promising and went to work on the advertisements. One of the first ones they produced was an animation for the Internet. In the ad, one of those yellow "Idea" balloons drifted near an X300, the balloon's string caught on the ThinkPad, and the balloon lifted the laptop into the air and floated off with it. The message: ThinkPad X300 is lighter than air. And MacBook Air, too.

Lenovo's Olympic marketing hit a major snag long before the games actually began. The problem: China's crackdown on Tibet. Riots had erupted in the Tibetan capitol of Lhasa on March 14 after protesters took to the streets demanding independence from China. The Chinese army cracked down, and a number of people were killed—which provoked pro-Tibet demonstrations throughout the western provinces of China. When the Olympic torch relay began on April 1, it became a magnet for protests. In London,

Paris, and San Francisco, demonstrators disrupted the relay. Lenovo, which had sponsored the relay in addition to the Olympics themselves, was in an awkward position. It had hoped to get favorable press in each place where the torch was carried. The company had handed out a slim X300 laptop to each of more than two dozen members of the torch relay entourage to help connect the dots in journalists' minds between the Olympics, the torch, and Lenovo products. Instead of the halo effect, though, each stop along the relay route was yet another blow to China, the Olympics, and, by association, Lenovo and its computers.

Yet by the time the Olympic Games kicked off, the Tibet protests seemed to have faded in importance. An awe-inspiring opening ceremony, favorable TV coverage, and the excitement of U.S. swimmer Michael Phelps's quest for gold medals created a feel-good environment for Lenovo to establish itself as a global brand. The company spread its message on more than 1,000 billboards throughout Beijing, on 500 buses that were cruising the city's streets, and via TV ads. Everywhere there were Lenovo computers—12,000 desktop machines, 800 notebooks, and 700 server computers—running every aspect of the giant operation. And ThinkPad X300 was featured prominently.

By then, the X300 had been on the market for about six months. While Lenovo would not provide sales numbers, Peter Hortensius, head of the laptop business, declared it a roaring success. Many more X300s were sold than the company had forecast. In fact, it couldn't keep up with demand. Beyond the sales tally was the value of the impression the product had made. In the media, it had been favorably compared for months with Apple's superthin MacBook Air. "There was a lot of brand lift for Lenovo because we had in some ways beaten the strong industry innovator, Apple," says Hortensius.

But the X300 had not produced an immediate halo effect on the sales of other products. Revenues for the second quarter of the year came in with a solid but unspectacular 10 percent growth—restrained by slowing economies worldwide. This superior machine, well received, had not single-handedly boosted Lenovo's sales. And now other PC companies were coming out with similar models. The best Lenovo could hope for was that X300 had helped build its image in the minds of consumers as a maker of cutting-edge computers. It would be a long, slow journey to global brand nirvana.

9

VERY SMALL COMPUTERS

In late January 2008, Lenovo Chief Executive William Amelio spoke on a panel at the World Economic Forum, in Davos, Switzerland. This high-powered gab fest, which was held every year in the tiny ski village, attracted many of the world's leaders from business, government, entertainment, and the nonprofit sphere. The topic at Amelio's session was the future of technology, and, when one of the other panelists made a passing reference to it being the "post-PC era," Amelio fired back with a blitz of statistics demonstrating just how big and fast-growing the PC market was—especially laptops. "I feel like Mark Twain when people talk about the death of the PC," he said. "I'm not feeling like a dinosaur just yet."

True, the PC was far from dead. HP, Dell, Lenovo, and others would pump out 300 million of the machines that year. The laptop was gradually replacing desktop PCs in corporations and in homes, and on some college campuses laptops had largely replaced paper notebooks and obviated the need to go to the library to do research. Lenovo's X300 and Apple's MacBook Air were wonderful refinements of a form that had been improving, though in fits and starts, since John Ellenby and Bill Moggridge had collaborated to create the GRiD Compass, in 1982. The laptop was edging ever closer to perfection.

But the X300 and Air were evolutionary rather than revolutionary devices. For many tech mavens, the thrill was gone. As

Amelio spoke, much of the excitement in the industry surrounded the latest handheld devices that were just then coming to
market, so-called mobile Internet devices. These sleek little gadgets were being designed to make it easy for young people to click
to the Facebook or MySpace social networking Web sites, to
thumb-type instant messages to friends, or to tap in a blog comment. A whole new use for computing had been discovered, and
new specialized devices were being created to address it.

In fact, on that day in Davos, Amelio held a prototype mobile
Internet device on the table in front of him. He proudly showed it
off when invited to do so by the moderator. The little black device looked like a miniature TV. You could hold it between your
thumb and forefinger and navigate with the touch of a finger on
the display screen. There was more computing power in that tiny
device than there had been in a desk-drawer-sized PC a few years
before.

A powerful computer that could fit in the palm of your hand. It
was a natural progression of the march of digital technology. But,
even more than with laptops, the quest to design excellent handheld devices had long confounded the tech industry's entrepreneurs, designers, and engineers. That's because all of the critical
challenges of creating a successful portable were exaggerated.
These devices had to be small enough to be easily carryable, yet
have a large-enough display screen and keyboard to be useful.
They needed to be packed with the latest technology, yet affordable. And, given the demands of consumers and pressures of competition, they needed to look and feel good.

This quest for the ultimate handheld computer began in an odd
way. In 1984, just after Apple's Steve Jobs launched the Macintosh
computer, he hired a Hewlett-Packard engineer named Steve
Sakoman for a special project. The task Jobs had in mind was to
design a Macintosh telephone—a phone that was also a computer.

Sakoman brought to mobile computing a deep knowledge of
what it takes to make really small computers. He grew up in
Youngstown, Ohio, the son of a steel mill worker. He got inter-

ested in computers because Youngstown State University ran a computing program in the city's high schools. These were huge mainframes that the students rarely actually saw, but Sakoman got a sense of how computers could empower individuals. After starting out as a physics major at Case Western Reserve in Cleveland, he switched to engineering. This was the early 1970s, when engineers and engineering students still used slide rules to make calculations. Hewlett-Packard was about to change that. It produced the first battery-powered programmable calculator, the HP 35, in 1972, and the era of the slide rule was over. "I was bitten by the handheld calculator thing," says Sakoman. "It was the idea of a portable computer, battery powered, that you could program—as opposed to a huge machine in an air-conditioned room."

At Case, Sakoman built a couple of prototype computers with microprocessors that were just then becoming available. Then, as an employee of the university's engineering design center, he helped design medical monitoring devices—really, tiny computers—that were to be implanted in people's bodies. But he dreamed of getting a job at HP and working on programmable calculators.

He got his foot in the door at HP in 1975 when the company hired him to work in its minicomputer group. Minicomputers were actually very large computers, some as big as a refrigerator, but were called minis because they were smaller than mainframes. Working on that scale didn't interest Sakoman, so he was relieved when he got a chance to transfer to the calculator division in Corvallis, Oregon. While other companies and entrepreneurs, like Apple's Wozniak and Jobs, were shrinking computers down to personal proportions, the folks at HP were gradually giving calculators more and more capabilities until they, too, were essentially personal computers. When Japanese manufacturers flooded the world with cheap basic calculators, HP moved upstream. In the early 1980s, Sakoman took HP's most advanced technology for calculators and created one of the early portable computers: the HP 110. Introduced in May 1984, just four months after Apple's

Macintosh came out, it weighed nine pounds (4.08 kilograms) and was the first battery-powered computer based on IBM's and Microsoft's blueprints. Because it didn't have a mechanical disk drive, all the programs were loaded onto memory chips, and the computer turned on and off instantly. But, with a price of $2,995, the HP 110 was a flop in the marketplace.

The computer did have one lasting effect; it connected Sakoman and Jobs. During the summer of 1984, according to Sakoman, Jobs had visited computer stores to size up the competition. In one store, when Jobs asked a clerk what was the coolest personal computer on display, he expected to hear that it was the Mac. Instead, the clerk started raving about the HP 110. Then he showed Jobs how it worked. Jobs was impressed enough to ask around about who had created the HP 110. One of Apple's marketing people had formerly been a college intern at HP and knew that Sakoman had designed the computer, so he offered to make an introduction. Sakoman interviewed with Jobs, but he turned down the first employment offer. He was reluctant to leave HP. But Steve Jobs can be very persuasive. "He told me, 'You can't say no. I want you here.' And he made a better offer. So I went," recalls Sakoman.

His first task was to make a prototype of what a Macintosh phone could be. The idea was to design a machine that would serve multiple purposes—as a telephone, answering machine, and e-mail terminal. So it would have a handset, a modem for transmitting data, and a small display screen. Sakoman built a couple of circuit boards and tried packing all of the electronics in a case, to prove the concept. He and Jobs traveled to Japan together to talk to display makers.

On that trip, traveling around Japan by train with Jobs, Sakoman learned that relations between Jobs and Apple Chief Executive John Sculley were starting to go bad. The company's product development efforts were in disarray, and since Jobs was largely responsible, he was under a lot of pressure to sort things out. Back in

California, Sakoman kept working on the Mac phone, but politics were swirling all around him and it was hard to concentrate. A sales slump that hit the entire computer industry in late 1984 took Macintosh sales down, too, and in May 1985, amid layoffs, Sculley replaced Jobs as the head of the Macintosh division with Jean-Louis Gassée, who had formerly been the head of Apple Europe. Jobs gradually drifted out of Apple, and with him went any interest in the Mac phone. The project was dead.

Fortunately for Sakoman, he found a new patron in Gassée. The Frenchman earned tremendous loyalty from Apple's engineers because he respected them and was passionate about creating great products. Gassée talked Sakoman into heading the Macintosh hardware division. In that role, Sakoman assembled a team to build Apple's first mobile computer, the ill-fated Macintosh Portable. But he spent much of his time and energy on the desktop Macintoshes, Apple's bread-and-butter products.

Meanwhile he had his own pet project, code named Newton. Even back in his days at HP, he had played around with the idea of using a stylus to write or draw on a computer display, as an alternative to the keyboard. At Apple, in 1987, he started thinking about pen computing again. Even though Apple didn't yet have a portable computer, some of its executives bought laptops made by other companies, brought them to meetings, and typed notes. Sakoman found the clicking of the keys quite annoying. He envisioned creating a tablet computer the size of a steno pad that would be operated with a pen rather than a keyboard. The Macintosh operating system had been designed for running desktop computers, and was unsuitable for a tablet, so Sakoman decided to wipe the slate clean and start from scratch to design an operating system for an altogether different style of computing. He chose Newton as the code name for the project because the original Apple logo featured Isaac Newton sitting under an apple tree, and part of his motivation for designing the Newton products was he wanted to get Apple back to its innovative roots. When Sakoman took the idea to Gassée, he found that Gassée didn't just like the idea, he *loved* it. In fact, he wanted to quit Apple and build a new company of his own around the Newton concept.

One of the recurring patterns in the story of portable computing is that, often, more than one person or group has a big new idea at any given time. That was true of the luggables and the laptops, and it was also true of pen computing. It's not surprising, since technologies advance in waves, with many hands helping, and smart people who are deeply involved in efforts like those can look into the future and see what, logically, might come next. While Sakoman and Gassée were scheming about Newton, another pair of entrepreneurs was having similar thoughts. And, in fact, their idea would take shape first—beating the Newton products to market by more than a year. The two entrepreneurs were Jerry Kaplan and Mitch Kapor. Kaplan was a bona fide computer scientist. He got a Ph.D. in artificial intelligence at the University of Pennsylvania and was a researcher at Stanford University before taking the start-up plunge in 1981 with an artificial intelligence software company called Teknowledge. It was while he was there that Kapor, the founder of Lotus Development, the first wildly successful PC application company, sought him out. Kapor wanted to know if artificial intelligence could be used to help manage individuals' personal information, such as calendars, diaries, to-do lists, and phone messages. Kaplan thought it could, and, before long, Kapor hired him as a consultant to develop a flexible database of personal information for Lotus, which was based in Cambridge, Massachusetts. Eventually, this work would result in the Lotus Agenda personal information manager, or PIM. It was on a flight that Kaplan and Kapor took together from Boston to San Francisco in February 1987 that their pen computing idea was born.

They were flying in Kapor's private jet, so it was just the two men in the cabin. There was plenty of time to chat about business and to compare notes on the latest technologies. Right away, Kapor pulled out a Compaq 286 notebook computer, one of the first notebooks to pack the power of a desktop PC. While Kaplan watched in amazement, Kapor fished through the pockets of his jacket, shirt, and pants and pulled out notes on all manner of scraps of paper, including napkins. He started up the Lotus Agenda prototype program and began typing the information from his notes into his computer. In his 1995 book, *Startup: A Silicon Valley Adventure*, Kaplan quotes Kapor: "You know, this is really the pits. It doubles the time it takes for me to keep organized. I wish there was some way for me to get all this stuff directly into the computer and skip the paper." That wish launched them into a half-hour of musing on what it would take to make a portable computer small and light enough to be a person's constant companion. But if you shrunk a computer down far enough to carry with you everywhere, how would you type on it? There were limits to how far you could compress the keyboard and still keep it usable.

Without reaching any conclusions, they took a break for a dinner. Then Kaplan tilted his seat back and took a nap. A half hour later he woke up with a fully formed idea in mind. As Kaplan shook off sleep, Kapor looked up from his typing and asked if he was okay. Kaplan's response, as he recounted in *Startup*: "Mitchell, suppose you used a pen instead of a keyboard?" He explained to Kapor how instead of typing text you would write with a stylus directly on a screen in electronic ink, and then a program in the computer would translate the handwriting into regular text and numbers. The two concluded that the next big thing in computing would be create devices that worked like notebooks instead of typewriters.

That was the beginning of Go Corp., one of the first companies dedicated to pen computing, and the beginning of a pen computing craze. Pen mania peaked in the early 1990s and then crashed on the rocks of disillusionment just months later as long-dreamed-of products finally came to market and the limitations of the technology became embarrassingly obvious.

The ah-ha! moment for Go provides a view into the mysteries of the creative process for high-tech inventors. After running Go,

Kaplan started two more companies, onSale, the first Internet-based auction service, and Winster, a social networking Web site where people make friends by helping each other win prizes. In each case, the kernel of the idea that became the company came to Kaplan in a flash. "Usually, what happens is I go to sleep and I wake up and I know the answer," he says. "We don't have the ideas. The ideas have us. You can't control it."

So, separately, Kaplan and Sakoman had dreamed up essentially the same idea. They soon crossed paths. Back in those early days of the PC industry, the people who ran things and invented things still made up a fairly small and tight-knit community. They knew each other from way back, often from attending the Homebrew Computer Club, meeting at the West Coast Computer Faire, or mingling at conferences that were springing up to serve as idea-sharing and marketing forums for a booming young industry. Gradually, the annual COMDEX trade show in Las Vegas became the economic and social nexus for the community. There, at "Spencer the Cat" parties hosted by the trade magazine *PC Week*, the giants of a still-small industry would dance to live rock and roll and drink beer together. ("Spencer" was *PC Week*'s industry gossip columnist.) So it's not surprising that the people who were envisioning pen computing would be acquainted. Kapor and Sakoman got to know each other when Sakoman licensed the Lotus 1-2-3 spreadsheet program for inclusion in the HP 110. After that, they met from time to time. Soon after the two pairs had their big ideas, Kapor visited Sakoman in his office on the Apple campus. They mulled over their ideas on pen computing. Maybe, they decided on the spot, they should consider collaborating. Within days, the four entrepreneurs were talking seriously about starting a company together.

These kinds of flirtations were happening all the time back then. A handful of bright people bubbling over with ideas would get together and explore the possibilities of forming a business. It was like a courtship. They'd date for a while, maybe even get engaged, and, in a few cases, consummate a marriage. In this case, things didn't get very far before the breakup. A few weeks after talks started, Kapor invited a handful of confederates to a meeting at the Kendall Square Marriott in Cambridge, near the Lotus offices. In addition to Kaplan, Sakoman, and Gassée, he invited Peter Miller, a colleague from Lotus. At that meeting, Kapor was wary of the potential for a power struggle between him and Gassée. A second, crucial meeting took place a few days later at Kapor's mansion in Brookline, Massachusetts, just a few miles away. They met in a wood-paneled den. Kapor was known for wearing Hawaiian print shirts all year round in spite of Boston's nippy winters, and Sakoman recalls that all five of them wore Hawaiian shirts that day in a show of camaraderie. But, it wasn't very long before Sakoman began to have second thoughts. He was an engineer at heart, but, watching his potential partners interact, he realized that any one of the other four people in the room might want to be the new company's chief executive. He hated office politics, and he foresaw a huge battle shaping up over who would lead the company. "I started to get really nervous," he said. "I was trying to escape all of the politics at Apple, and saw a recipe for a continuation of all of that."

After arriving back home in California, Sakoman called Kapor and told him he didn't think their project was going to work. He wanted out. Meanwhile, he had already told Gassée about his misgivings, and his boss had suggested that they take the idea to Apple CEO Sculley to see if he would be interested in making their pen computing idea an Apple project. So that's what he did. In a fateful meeting in Sculley's office, Sakoman described the Newton idea to him, and Sculley loved it. "He said, 'Perfect. Do it. That's just the kind of stuff that Apple needs to be doing,' " Sakoman recalls. So Sakoman and Kaplan set off on different tracks. Newton would be an Apple project, and Kaplan would go off and start Go with a handful of partners—with Kapor investing and sitting on the board. The Newton and Go computers would eventually emerge in the early 1990s as the two most celebrated pen devices. They would also go down as two of the biggest flops in computing history, though, in both cases, they paved the way for major technology advances that would come later. The Newton project also played a role in Sculley's high-profile fall from grace at Apple.

The reason Sculley was so receptive to Sakoman's idea was that it fit with a new vision of computing he was developing with Alan Kay of Dynabook fame. In 1984, Steve Jobs had hired Kay as an Apple Fellow to work in the company's Advanced Technology Group. After the Macintosh came out, Kay had approached Sculley and told him that while technology breakthroughs like his at Xerox PARC had helped make the Mac into a hit, Apple would have to rely on itself for the next round of innovations. So the two had worked together on a concept called Knowledge Navigator. They envisioned a portable computer that would be as much about communications as computing, and would be a personal empowerment device, helping people learn, think, and express themselves more effectively. (Sakoman later derisively called it "Dynabook on steroids for adults.") Knowledge Navigator would harness the power of Moore's law, named for Gordon Moore, one of the cofounders of chipmaker Intel, who posited that because of advances in semiconductor technology, chips would get twice as powerful or shrink by half every 18 to 24 months. That meant incredibly powerful yet very small devices would be possible in a matter of years. Sculley and Kay visited some university labs to peek at the technologies that were coming down the pipeline. And, with the help of movie director George Lucas at Industrial Light & Magic, they made a short special-effects-laden movie about what Knowledge Navigator would look like and what it could do. "I wanted to get people excited about where mobile computing could go in the future," recalls Sculley. He saw Newton as a step along the path to Knowledge Navigator.

From the start, Newton was laden with great expectations, and that turned out to be a great big problem. Since it was one of the most exciting projects at the company, all the big shots wanted a piece of it—including Sculley, Kay, Gassée, and a handful of others. Almost immediately the politics got intense. Kay thought the machine should have a keyboard, and not just rely on the pen for input, but some of the marketing people insisted that it should not have a keyboard because that would make it too much like Macintosh, and they wanted this to be a radical departure. Also, Kay and Sakoman argued over what was the right microprocessor to use. Says Kay: "The worst person you could be at Apple, from a technical point of view, was somebody who was at Xerox PARC. There was a lot of jealousy, a lot of politics. I went in and out of the project." For his part, Sakoman thought Kay was a prima donna and called the hold he had on Sculley "the Alan Kay reality distortion field."

So the Newton project was begun in a chaotic Apple. Sakoman hand-picked a small team of engineers, and, in an attempt to shield them from distractions, he found an old warehouse on Bubb Road in Cupertino, California, back by the railroad tracks, and Sculley gave him permission to remodel it. At that time, most engineers at Apple worked in cubicles, which was then the normal practice in Silicon Valley, but Sakoman wanted to signal that this would be a different kind of project, so he built private offices for each engineer with glass walls around a central gathering place where there were couches and overstuffed chairs. He wanted his engineers to have quiet places to work, but also to see and interact with each other in a friendly, comfortable setting.

Once the carpentry was done, Sakoman and a small team moved in and began the audacious process of rethinking portable computing. Originally, they didn't plan to make a pocket-sized device. Instead, Newton would be a large tablet most suitable for artists, architects, and other creative types for whom drawing was an important form of expression. They decided to build a new operating system, a new software programming language, and new applications. They also planned on codesigning a new mobile computing microprocessor with AT&T called Hobbit. Plus they meant to create a handwriting recognition system. It would have been a daunting set of tasks for any organization. For a team of just a dozen people, it was impossible.

One of the key members of Sakoman's team was Steve Capps, who had been a designer of the Macintosh user interface. He had quit Apple after Steve Jobs left, but went back when he learned that Sakoman was working on a pen computer. He wrote a long memo to Sakoman about handwriting recognition, and that landed him a spot on the Newton team. When he arrived at the warehouse, he appreciated the spirit of community Sakoman had established. Capps bought an espresso machine, and Gassée came up with money to install a small basketball court out by the tracks. The engineers would pick up games when they needed to blow off steam. So the team had plenty of camaraderie. What it lacked was discipline. The engineers did a lot of talking about their big plans to invent everything from scratch, but, it seemed to Capps, very little progress was actually being made. Things went like this for two years.

On the politics front, the situation got worse. By 1989, Sculley had fallen out of love with Gassée, his product development chief. The failure of the Apple Portable was a major factor, but their personal chemistry went bad as well. It was clear to many of the engineers and product development managers that tensions were increasing between the bosses, and many of them sided with Gassée, who stopped bothering to be diplomatic in his dealings with Sculley. "I was unhappy. I was a thorn in his side," explains Gassée. "I showed considerable and repeated lack of respect for him." Finally, Sculley fired Gassée, but gave him six months to stay on as a minister-without-portfolio. When Gassée's engineers learned that their beloved boss was leaving, they staged a demonstration—complete with protest signs and chants—in the center of Apple's campus. When Gassée finally left, to start Be Inc., with the goal of building a new consumer multimedia PC, Sakoman joined him. "Apple wasn't the place for me anymore," said Sakoman. "It was big and political, and it was really hard to get things done." After Gassée's departure, Sculley decided to take on the role of Apple's chief technology officer (CTO). He had read an article in the *McKinsey Quarterly* that argued in favor of business leaders, rather than hard-core technologists, being CTOs. That way, a company's innovations would serve its business and marketing agenda rather than being led by technology considerations. With his move, Sculley alienated some of Apple's best engineers. "In hindsight, it was really dumb of me," he says.

The person who picked up the pieces of the Newton project was Larry Tesler. He had worked at Xerox PARC in the 1970s alongside Kay, where he was one of the designers of the Note-Taker portable prototype. He had moved over to Apple in 1980. When Gassée left, Tesler was vice president of the Advanced Technology Group. At first, when he visited the Newton team's lair on Bubb Road, his assignment was to scavenge any good technology he found and shut the project down. Instead, according to Capps, he became intrigued and decided to keep it going. Still, he spent a lot of time in the early days moderating debates between Newton engineers about practically every aspect of the project, from the microprocessor, to the size and cost of the machine, to the programming language.

Capps was so discouraged that he considered quitting. But his optimism was rekindled after a new member was added to the team: Michael Tchao, a young product marketer who had been the launch manager of the ill-fated Apple Portable in 1989. Tchao knew first hand about the bad things that can happen when you try to pack too much into a portable computer. Tchao got the office next to Capps, and the two struck up a friendship. Late at night, they would go on long walks along the railroad tracks in back of the warehouse and talk about what it would take to clean up the mess that Newton had become and actually deliver a product. Finally, they concluded that they needed to make it smaller and more portable, cheaper—costing about $700, and less complex. Some of the built-from-scratch software components would have to go. Instead, they could use some software that had already been created.

They got their opportunity to change the direction of Newton by serendipity. During the first Gulf War, Sculley was scheduled to fly to Tokyo to make a presentation at a multimedia conference. He had asked Tchao, who was one of Apple's experts on multimedia technologies, to tag along and help him develop his presentation. Sculley was nervous about using a commercial airline because of the danger of terror attacks, so Mike Markkula, then an Apple board member, lent him a private jet, a Dassault Falcon 900. Before Tchao boarded the plane, he called Capps and said, "Shall I tell him about what we want to do with Newton?" Capps said yes. It meant going over their bosses' heads, but they decided it was worth the risk. On the plane, the only other passenger was C.J. Maupin, Sculley's speechwriter, who later became the model for the character C.J. Craig on NBC's *The West Wing* TV drama. Early in the flight, when Tchao and Maupin had a moment alone, Tchao asked for her advice. Should he talk about Newton with Sculley? She encouraged him to go ahead. After a refueling stop in Cold Bay, Alaska, Sculley made things easy for Tchao. He asked how the Newton project was going. Tchao's answer: "It's going great, but we have some ideas that could make it better."

Tchao spent 20 minutes laying out his and Capps's vision of a smaller, simpler Newton with an emphasis on free-form note taking. Sculley was receptive. He asked questions. While they spoke, he grabbed a copy of the *New York Times* Sunday Magazine that sat nearby and started doodling on the cover next to a photo of then New York governor Mario Cuomo. He drew a traditional notebook PC, and, then, next to it, a small tablet with a pen. He jotted down the target price of $650 and listed the uses for the tablet. Then he circled the tablet and drew an arrow pointing to it. Tchao knew then that he had made the sale. "I was over the moon," he says. "I had been very nervous about the way things were going. I thought it could go on forever and it would end up not ever shipping. That's a product manager's worst nightmare."

Tesler took Tchao's maneuvering well. Back in Cupertino, Tchao met with him and laid out his scheme and told him Sculley was for it. Tchao recalls that Tesler was reluctant to give up some of the cutting-edge technologies, such as the new programming language. But, ultimately, he relented. They were on track to build two versions of Newton, the small one advocated by Tchao, which was ultimately released, and the larger version, which never shipped.

To make matters even more complicated, there was yet another handheld computing project in the Apple solar system. In 1990, Marc Porat, who was in Apple's Advanced Technology Group, came up with the idea of writing software that would connect mobile devices and make it possible for relatively simple handhelds to possess a lot of the capabilities of a desktop computer. The idea was that the software would be licensed to computer and consumer electronics companies, who would build and sell handhelds based on it. The project got two code names: Paradigm for the software and Pocket Crystal for the hardware. Porat recruited Andy Hertzfeld and Bill Atkinson, two of the programming geniuses who helped produce the Macintosh operating system. And he drew Sculley into his small circle of confederates, which also included Pierre Omidyar, who would later found Web auction site eBay. It wasn't clear whether this would become an internal Apple project or would spin out as an independent company. Capps recalls being invited to meetings about the concept that were held at people's houses rather than on the Apple campus. This troubled him. He was an Apple employee and an engineer on the Newton project, and he was also being invited to help plan something that would compete with Newton. Even more worrisome, Sculley attended some of the gatherings, too. Capps recalls that after one meeting he confronted Sculley when they were both outside. "Why are you involved in this? If you don't support Newton, tell me and I'll come and work on this," Capps told Sculley. "John patted me on the shoulder and said: 'I just don't know yet.'"

Ultimately, Sculley decided to invest some of Apple's money in Porat's project, which spun out of Apple as a new company, General Magic. So Apple had a finger in General Magic, but both feet were committed to Newton. Dozens and then, ultimately, hundreds of people worked on Newton as it approached the marketplace, but, from the Tokyo flight onward, Sculley really made it his own. He took a big gamble and, on the advice of Tesler and Newton hardware maven Mike Culbert, chose the new ARM processor over AT&T's Hobbit. Apple made a substantial investment in the Acorn RISC Machine, the company that owned ARM, a chip designed to provide the low power consumption necessary for small portable computers.

Inspired by the Knowledge Navigator and all the advances in multimedia technology and wireless communications, Sculley wanted to take the role of visionary not just for Apple but for the entire PC industry. He had been asked to make a keynote address at the Consumer Electronics Show (CES) in Las Vegas in January 1992, and decided to make this the launchpad for his new vision. Apple was just then overtaking IBM as the market share leader in personal computers, so Sculley commanded respect and attention. He had his bully pulpit at CES. The message he planned on delivering was audacious: the era of the conventional PC was passing. Those oh-so-ordinary machines would be overtaken by a new generation of highly portable machines that were part computer and part communications device. In the end, this would enable a great convergence of three industries—computing, communications, and entertainment—and, according to market researchers at Apple, the convergence represented a $3.5 trillion-per-year sales opportunity by the end of the decade. On the flight to Las Vegas, when Sculley was putting the finishing touches on his speech, he struggled to come up with a catchy name for one type of device he envisioned—handheld portable computers like Newton. At first he considered calling it the PC personal communicator, and then he tried other combinations of words and letters. Finally he settled on personal digital assistant, or PDA.

Sculley's speech was electrifying. The media and the industry were ravenous for something new, and he had just handed them a giant slab of red meat on a table. The convergence of computing and communications would be huge! A thousand articles were written about the digital convergence and PDAs. Everybody wanted to get in on the act. Even Bill Gates started using the PDA term. In this new world, Apple and Sculley, rather than Microsoft and Gates, seemed perfectly positioned to come out on top. "This will be the measure of the man," venture capitalist Nat Goldhaber told the *San Jose Mercury News* for an article that was published on May 24, 1992, just five days before Sculley was to show Newton to the world at another CES conference, this time in Chicago. "Apple could be the premier consumer electronics company in the United States."

Yet just as Sculley and Apple and Newton seemed poised to take over the brave new digital world, behind the scenes, their plans were about to unravel. In 1990, Sculley had handed off day-to-day command of Apple to one of his lieutenants, Michael Spindler, a hard-driving German who was nicknamed "Diesel." That left Sculley free to dream of a new era of computing and fly off to Tokyo and Hollywood to talk to industry kingpins about the convergence of computing, communications, and entertainment. He even dabbled in politics, appearing with Bill and Hillary Clinton at public events. Sculley was restless. He had been running Apple for nearly ten years and had built it into a $6.6 billion company that was respected all over the world. Yet he had lost interest in the company's bread-and-butter business—PCs. In late 1992 he had come up with a radical idea. Why not split Apple into two pieces? One, the Macintosh piece, would keep the name Apple and stay in California. Meanwhile, Sculley would move back to the East Coast and run a second company that would include Newton and other technologies not related to the Mac. Maybe they'd even sell the Macintosh company. He floated the idea to the board in early 1993 and the directors gave him the go-ahead to hire the investment banking company Goldman Sachs to explore options. This was all top secret. Nobody outside of Sculley and the board knew about it at first. Two companies, AT&T and IBM, sent teams of executives to Silicon Valley to talk to Sculley about buying Apple. But, ultimately, neither company bit.

Still, Sculley's scheme carried serious consequences for him and for Apple. As the members of his executive staff learned about the plan, they didn't like it. Their jobs were being put at risk. "The executives hated the idea. So they revolted," says Sculley. He believes Spindler and others began criticizing him to board members, but he wasn't aware of what was going on behind his back until Apple's financial performance fell off precipitously in the third quarter of fiscal 1993. The board called an emergency meeting on June 17, 1993, and, in a matter of minutes, a stunned Sculley was replaced as CEO by Spindler, though Sculley retained the chairman title for another few months. Within a matter of weeks, in the midst of a general slowdown in the PC industry, Apple announced a $188.3 million third-quarter loss, its largest ever loss up to that time, and it laid off 2,500 employees. Markkula would not comment on the reasons for Sculley's removal as CEO. Spindler couldn't be reached for comment. But Al Eisenstat, who was then the company's general counsel and held a board seat, confirms Sculley's version of events. "We were disenchanted that the company didn't have a clear path for the future," says Eisenstat. "Some executives had laid out complaints about Sculley to the board. The board wanted a clearer strategy, and John didn't seem to have the stomach for it anymore."

Amid all the tumult and political infighting, the Newton project went astray again. Though Tesler had pared down ambitions and focused on making a reasonably priced handheld machine, engineers kept adding features. At the same time, the pressure was intense to ship a product at long last. Gaston Bastiaens, who had formerly worked for European consumer electronics giant Philips Electronics, was put in charge of bringing Newton devices to market. In the spring of 1993 Tchao led the marketing team through an item-by-item readiness analysis, and, when it was finished, they gathered in a conference room in Building Number 3 on the Apple campus to review the results. There were still plenty of bugs, and not just in the handwriting recognition software. Even the fax and print features didn't work smoothly. During the meeting, Bastiaens walked into the conference room and inter-rupted. He asked: " 'How's it going? Do we have something to ship?' " Tchao recalls. When Tchao told him that if they shipped the product they'd have serious quality issues and customer com-plaints, Bastiaens threatened to fire him. He said, "If you say it can't ship, I'll find a product manager who will say it can ship," re-counts Tchao.

Apple MessagePad, the first of the Newton project products, was launched at the Macworld Boston trade show in Boston Sym-phony Hall on August 3, 1993. Six years had passed since it was first conceived by Steve Sakoman. Apple enthusiasts gobbled the machines up, buying 5,000 within hours. The $800 price tag was no deterrent. But while MessagePad was innovative, with a great user interface and useful applications for people on the go, it was also deeply flawed. Four AAA batteries didn't give the machine enough oomph. It was too wide for people with small hands to hold comfortably in one hand, and too wide to fit in a shirt pocket. The handwriting recognition feature, while better than anything else then on the market, still wasn't good enough. Car-toonist Garry Trudeau drove a stake through Newton's heart in a Doonesbury strip published a few weeks later. In the strip, Michael Doonesbury writes "I am writing a test sentence" on the display of a MessagePad, which is interpreted by the handwriting recognition software as, "Siam fighting atomic sentry." Donald Norman, the user-centric design guru who had recently arrived at Apple as an Apple Fellow, said the Newton fiasco was the result of how product development teams worked in the early days of the personal computing industry. Product development was driven by engineers. "The Newton was brilliantly designed in many ways, but everybody was so thrilled by the technical hurdles they had overcome that they didn't notice that, for the average user, it didn't work," said Norman. "The user doesn't care how hard it is to do. They just want it to work."

So Newton was a laughingstock, as was Sculley, whose name and reputation were inextricably tied to the little machine. "It was very painful," said Sculley. "I had always succeeded in everything I had done. This was the first time I was being labeled as a failure. I was kicked out as the CEO of a high-profile company, and then I was stapled to the Newton. All those things hurt. I was suffering for many years."

Still, looking back, Sculley said he learned from the experience. The main lesson was to reflect back on what Steve Jobs had taught him in their early days together at Apple. Jobs's first principle of product development was to focus on creating an excellent user experience and then choose the technology and features that help you accomplish that goal. Newton, in contrast, was all about grasping for the latest technologies and then trying to pack them into a useful container. That's why it failed.

Lesson number 2 was to be wary of hype. PC industry marketers had gotten into the habit of touting the virtues of gee-whiz new products months and sometimes even years before they were ready to ship. The goal was to whip up consumers into a frenzy of desire that would peak when the products were finally ready for the market. Sculley saw a need to evangelize the PDA. Nobody had ever seen one before, so he had to tell people what these machines were and what they could do for you. But he admits that in the case of Newton, he overdid it: "It was a big mistake. We shouldn't have let the hype get way ahead of the product. It took on a life of its own." And when MessagePad failed to live up to all the hype, critics like Trudeau—and Apple's rivals—were ready to pounce.

Newton was by no means alone. Every pen computing project launched at around that time failed, including products from Go, Momenta, Slate, Casio, and Microsoft. Miniaturization of electronic components still had a long way to go to make it possible to pack a lot of computing and communications capability into a package small enough to comfortably hold in your hand. And handwriting recognition was nowhere near ready for main street. People wouldn't tolerate handwriting recognition that was anything less than perfect. Tom Perkins, the legendary venture capitalist whose firm, Kleiner Perkins Caufield & Byers, lost a ton of money in the pen computing bubble, says: "We were just too early. And we still may be too early now."

Kaplan's adventure at Go Corp. lasted until 1994, when AT&T bought the struggling company and, ultimately, closed the business down. By Kaplan's calculations, he and his Go colleagues had burned through $75 million in venture money and advances against royalties. The entire industry may have spent as much as $1 billion on its pen computing misadventure. There were some thrilling high points for Kaplan, like when State Farm agreed to work with Go, and when IBM licensed Go's Penpoint operating system in 1990, and when Penpoint 1.0 was released in April 1992. But most of Kaplan's memories were unpleasant. He was dismayed at how small start-ups get wound up in the machinations of big companies like IBM, AT&T, and Microsoft, and get ground up by the giants.

While AT&T usually gets blamed for killing Go, it's clear that Microsoft contributed to its demise, as well. Bill Gates first met with Kaplan and his colleagues to talk over their technology in July 1988. By 1991 the software giant was laying out plans for its own pen software, Windows for Pen Computing, at industry conferences. It introduced an early version a year later. Even though Windows for Pen Computing didn't catch on, Microsoft's power in the industry was enough to spoil the market for Go. Kaplan's software was initially aimed at very specific corporate applications, like on-the-scene data collection for insurance companies. The pen was perfectly suited for things like that, which didn't require perfect handwriting recognition. But the technology wasn't ready for mass consumption. "The entry of Microsoft into the field made it necessary for others, including us, to immediately go after a broader market, and it was really too early for that," says Kaplan. Go's coffin was firmly nailed shut when PC makers opted for Microsoft's software when they set out to design pen computers. Kaplan believes that Microsoft intimidated them into choosing its technology, and he filed an antitrust suit against the software giant in 2002, but Microsoft denies it. The case was not resolved when this book went to press.

There's another reason why pen computing didn't take off. Back in the mid-1980s when dreamers like Kaplan and Sakoman first laid out their plans, many men didn't know how to type. They considered placing text on paper to be women's work. So it seemed logical and plausible that men, who were the early adopters of personal computers, would feel more comfortable with an electronic pen than they would with a keyboard. However, by the early 1990s, a social and technological revolution had taken place. PCs had become the ubiquitous tool of the information age, and men had been forced to learn to type.

In fact, pen computing didn't celebrate its first significant successes until after Microsoft introduced its Windows XP Tablet PC Edition in 2002. Bill Gates had championed the pen from the early days as part of his vision of PCs putting information at people's fingertips wherever they may be. But, throughout the mid- and late 1990s, Microsoft's pen technologies came and went without stirring a breeze.

The seeds of change were planted in 1998, when Microsoft Research hired Bert Keely, a pen computing pioneer, to give the technology another try. Keely, who studied engineering at Stanford University, had always been interested in ergonomics and human interactions with computers. "I believed that electronic information should be as handy as paper and as portable as a book," he says. After graduating from Stanford in 1980, he went to work at Convergent Technologies, where he helped develop one of the first handheld computers, called WorkSlate, an 8-by-11-inch (203.2-by-279.4-millimeter) device for filling out forms that promptly bombed in the market. Keely's next stop was at Agilis, a company started by laptop instigator John Ellenby, maker of the GRiD Compass, after he left GRiD in 1987. Agilis's products, which used a touch screen, were among the early attempts to use wireless networking technologies in a handheld computer. Agilis got a decent pickup from military and public safety organizations, but couldn't sell enough machines to stay in business. So in 1990 Keely moved to Silicon Graphics where he developed a series of prototypes of pen computers for engineers and designers. In spite of years of work, he couldn't convince his bosses to build any of them. So, in frustration, he tried to raise money from venture capitalists and start his own company. It was on a market-scoping trip that he met Michael Dell and woke up to the realities of creating cutting-edge technologies for a mass market. At a meeting in Round Rock, Texas, where Dell is based, the PC company CEO listened patiently while Keely showed his prototypes and explained his ideas. Then Dell asked if the computer would run Office, Microsoft's ubiquitous package of word processing, spreadsheet, and presentation management software. The answer was no. "If it doesn't run Office, nobody will be interested," Dell told Keely.

Like many technology purists in Silicon Valley at the time, Keely looked down his nose at Microsoft. He considered its technology to be second rate. But Dell had woken him up to the cold facts. If he wanted to create mass-market pen computing products, he had to build something that ran Microsoft Office. He didn't know anybody at Microsoft headquarters in Redmond, Washington, but Forrest Baskett, Silicon Graphics' then chief technology officer, offered to make introductions. So Keely took his prototypes to Redmond and showed them to Nathan Myhrvold, who was then Microsoft's chief technology officer. The two men immediately hit it off. Myhrvold wanted to bring Keely and his team of 25 engineers into his organization to develop technologies for electronic books and pen computing. But when Keely went back to Silicon Valley and asked the rest of the team if they'd be willing to join Microsoft, they refused. "Not a single one was willing to cast their fate with Microsoft in Redmond, so I went alone," he recalls.

Keely started his career at Microsoft by taking small, sure steps. At the time, Sony and other companies were designing special devices for electronic books. So Keely designed software for reading e-books and an electronic typeface technology to make text on a screen easier on the eyes during long reading sessions.

But pen and touch-screen computing ideas were always buzzing around in his head. In 2000, he wrote a white paper in which he proposed taking advantage of the latest advances in processing power and display technology and using the pen to capture freeform notes and diagrams. Each year, Bill Gates went on an annual "Think Week" where he stayed at his family's compound near Hood Canal, 90 minutes west of Seattle, and ruminated on the future of technology. He invited Microsoft employees to send him memos about the things they thought were important for him to consider. So, in 2000, Keely sent his paper. Gates had been fascinated with pen computing for more than a decade, and, during Think Week, he was excited by Keely's ideas. When he returned to Redmond, he gave Keely the go-ahead to develop new pen and touch-screen technologies.

Keely started a project team in Microsoft Research along with Charles "Chuck" Thacker and Butler Lampson, former Xerox PARC scientists who had built the Alto computer in 1973. Gates took a personal interest in the project, checking in with Keely from time to time and giving him advice about how to navigate Microsoft's bureaucracy. When the new pen technology was ready to be turned into a product, Gates made a radical proposal: put the organization under the Office group rather than the Windows organization. His idea was that while Keely and his colleagues were indeed building an extension to Windows, they'd be more successful if they thought about it from the office worker's point of view. Also, it would be easier to keep focused if they worked with a group, Office, that lived and breathed the user experience every day. Another plus: the Office group was run by Jeff Raikes, who had a history with pen computing. He had run the initial Windows for Pen Computing project back in the early 1990s.

Keely thought hard about what it would take to improve the pen computing experience. A major consideration was getting the electronic ink right. It had to flow smoothly and quickly as people wrote or drew on the surface of the display. Another crucial element was handwriting recognition. They had to consider all sorts of writing styles. Early on, when Gates tried a version of the software, it did a really poor job of recognizing his script. The engineers talked it over and concluded that the system wasn't working well because Gates was left-handed, and it had been designed by a bunch of right-handers. So the developers went back to the lab and tweaked their software so it would work well for left-handed people as well. Keely also reconsidered some of the conventional wisdom about how to make successful handwriting recognition software. Most scientists thought that the larger the dictionary you had, the better the software would be. He disagreed, and pushed for culling rarely used words. Eventually, the software focused on automatically learning not just the cursive writing style but the vocabulary of the individual users. It even scanned sent e-mails to build an individual dictionary of frequently used words.

When Microsoft introduced Keely's Tablet PC software in New York on November 7, 2002, Raikes and Gates were onstage. It was something of a vindication of all of their years of effort. "The tablet has been a dream that I and many other people have had for years and years," Gates told the crowd. "Even when Paul Allen and I first talked about starting Microsoft and how we'd take computing from being something that large businesses use to moving it down to something that was personal in nature, we thought of reading and note taking as things that would eventually be in the realm where the PC would have software that would help out with those things."

Ultimately, Microsoft's Tablet PC software created a market for pen and touch-based computers. It wasn't huge—nothing like what the early champions of pen computing imagined in the early 1990s. But, by mid-2008, three million Tablet PC devices were in use, many of them "convertibles" that could be used either as a regular notebook PC with a keyboard or as a pen-based tablet. "The lesson we learned is you don't stop using a keyboard just because you also want to use a pen," said Keely. With the release of the Windows Vista operating system in 2006, handwriting recognition became standard equipment in most new PCs. Still, Keely wasn't satisfied. For Tablet PCs and convertibles to become more popular, they'll have to be lighter, thinner, easier to use, and less expensive. "My white-paper vision hasn't yet been fulfilled," he said.

Back in 1998, when Keely was shopping around his pen-computing ideas, one of the wise people he tapped for advice was Jeff Hawkins. This made a lot of sense, since Hawkins had played a seminal role in pen and handheld computers starting in the mid-1980s. Hawkins was a technology genius. He had long dreamed of rethinking the entire computing paradigm and creating a new generation of computers whose circuitry mimicked the workings of the human mind. But, even more important, he had something that eluded some of portable computing's other pioneers: a lot of common sense. Rather than pushing the latest cutting-edge technologies, he kept a sharp focus on the needs and wants of the people who use computers. He also had a knack for learning from other people's mistakes. That's how he emerged in the mid-1990s as the first person to make handheld computing a mass phenomenon, with Palm and the wonderful little handheld gizmo, Palm-Pilot.

Hawkins was born with the innovator gene. His father, Robert Hawkins, was a professional inventor, and the family's home near the north shore of Long Island was like Santa's Workshop, with dad, mom (Marion, a teacher who brought in the dependable income), and three sons all engaged in family projects. Hawkins recalls that when he was in third grade, his father's picture was on the cover of *My Weekly Reader*, the popular kids' magazine that was distributed through schools. His dad had invented pattern recognition technology, and, on the magazine cover, he was pictured holding a microphone to the mouth of a dolphin. He planned on decoding dolphin speech so people could learn to talk to the animals. But speech recognition was just a sidelight. The family obsession during the 1960s, when Hawkins was growing up, was building a round boat that was kept afloat on a cushion of air. Hawkins' father had hoped to sell the boats to the U.S. Navy. That never happened. But he eventually sold the only boat he finished to a touring orchestra that put on waterside concerts. Through these projects, Hawkins learned carpentry, industrial sewing, and how to operate machine tools. He wasn't afraid to experiment with new ways of doing things. "This was an excellent background for my career," Hawkins says. "I got very good at knowing a lot about a lot of things, so I'd be willing to make a decision that others would not be willing to make."

His first chance to invent something himself was when he began working for John Ellenby's GRiD Systems. Hawkins had studied engineering at Cornell University and worked for chipmaker Intel right out of college. Then GRiD hired him to help market the Compass, the first true laptop computer, which had been designed by Ellenby and industrial designer Bill Moggridge. Hawkins saw that one way to make the Compass more popular would be to create a programming language that other companies and individuals could use to write their own software applications to run on the computer. So he wrote a language, GRiDTask, that had a lot to do with the Compass's early successes. He left GRiD in 1986 to study biophysics at the University of California at Berkeley. While at Berkeley, he invented some rudimentary handwriting recognition software and patented it. Even while studying biophysics, he kept watch over advances in pen computing. He even interviewed for a job at Go Corp., just after the company got its funding from Kleiner Perkins, but he turned down an offer to be a pen-computing evangelist for Go. "I thought they'd fail. They were being too grandiose," he says. "Their motto was that the pen was the point. I saw the pen just as another input device. For me, mobile computing was the point."

So, instead of joining Jerry Kaplan on his ill-fated quest, Hawkins focused on more practical and doable uses of pen technologies. He returned to GRiD with the goal of building the first tablet computer. It would be operated with a pen, but would not depend on cursive handwriting recognition. Instead, people like warehouse operators and package delivery people would use the tablet to track inventory and fill in forms. The GRiDPad caused a sensation when it came out in 1989. It seemed to open the door to a flood of more versatile pen-based computers that would come into the market.

Thanks to GRiDPad, Hawkins was suddenly in computing's big leagues. With Ellenby gone from GRiD, and the company owned by Tandy, it was no longer an incubator for innovative portable computers, so Hawkins began shopping around for his next gig. He had an idea for creating a new consumer-oriented handheld computer that would use a pen, called Zoomer. He was wary of starting up his own company because friends of his had started companies and he had seen all the hard work and stress that came with it. Still, with venture capitalists badgering him, he took the plunge. He quit GRiD in early 1992, hired two engineers, and set up shop in a spare office at the venture capital firm of Merrill, Pickard, Anderson & Eyre, which had arranged the first round of funding, $1.3 million, for Palm Computing. The focus was to be on the Palm, not the pen. When Palm had just eight employees, Hawkins made a move that would prove its value repeatedly over the next decade: he hired former Apple executive Donna Dubinsky as the company's CEO.

Palm's first project was Zoomer, and it almost wrecked the company. The plan was for Palm to build its software on top of an operating system created by another company, GeoWorks, and for Tandy and Japan's Casio, the digital watch company, to build and brand the Zoomer. When the first Zoomer models were announced at the Consumer Electronics Show in Chicago in June 1993, the initial reviews were favorable. Sales were strong when the products arrived in stores that October, but then dropped off quickly. The Zoomers were too large and heavy, their performance was sluggish, and the handwriting recognition was lousy. Both Newton and Zoomer had crashed. Hawkins and Palm marketing chief Ed Colligan wanted to know why, exactly, so they took the unusual step of conducting interviews with dozens of Newton owners, in addition to surveying Zoomer buyers. What the Palm team discovered was that customers hadn't been attracted by all of the hype surrounding Newton. They simply wanted a device that would help them organize their lives by keeping track of their contacts and appointments. They didn't even want e-mail. "They wanted a better Daytimer. We said, 'If that's what they want, why don't we build it?'" Hawkins recalls. But improving on the Newton and Zoomer products wouldn't be a snap. Hawkins and Dubinsky were frustrated by the difficulties of depending on partners to produce the devices on which their software would run. Worse yet, they were just about out of money.

A key turning point for handheld computing came at a meeting that Hawkins and Dubinsky had with venture capitalist Bruce Dunlevie of Merrill Picard in April 1994. The encounter took place in Dunlevie's office on Sand Hill Road in Menlo Park, where most of Silicon Valley's venture capitalists had set up shop. Dunlevie had been the first financier to back Palm, and Hawkins wanted his advice about which way the company should turn. Zoomer had been a failure, money was hard to raise, and Palm's partners were losing interest. Hawkins remembers the conversation vividly.

"Do you know what product you ought to be building?" Dunlevie asked them.

Hawkins said yes.

"Why don't you build it?"

His answer: "We're a software company. We don't have the resources to also build the hardware and the operating system." Indeed, the company had only 27 employees at the time.

Then Dunlevie issued a challenge that changed the direction of computing history. "What else are you going to do, just go out of business?"

For Hawkins, Dunlevie's comment was like a slap across the face. He was stunned into silence for a few seconds. Then he calmed himself. He knew what people wanted in a handheld computer, and he felt he and his team were capable of making it. Why not give it his best shot? Suddenly, he felt confident. "I know what to do. I'll come back with some ideas," he told Dunlevie and Dubinsky.

Hawkins lived in a modest house in Redwood City, 10 miles from Dunlevie's office, with his wife Janet and two kids. By the time he got home that day it was early evening and he was alone in the kitchen. He gathered a pad of paper, a millimeter ruler, and a pencil and sat at the kitchen counter. There was still daylight, and out the window in front of him he could see the San Francisco Bay and, beyond it, a line of grass-covered hills that rose steeply on the other side of the water. But Hawkins spent most of his time with his head down, concentrating on his pad of paper. He was back to being an inventor again. Ideas flowed quickly. He knew that the device had to be smaller than Zoomer or Newton so it could be conveniently carried around all the time. That meant it had to fit comfortably in a person's shirt pocket. He also wanted the machine to cost less than $300, to synchronize with a PC through the use of a docking station, and, lastly, it had to be better than a paper Daytimer.

What Hawkins faced was a three-dimensional puzzle, a Rubik's Cube for computing. He knew how big the various components had to be—starting with two AAA batteries. He'd put the display over the batteries, placed a tiny circuit board next to the battery compartment, and so on until he had all the pieces arranged so they could be contained in the smallest and thinnest package. It took just about an hour to sketch out the device on paper.

The next step was building a model. Hawkins had a workshop in his house equipped with all manner of tools and equipment—including an old table saw from his parents' home on Long Island that the family had used to build the big round boat. He fashioned the model from two layers of plywood and one layer of cardboard. That was just the right thickness. He gave the rectangle some slight curves with an Exacto knife. Then he covered it with printer paper, and he drew the display and other features of the user interface on the paper. He taped together a crude docking station out of cardboard. He even whittled a stylus out of a chopstick that he found in a kitchen drawer. Just like that, the basics of the PalmPilot fell into place.

Hawkins remembered this whole process being done in time for him to go to bed by 11 p.m. However, in their book, *Piloting Palm*, published in 2002, authors Andrea Butter and David Pogue reported that his binge of creativity lasted a day and a half. Hawkins, later, didn't dispute that account. He said his memory was foggy on the details.

When Hawkins showed his model to Dubinsky and Dunlevie, they were enthusiastic. But Palm's board of directors didn't like the idea of Palm building its own device. The board was mainly made up of people who had invested in the company. "They thought it was nuts. Anybody who built consumer electronics hardware was nuts. I was going in the wrong direction," says Hawkins. Still, the board didn't have any better ideas. They weren't planning on investing more of their money, but they gave their approval to Hawkins and his colleagues to spend Palm's last $3 million trying to see how far they could get on his new project, which was code-named Touchdown.

A key to making this gambit work would be handwriting recognition—or, rather, the lack of full handwriting recognition. After the failure of Zoomer, it was clear that PalmPrint, the company's recognition software, wasn't good enough. Hawkins saw that to design a successful handwriting input system, he had to create a situation where if there were mistakes, consumers would blame themselves rather than the machine. "I wanted to make a system where you train the user rather than the computer," Hawkins says. So he had come up with the idea of creating a method for putting information into a handheld device with a stylus that would be simple enough for consumers to learn and simple enough for the machine to process. His solution was Graffiti, a system where users write uppercase letters on a stylus-sensitive screen, but a handful of the letters are simplified to the point where recognition mistakes are rare. (Hawkins had seen a demonstration of similar software at Xerox PARC, and, after the PalmPilot came out, Xerox sued for patent infringement. After several rounds of court decisions, the two companies settled their differences out of court.) Hawkins wanted to use Graffiti in the PalmPilot, but got resistance from others on the Palm team. "Half the company said we shouldn't risk the Pilot by putting it in," he says. "But we went with it. I promised it would work. We took the risk."

Taking the PalmPilot from concept to product was no easy task. Strapped for cash, the company outsourced some of the electrical and mechanical engineering work as well as some of the software programming. Finally, in a little over a year, they had a working prototype. Armed with something tangible, Dubinsky made the rounds of the industry looking for new investors.

The search for cash led Palm to Compaq. It had emerged in the mid-1990s as the most formidable PC company in the world. It had a full line of desktop and laptop PCs, but no handheld devices. Ted Clark, who had worked at GRiD, was by then running portable products for Compaq, and he called up Hawkins to explore the idea of Palm and Compaq collaborating to develop a handheld computer. That started months of conversations between executives and engineers at the two companies over how they might work together. Clark was for it. He even thought Compaq should buy Palm, but in the end, Compaq's top brass nixed even a strategic partnership. "If there was ever a strategic blunder, that was one of the top five computing blunders of all time," says Clark. He figures that with Palm's innovators and Compaq's money and marketing muscle, they could have built a huge business in handhelds.

In the end, Palm was sold to US Robotics for a mere $44 million. The Newton and Zoomer disasters were still fresh in peoples' minds and the PDA term was almost a dirty word. Few in the tech industry saw much promise in handhelds. US Robotics, whose main business was building computer modems, provided the Palm team with the money they needed to bring PalmPilot to market in 1996. Within a year, they had sold several hundred thousand devices and the PalmPilot was the number one selling PDA, with a 70 percent market share. But, by then, a troubled US Robotics was bought by 3Com, and, a year after that, Hawkins and Dubinsky, frustrated with 3Com's management, left to start yet another company, Handspring, which built handhelds based on Palm's operating system. Palm was valued at a whopping $53 billion at the end of Wall Street trading on March 2, 2000, when it went public as a spinout of 3Com. By the end of that year, more than five million Palm handhelds had been sold and its annual revenues topped $1 billion.

But even though Palm's stock soared, there was already a hotter handheld on the block: the BlackBerry. Introduced in 1999 by a little-known Canadian company, Research in Motion (RIM), it dispensed with the pen entirely and replaced it with a small keyboard for putting in words and numbers and a so-called track-wheel for quickly sorting through items on the display screen. The genius of BlackBerry was in how it handled e-mail. Even though Palm and Handspring had offered messaging earlier, BlackBerry's e-mail experience was dramatically better. Instant e-mail updates were available through major mobile telecommunications companies' networks, and RIM had developed software that made it easy to forward mail from corporate networks and personal accounts to its devices. At last, people could be constantly in touch with friends or business associates no matter where they were.

The inventor behind the BlackBerry was Mihal "Mike" Lazaridis, who grew up in a blue-collar neighborhood in Windsor, Canada, across the river from Detroit. His interest in electronics had emerged very early in life. He was born in Istanbul, Turkey, in 1961 to Greek parents who soon moved to a small town in southern Germany, where his father and uncle apprenticed in a tool-and-die machine shop. When Lazaridis was just four years old, his father bought him an electric train set, but, because their landlord couldn't stand noise, the youngster was not allowed to run the locomotive whenever he wanted to. His father showed him how to turn on the train's lights using a battery and two wires. "I was fascinated with how the battery could turn on the lights. The idea of completing an electrical circuit was a big deal. It transformed my life," Lazaridis says. After the family moved to Canada, he became a sponge for scientific knowledge. He was impressed by anything electrical or mechanical. He remembers his father taking him to the factory where he worked, Canada Bridge, which made parts for bridges, and showing him a 12-foot gear that would be used in a drawbridge. It was awesome. At age 12, he won a prize for reading every science book in his local branch of the Windsor Public Library.

None of the books were about computer science for the simple reason that it was still a relatively narrow field practiced by university scholars and corporate technology druids. It wasn't yet personal. But that was about to change. By the time Lazaridis was in his mid–teen years, computer technologies had joined radio and TV as popular hobbyist playthings for bright young nerds who tinkered away in their families' basements. Lazaridis's main tinkering partner was a neighbor, Douglas Fregin, whom he had met in grade school. Fregin was the president of Windsor's amateur TV club. In 1975, when Lazaridis was 14, a watershed event occurred that would change many lives and launch the personal computer industry. MITS, a tiny electronics company in New Mexico, began selling a kit to hobbyists that had all the parts and instructions they needed to assemble a rudimentary computer. The Altair 8800 is widely considered to be the first personal computer. It was an article about the Altair in the magazine *Popular Electronics* that inspired Bill Gates and Paul Allen to quit college and form Microsoft, which became one of the first PC software companies. The kit was snapped up by members of Silicon Valley's Homebrew Computer Club, as well. Lazaridis didn't have enough money to buy an Altair kit, which cost $397, a considerable sum for a blue-collar kid growing up in Windsor. But the Altair inspired Lazaridis and Fregin to build their own personal computers from scratch. Instead of Intel's microprocessor, they chose the Z80A processor from Zilog, which was later used in the Osborne 1 and Kaypro PCs. So, picture two boys at work in the basement of Lazaridis's house in Windsor, with PC, radio, and TV parts scattered around them. For them, radio and computing technologies were woven together. High school electronics teacher John Micsinzki planted a seed in Lazaridis's mind that germinated many years later. "He told me that the person who combines wireless technology with computers would come up with something special. I stored that away," says Lazaridis.

Lazaridis went to college at Canada's most prestigious technical school, the University of Waterloo, just outside Toronto. But, from the start, he was as much an entrepreneur as he was a student. The university fostered entrepreneurial thinking. It offered a joint major in electrical engineering and computer science, and Lazaridis was immediately thrown into an environment where students used giant mainframe computers, a network, and e-mail to gather information, write their papers, and communicate with each other and their professors via e-mail. The school also ran a cooperative education program that placed its students in technology companies so they could learn by doing. Lazaridis's first such posting was at a nearby office of Control Data Corp. (CDC), headquartered in Minneapolis, which was one of the early manufacturers of number-crunching supercomputers. He was assigned to a group that was designing a new generation of computers that would do the same amount of data processing in a box one-quarter the size of CDC's existing computers, and for one-tenth the cost.

It was his first lesson in the ability of new technologies to radically reshape the geometries and costs of computing in a short period of time. Executives at CDC were frightened by the implications of their engineers' invention. It threatened to undercut their existing business. So, Lazaridis claims, they actually decided to slow down development of the new machines. CDC eventually lost its competitive edge and broke into pieces. So

Lazaridis learned another valuable lesson: "If you don't innovate, somebody else will eat your lunch," he says.

Lazaridis was innovating like crazy. His specialty was writing software to make processors and other chips perform new tasks. Working as a consultant, he performed one job after another until he landed a contract with General Motors to build an add-on computer control system for some of its manufacturing equipment. He hired a small team of engineers to help him out, and, gradually, the GM contract took over his life. There was no longer time for him to go to classes. So he quit school just a few months before he would have graduated. Fregin soon joined him, and they set up RIM in 1984.

The company was anything but an overnight success. From 1984 to 1999, the year when they launched the product that would make them rich and famous, RIM gradually migrated from developing technologies for others in the sphere of wired networks to becoming a leader in advanced paging technology. Lazaridis discovered the potential of wireless data communications in 1987 when he attended a conference and learned about a wireless system that was being used in Japan to monitor soft-drink vending machines and send alerts when they were running empty so trucks could be sent out to reprovision them only when needed. At the time, there were only a smattering of wireless data technology companies in North America.

RIM got into the business when Cantel, now part of Rogers Communications, invited Lazaridis in to help with some technology it planned on using in a new data communications service. Cantel already offered mobile phone services and basic paging services. The new technology was called Mobitex, and it was made by Sweden's Ericsson. The problem was, when Cantel received its first shipment of Mobitex equipment, all of the documentation came in Swedish, and nobody there knew the language. Lazaridis and his engineers found electronic parts scattered around a basement storage room. It was chaos. But Lazaridis had a secret weapon. One of his engineers could read Swedish. Within an hour, they had the equipment assembled and working. That feat landed them a contract with Cantel to write key pieces of software for connecting the Mobitex paging system with computers. "That's where it all started," says Lazaridis.

From there, RIM branched out into designing and building modems and other paging equipment. By the mid-1990s it was building some of the first two-way messaging pagers, which required new methods for crafting short messages. Lazaridis had watched how people had struggled with handhelds such as Hewlett-Packard's 95 LX and 100 LX, shrunk-down versions of notebook computers that had small QWERTY keyboards, organized just like a typewriter. The keys were too small and too close together for touch typing, so people hunted and pecked with their index fingers. It was slow going. But Lazaridis found that if you made the keyboard even smaller, and people used their thumbs for typing, they could type faster. With practice, they developed something he calls "muscle memory." Their thumbs were able to maneuver over tiny pieces of real estate without making many mistakes. Based on this observation, RIM produced the Inter@active Pager, which looked like a toy clamshell notebook computer. It had a miniscule display on the inside of its lid, and an ultracompact QWERTY keyboard.

A turning point in the development of BlackBerry was when engineers from Intel traveled to RIM's headquarters in Waterloo to have a little talk about microprocessors. Intel had been an early financial backer of RIM, and the company was always on the lookout for new markets for its processors. At this meeting, an Intel executive suggested that RIM put an Intel 386 processor—a type used in personal computers—into some of its most advanced pagers. "Their proposal was so wild that I thought it was a joke. I laughed out loud," recalls Lazaridis. In fact, it was this idea that ultimately spawned the BlackBerry. In a series of discussions and experiments, engineers at RIM found that they could use software to alter a 386 processor so it consumed much less electricity than normal yet packed the processing power of a personal computer in a pager. Another way to think about it: Intel made it possible to create an interactive pager on a single chip. That meant a powerful computing device could be placed in a very small package.

The other key advance that made the BlackBerry so successful was RIM's decision to craft a messaging service that connected seamlessly with corporate e-mail systems. E-mails received by corporate e-mail equipment would instantly be pushed out to the BlackBerry. And when people replied with messages of their own on their BlackBerrys, they were essentially instructing their corporate e-mail system to send a message. By 1999, e-mail had become ubiquitous and the telecommunications carriers had dropped their prices, so it was suddenly ultracheap to send and receive e-mails on a mobile device. Technology met opportunity, and the BlackBerry phenomenon was born.

Lazaridis never considered using a pen as an input device for the BlackBerry. That's because, coming from the paging world, he wanted people to be able to use his little machines with one hand. The goal was to keep things simple.

The major key to BlackBerry's success, according to Lazaridis, was that everything he and the RIM engineers put into it was based on a fundamental principle: they were creating a "connected appliance" that would do one thing—e-mail—very well. They didn't attempt to create a replacement for the laptop computer. The technology was optimized to create a small, easy-to-use, and secure device with long battery life. "It's compelling. Some would even say it's addictive," he says. In fact, the Black-Berry proved to be so popular and addictive that it got the nickname "CrackBerry," because the office workers and professionals who bought them up by the hundreds of thousands couldn't seem to pry their hands off the little blue machines.

While those CrackBerrys were mighty popular, within just a few years the early models already looked quaint and out of date. The simple reason: you couldn't make a phone call on one. The BlackBerry's main attraction, doing one thing, e-mail, really, was suddenly a limitation. Ever since Sculley's speech at CES in 1992, leaders and pundits in the tech industry had spoken confidently about the convergence of computing and communications. Things hadn't advanced as quickly as many had predicted or hoped, mainly because the enabling technologies were slow to arrive or they weren't available at low-enough prices. But, finally, early in the new millennium, the convergence was happening for real.

By then, Sakoman, who first dreamed of making a handheld computer, had moved to a parallel universe. After leaving Apple, he had had a series of jobs running product development for Silicon Valley hardware and software companies. Later, he returned to Apple as vice president of software technology. But after a few years he retired from Apple and moved to remote Redding, California, in the far north end of the state, and ran a small solar energy firm. "My life is very different now," he says. "My cell phone sits in a cradle for six days out of seven. There are not a lot of people calling me." For Sakoman, the consummate engineer, all the politics he hated are a thing of the past. But so, at least for the time being, is his quest to design the ultimate portable device.

10

THE CONVERGENCE CONVERGES

R ight in the middle of Lenovo's X300's journey to the market-place, something had happened that signaled the dawn of a new era in mobile computing—and, to some people, raised questions about the future role of laptop PCs. The event was Apple's launch of the iPhone. This was Apple's first entry into the up-and-coming segment of portable computing called smartphones: mobile tele-phones that also did a bunch of other fun or useful things, including instant messaging, music playing, e-mail, and Web browsing. It was plain to see that the iPhone was a portable computer. Also, while the concept of a smartphone had been around since the early 1990s, Apple's introduction of the iPhone was to smartphones what the advent of the Apple's Macintosh was to desktop PCs in 1985. It took a powerful idea and turned it into a wonderful experience.

Apple's loyal fans were ecstatic. They lined up by the thousands at Apple stores starting three days ahead of the June 28, 2007 re-lease date. "This is this generation's Woodstock. They'll remember where they were on this day 20 years from now," predicted John Sculley, the former Apple CEO. At the Apple Store in the ultrahip SoHo section of Manhattan, which is essentially an upscale, open-air shopping mall, the line of people waiting to get into the store wound around a whole city block. This was a Friday afternoon, and the earliest of the early birds had staked out their spots at the front of the line on Tuesday. By Friday at 5:30 p.m., many were sunburned and bleary-eyed. They sat in folding beach chairs or on the pavement surrounded by suitcases, sleeping bags, umbrellas, yoga mats, and articles of clothing. Up front were some celebrities who had bought places in line: comedienne Whoopi Goldberg, with her dreadlocks, and movie maker Spike Lee, in his ever-present Yankees cap.

As the 6 p.m. opening time drew near, people who filled a closed-off Prince Street crushed in close around the front door of the Apple Store. A phalanx of bouncers with bulging muscles and black t-shirts blocked their way. Somebody in the street shouted "It's an historic event!" At 6 p.m., the huge crowd counted down from ten to one and gave a huge "whoop!" as the doors opened and the first group of shoppers rushed in. People in the crowd held video cameras and camera phones over their heads to record the event, and some of those who filed in videoed themselves as they went. A group called iPhonelaunch.TV was videoing everything and streaming it live on the Internet. A young woman in the crew explained breathlessly: "We have been taping all day and we'll be taping all night."

Inside, dozens of Apple Store employees lined up alongside the steps that led to a first landing and then upstairs again to the main floor. They applauded as the customers filed in and dashed up the stairs. Minutes later, when the first happy customers came bounding down the steps with their $600 purchases in little black bags, the clerks gave them ovations, and, outside, the crowd would cheer. It was like the scene at the finish line of the New York City Marathon, where exhausted but triumphant runners are egged on by a wildly enthusiastic crowd.

A young woman in the street laughed at the goings on. Rosina Genao, a 34-year-old fashion buyer, was on her way home from work in the garment district, but stopped to see what the commotion was about. "I live next door, and I wouldn't wait 15 minutes on line for this," she said. But, it turns out, her attitude wasn't a reflection on the desirability of the iPhone itself—just the notion of waiting in line for one. Would Rosina buy an iPhone after the lines melted away? "Yeah, for sure," she said.

This was Steve Jobs's genius. Apple products on his watch had only occasionally been true technology innovations. What he was really good at was glomming onto important tech advances by others, understanding the wants of customers, designing products that were easy to use and pleasing to the eye, and then marketing the hell out of them. The essence of his marketing message was simple and hard for many people to resist: you're smarter, hipper, and more creative than other people, so buy an iPhone, iPod music player, MacBook laptop, and so on. For many, buying Apple products was like a Catholic taking communion or a sugar addict eating cake.

What was so great about the iPhone? To be sure, it packed plenty of features, including a cell phone, music and video player, personal organizer, e-mail program, and Web browser. But other smartphones from the likes of Nokia and Samsung offered all of that—plus better networks with faster downloading and Web browsing. Some of them even had global positioning technology packed in so you could orient yourself via maps on their displays. The iPhone didn't have that. What it had was great software that made it extremely easy to use and delighted consumers with little flourishes—like the fact that you could turn "pages" on the roomy 3.5-inch (88.9-millimeter) screen by flicking the screen with your finger. Instead of the mechanical keys that were popular on other smartphones, you typed by touching graphical keys on the display. Some particularly reverential or sarcastic people called it the "Jesus phone." iPhone hype would crest again with the introduction of iPhone 3G in July 2008. Not only was Internet access much faster but, within a month, iPhone owners had downloaded 60 million applications written solely for iPhone.

The iPhone launch and relaunch were arguably Steve Jobs's finest performance ever in three decades under the PC big top. He and pal Steve Wozniak had started Apple in 1976 and, for nearly a decade, Jobs had been the company's visionary leader and marketing genius while Wozniak, an engineer at heart, had gradually faded from view. Jobs made his mark as a consummate product developer and marketer with the Macintosh, which he introduced with great fanfare in 1984. The PC was a good tool for individuals, but it was hard to use. The Macintosh was a revelation—with its mouse, graphical user interface, and pleasing shape. For the first time ever, people fell in love with their computers. In spite of the success of the Macintosh, the volatile Jobs was pushed out in 1985 in a power play engineered by John Sculley, whom he had lured to run Apple from Pepsi in 1983 with the challenge to help change the world. During Jobs's decade-long exile from Apple, he continued to develop his skills as a design tastemaker, first with the elegant black, pizza-box-shaped NeXT Computer and then with Pixar Animation Studios, maker of the delightful movies *Toy Story*, *Cars*, and *Monsters, Inc.*

By the time Jobs returned to Apple in 1996 with the company's acquisition of NeXT, he had developed truly exquisite taste. He put it to use in collaboration with Apple's skillful design chief, Jonathan Ive. Together they produced one stellar design after another, including iMac, where they integrated the display and electronics of the PC in a curvaceous, candy-colored body; iBook notebooks, which were colorful and curvy; and the first MacBooks, which replaced iBooks in 2006 and, with their simple, squared-off forms, resembled the original ThinkPad design concept. The duo truly hit their stride with iPods, the tiny music players that borrowed their rounded-off shapes from the work German designer Dieter Rams did for the consumer electronics and appliance maker Braun.

Jobs and Apple proved once and for all that design mattered in the computer business, and that woke up the rest of the industry. Yet while a number of products from the likes of Sony, Hewlett-Packard, and ASUSTeK stood out, and while Lenovo kept renewing its strong ThinkPad design, the rest of the PC world couldn't seem to catch up with Apple. There were plenty of excellent designers around. Apple didn't have a monopoly on them. The only explanation for this phenomenon was Jobs himself.

In the late 1980s and early 1990s, during his banishment, Apple was chaotic. Donald Norman, the user-centric design guru and Northwestern University professor, who headed Apple's Advanced

Technologies Group (ATG) in the mid-1990s, tried to impose discipline. He set up a process requiring product marketers, engineers, and industrial designers to work together as a team from the beginning of projects. When Jobs returned in 1996, everything changed. Apple was in deep trouble; in danger of going out of business. He fired hundreds of people, including Norman and most of ATG. And he imposed a new discipline, which was basically the discipline of Steve. "Steve was just a nasty person, which is exactly what Apple needed," said Norman. "He had a strong commitment to do things one way. If you disagreed, tough." The wrath of Steve was to be avoided at all costs. *Wired* magazine, in its January 2008 issue, recounted an early demonstration of a prototype of the iPhone that was so bad that Jobs terrified his engineers not by throwing one of his usual tantrums but just by staring at them and saying levelly, "We don't have a product yet."

Jobs waited for mobile phone and handheld computer technology to become robust before he produced his own smartphone. In that way, he had avoided a lot of the hard work that had to be done to make smartphones work well, and, in essence, skipped to the head of the line after the rest of the industry had completed that job.

The smartphone was, truly, a long time coming. What could be more natural than combining contacts, calendaring, and e-mail, with a mobile phone? Yet, here, the challenges that confront all portable computer developers are compounded. It had proved difficult to produce small, single-purpose mobile phones that worked seamlessly across networks and country borders, and delivered good voice quality and uninterrupted calling. Now try to pack all of that in a very small package with e-mail, Web browsing, and the rest to create the Swiss Army knife of computing. The early efforts produced Rube Goldberg-esque machines that were too big and didn't work as advertised.

The first of these experiments was the Simon Personal Communicator. This venturesome yet deeply flawed gadget was created jointly by BellSouth and IBM, and had its beginnings at the

COMDEX computer industry trade show in Las Vegas in 1992. That was a time of soaring ambitions for the former Bell operating companies, including BellSouth. In 1991, the U.S government had given them permission to offer online information services. Dan Norman, who had only recently been promoted to set up and run BellSouth Cellular's R&D lab, had conducted a series of marketing focus groups with customers in Georgia and Florida to find out what new services they wanted. One of the things they were interested in was combining phones with computers. (IBM had recently introduced a laptop with a cell phone attached, so the idea was in the air.) So Norman was on the lookout for technologies that bridged between the telephone and computer industries when he attended COMDEX that November. And he wasn't disappointed. A group of IBM PC division engineers was showing off a prototype of a product they were developing that was code-named Angler. It combined paging and global positioning technology, so people could fetch maps from over the airwaves. Next, they told him, they planned on adding cell phone calling.

Norman loved trying new things. Shortly after he went to work for AT&T in 1983, he landed an assignment with AT&T AMPS, the first cell phone business in the United States. This was even before AT&T's first cellular networks were switched on. So being on the ground floor of risky new ventures didn't frighten Norman. He arranged meetings with IBMers in Boca Raton, Florida, and, within a matter of months, they agreed to codevelop a product that would combine e-mail, fax, and phone. IBM supplied the electronics, screen, and handset housing. Norman's R&D engineers helped out with some of the software, and BellSouth agreed to market the product nationwide to wireless carriers. Neither of the two companies had ever designed a mobile handset, so they brought in Mitsubishi to engineer the cell phone electronics. Ultimately, Simon included a mobile phone, a pager, e-mail, a calendar, an address book, a calculator, and a pen-based sketchpad.

There were the inevitable delays. IBM discovered problems with faxing when it conducted manufacturing tests in early 1994.

But, amazingly, given the fact that three large companies were collaborating on a product that had never been tried before, BellSouth shipped the first models to customers in August 1994—a little more than a year and a half after Norman had stumbled upon Angler.

The first reviews were raves. Journalists and industry analysts were hungry for products that bridged between industries in those days, so they tended to overlook obvious flaws and accentuate the positive. You could do things with Simon that no device had done before. Some people loved the nifty touch screen, and their ability to press a button to switch from the landscape to portrait view on the oblong display. But, the fact was, Simon was a brick. It, literally, looked like a small black brick, and, at 20 ounces, it weighed too much to be very useful as a phone. Customers started feeling muscle fatigue after a few minutes of holding Simon to their ears. Beyond the size and weight, the device had a long list of deficiencies: battery life was short, only 30 minutes of talk time; it could receive e-mail, not send it; and; while you could receive a fax, reading it was another matter: it was nearly impossible. Initially, Simon cost $1,800, though BellSouth quickly dropped the price to $800. IBM produced 18,000 of them before word came to shut down the production line. In spite of all of Simon's flaws, Norman believes that the product was doomed by a flaw it didn't even have: handwriting recognition. You could draw on the Simon screen with a stylus, but that was it. The machine was not equipped to recognize handwriting. Yet, with the disaster of Apple's Newton fresh in the minds of consumers, those bad feelings rubbed off on other daring new digital products. The Newton phenomenon was toxic. "We didn't have handwriting recognition, but people thought we did," says Norman.

The Simon project was so fraught with bad feelings that nobody tried designing a smartphone again for years. Norman himself came up with a plan for a high-quality mobile phone with a touch screen and address book, but he couldn't get anybody to build it. Still, he's proud of what he and his colleagues did. After the iPhone was launched, he said: "I'm way past the point of complaining, but IBM and BellSouth were the first companies to mash all that stuff together and prove it could work."

The person who finally figured out how to make a good smartphone was also the guy who had done the same with PDAs: Jeff Hawkins. He had realized in the summer of 1998, when he and Dubinsky started Handspring, that the era of the stand-alone PDA would soon draw to a close. The big opportunity in the future would be in combining computers and telephones. "This thought depressed me," says Hawkins. "We were the leader in handhelds, but we had to get into the phone business, which was dominated by huge companies. We were a little nothing. But we had no choice. If we didn't build a smartphone, we'd be out of business." In 1998, it was too early for Handspring to develop a smartphone, however. For such devices to take off, they needed good wireless data networks, and those didn't exist yet. Also, at the time, handset makers designed their own chips. Handspring didn't have the resources to do that. So, in the meantime, Hawkins commissioned a mobile phone ad-on for Visor, the company's first handheld, but the VisorPhone was a flop. It was just too ungainly.

The technology landscape was changing rapidly, though. Carriers deployed new and improved networks, and a handful of independent companies that specialized in designing electronics for handsets started producing high-quality chips that Handspring could use in its products. So, as 2000's boom for handhelds turned into 2001's bust, Hawkins set about designing a new product that combined a mobile phone, Web browser, e-mailer, and organizer in a single compact device—the Handspring Treo.

The first Treo was something of a proof of concept. It was a flip phone, meaning you lifted the front cover to reveal the tiny keyboard and monochrome screen. This was the first time Hawkins and his team had used a keyboard, and it took a while to get it right. The keys had to be shaped just so, or else people using the device would depress more than one key at once. They also had to offer just the right amount of resistance to touch, so users knew by feel when they had successfully keyed in a letter or number. Hawkins decided that, since Treo had a keyboard, they could dispense with Graffiti, his system for writing on the screen in digital shorthand. But he got resistance from the marketing team, and, ultimately, Handspring shipped two versions. There wasn't much demand for the version that included Graffiti, though.

The introduction of the Treo 180 in early 2002 set off a race among the world's mobile handset makers to produce better and better smartphones. By then, with the market for handhelds swooning, Handspring had been bought by Palm, and Hawkins and crew produced a second smartphone that was a bona fide hit, the Treo 600. It was a color model with a so-called candy-bar design (no flip-up cover). The keyboard was also improved. Hawkins had discovered through experimentation that if you provided a strong backlight for a keyboard, people could find the keys much more easily and type faster. With brighter backlighting in subsequent models, Palm initially produced smaller keyboards—and thinner devices—than its rival, RIM, which had quickly followed Hawkins into the smartphone market.

Suddenly, mobile phones were emerging as the dominant portable gadget. At least they were getting most of the hype. And, based on the number of machines sold, mobile phone handsets were far outpacing sales of laptop computers. In 2007, for the first time, more than one billion handsets were sold in a year. That compared to about 100 million laptops sold. While the vast majority of those handsets were traditional mobile phones, devices that combine phone calling, entertainment, and computing were becoming more common. Handsets classified as smartphones came in at around 100 million in 2007, and analysts expected 250 million or more to be sold by 2010.

For the world's road warriors, the smartphone was a truly wonderful device. Jim Steele, president of worldwide sales at the on-demand software company Salesforce.com, spent an average of 200 nights away from his home as he hopped around the world visiting customers and salespeople. Before he got his first BlackBerry, when he was traveling on business, he'd call his secretary on his cell phone as soon as he landed at an airport and have her read his e-mail over the phone. If she wasn't in the office, he was just out of luck. He'd race to his hotel room and get online via his laptop. Steele was never a huge fan of laptops, though. Best to say he tolerated them. The reason was he had never mastered touch typing. He hunted and pecked, and not very rapidly. So when the Black-Berry came along it was a revelation to him. He found that he could type with his thumbs on the BlackBerry faster than he could type with his index fingers on a laptop. For a while, he carried a cell phone *and* his BlackBerry, but when RIM got its mobile phone technology right, he switched to an all-in-one. He could make calls, do e-mail, and get on the Web via one very small device.

The BlackBerry smartphone became a crucial tool for Steele and the entire Salesforce.com sales and management team. Thanks to always being in touch with one another, they could share information, confer, and make decisions rapidly. A huge deal that Salesforce.com signed with Citicorp in late 2007 shows just how instrumental the smartphone had become. They had been negotiating with Citi executives for several months about supplying the financial company with an online service for bank employees who managed money for wealthy customers. At last, it was time for a final push on what would be Salesforce.com's largest deal in its ten-year history. Over a period of two days, sales managers Wayne Like, Dave Orrico, and Dave Rudnitsky camped out at Citi's office in Manhattan negotiating the fine points of the deal. These sessions would last from 9 a.m. to 10 or 11 p.m. at night. They'd duck out of meetings and, standing in hallways, sent e-mails to Steele, Salesforce.com CEO Marc Benioff, and other company executives asking for their advice or approval of terms and conditions. Finally, on November 2, only a few last details remained. Steele was traveling in Europe. He weighed in via his BlackBerry from the airport in London and then again when he landed in Germany two hours later. That evening, when he and a customer were dining on wurst in a Frankfurt restaurant, Steele felt his BlackBerry vibrate in his pocket. Anticipating news on the Citi deal, he excused himself and checked his mail. An alert had come over notifying all top Salesforce.com executives that the Citi contract had closed. Steele shouted, "Yes! Yes!" and pumped his fist, startling his guest and other diners. If not for his ability to be in touch with his colleagues nearly constantly, the last phase of the deal-making process might have dragged on for weeks or even months. Instead, it was done in 48 hours.

This revolution in mobile communications gave rise to a raging debate in 2007 and 2008: which was the more important portable device, the laptop or the smartphone? Advocates for both sides weighed in. But, in the end, the fight was silly. It was the gadget-junkie version of medieval monks debating over how many angels could dance on the head of a pin. There would be uses where a smartphone would win hands down, such as phone calling, text messaging, basic e-mailing, and quick-and-dirty Web browsing. But if you wanted to create something, whether writing a letter or a longer e-mail, prepare a presentation, edit photographs or video, or even read a long e-mail, the notebook PC was still the best device for those uses—and it looked like it would remain so for the foreseeable future.

So, as Lenovo's X300 came to market, there were two hugely successful portable devices—the notebook PC and the mobile phone. But would people also want to use other gizmos that were smaller than a notebook PC but larger than a smartphone? The idea: offer businesspeople something very small—pocketable, in some cases—that's an alternative to carrying a laptop around town or on a short business trip. Samsung, Sony, Nokia, Fujitsu, and Vulcan Portals had all come out with such products, which were called "tweeners" by some people.

Palm's Jeff Hawkins had his own twist on the concept. During a digital products conference, in May 2007, he strode onstage to show a prototype of his latest brainstorm: Foleo. It was an ultra-compact computer with a twist. Palm was positioning the sleek clamshell device, which it planned on selling for $499 after a re-bate, as an alternative to carrying a larger, conventional laptop. It offered a nearly full-size keyboard, a 10-inch (254-millimeter) display, and a selection of applications including a word processor and spreadsheet. It ran the Linux operating system. Hawkins believed it would be most useful when people also carried smartphones, like Treos or BlackBerrys, and transferred e-mail to Foleo when they were in sit-down mode. "It's a companion to your phone and companion to you," he said during a briefing at the time.

Yet it wasn't clear if there would be a lot of demand for tween-ers. Most of the new machines, including the Foleo, were too large to fit into a pocket or not capable enough to replace a note-book PC. The priciest topped $2,900—far more than the average subnotebook. And Hawkins's demonstration of the Foleo, impressive as it was in some respects, left the computing cognoscenti scratching their heads: were people really looking for a companion to their phone? Would hard-core business types choose a computer that runs Linux rather than Microsoft's Windows? "The yet-another-device philosophy doesn't carry, so to speak, and it's sure as hell not the future of mobile computing," sniffed blogger Ryan Block on the popular Engadget technology Web site.

Perhaps Block's comment was prophetic. Three months later, Palm announced that plans to ship Foleo had been suspended in-definitely. The company had just been taken private in a lever-aged buyout by the private equity firm Elevation Partners, and it was conserving its resources. The top priority was completing a new operating system that would be optimized for combining mobile telephony and computing. So engineers were shifted from the Foleo project to work on the new operating system. Palm's move was a blow to Hawkins, who had dreamed of making a de-vice like Foleo for more than five years. He tried to shrug it off, though. "I think it's likely we'll ship it someday," he said at the time. "I still think the concept is one of the best I ever came up with."

By then, Hawkins was sitting on the sidelines of portable computing. He was a senior advisor to Palm rather than a regular employee. He spent most of his time developing theories of how the brain works, which he had laid out in a 2004 book, *On Intelligence.* He and Dubinsky had started a new company, Numenta, to develop computing products based on his neuroscience theories. The idea was to create software that, like the brain, knows nothing at the beginning of its existence, but which learns from what it experiences and builds a model of the world based on that knowledge. The software was designed to address problems that have been difficult for traditional computers to master, such as pattern recognition—the stuff Hawkins's father was working on with the dolphin and that Hawkins himself had wrestled with the handwriting recognition software at Palm. In his spare time, Hawkins built wooden boats.

It seemed like yet another chapter had begun in the saga of portable computing. Palm's market share was dwindling, and Apple and the iPhone were ascending. In October 2007, Apple announced an important strategic shift that positioned iPhone as more than just a nifty device that teenagers would die for. Jobs would allow independent software makers to create applications that could run on iPhones. This was the strategy that had helped make Microsoft's Windows the world's dominant PC operating system. Now Apple was in the game, too. The iPhone would be a "platform" for others to build upon, like Windows for PCs and like Microsoft's Windows Mobile software for smartphones. Apple had taken the early lead in the personal computing era only to be overtaken by Microsoft, with its superior business plan of building an ecosystem of other companies around its products. Now, Apple was back. And, if that wasn't enough excitement for the portable computing crowd, Google, the Web search engine giant, was getting into the mobile phone business, too. It announced in November 2007, just as Lenovo's Kodachi was going into its premanufacturing test phase, that it was creating a package of software, called Android, that handset makers could use to run their next-generation mobile phones. Google also created an alliance of companies, called the Open Handset Alliance, dedicated to using and promoting the software. Its goal was to rival the smartphone technology made by Apple, Microsoft, Nokia, Palm, and RIM.

Meanwhile, the tech industry was left to wonder what Apple's Jobs would come up with next. Even though dozens of reporters wrote about Apple regularly, the company had a knack for keeping its secrets under wraps. The company's purchase of a small chip design firm, P.A. Semi, for $278 million, in April 2008, suggested that it had huge ambitions for its smartphone business. P.A. Semi specialized in designing processor chips that required little electrical power—and so were well-suited for a device like the iPhone. It looked like Apple planned on becoming more vertically integrated—reversing a long-term trend in the computer industry. In the early years, computer companies had done everything for themselves—designing and making chips, manufacturing circuit boards and computers, and writing their own operating systems and applications. But, over the years, most companies had shifted. They gave up on being vertically integrated, instead buying hardware and software components from others. Apple had resisted. While other PC companies relied on Microsoft for their operating systems and other companies for applications, Apple kept designing its own software. And, though it bought microprocessors from others, including Intel and Motorola for PCs and ARM for iPhone, it kept designing some of the specialized chips that went into its machines.

With the purchase of P.A. Semi, it looked like Apple would take control over its own fate in microprocessor technology for smartphones and other handheld devices. As these machines become ever smaller, more and more of their capabilities are placed on fewer chips. And, continuously, more and more is added to the microprocessor chip itself. That means devices can be smaller and less expensive. So it looked like Jobs aimed to take the lead in the next generation of hardware miniaturization. Or maybe not.

An anecdote from 2001 gives a hint of just how inscrutable Steve Jobs could be. Remember Steve Capps and Michael Tchao of Apple Newton fame? Capps had left Apple in 1995 and went to work for Microsoft. Tchao ultimately found his way to Nike, where he became general manager of Nike TechLab, which focused on integrating digital technology with Nike's athletic shoes. In 2001, both were entrepreneurs-in-residence at Ignition, a Seattle-based venture capital firm. They had some ideas for improving the technology in smartphones and were casting about for a way to put them to use. They thought Apple should get into the mobile phone business, and hoped that, if it did, the company would license some of their technology.

Capps and Tchao believed there was an opening for Apple because the mobile phone industry wasn't doing a good job of serving its customers. The smartphones that were just then coming to market didn't work well with Web sites. What the industry needed was a disruptive force like Jobs, they thought. They figured that Apple could produce a great user interface and great mobile services coupled with great software—which would enable it to revolutionize the mobile phone industry.

The two friends felt the idea of Apple getting into the phone business was obvious, and suspected that Jobs was probably already working on it. So they arranged to meet with him at Apple's offices. They discussed the state of the cell business and some generic ideas for improving the customer experience on mobile phones. But, ultimately, after a wide-ranging discussion, Jobs said he wasn't interested. He didn't seem to understand the phone business. Or maybe he was just pretending not to. Tchao remembered Jobs saying: "Why would we get into this business? We don't know this space. What could we add?' " Well, it turned out that Apple could add quite a lot. Six years later, Jobs introduced iPhone, and a new era in portable computing was begun. "One thing Steve is incredibly good at is not necessarily being first to enter a space, but entering at the right time in the right way," says Tchao.

In late 2008, Apple and the rest of the tech industry seemed poised for a new wave of innovations. Some of the new capabilities that would come to portable computing were predictable—driven by relentless improvements in chips and networks. Others were unknowable. They were still inchoate dreams in the heads of countless designers, engineers, and entrepreneurs. But their time, too, would come.

11

THE FUTURE OF PORTABLE
COMPUTING

Even before the first X300 test models had come off the assembly line at the Lenovo factory in China in December 2007, the ThinkPad design team was turning its attention to the next generation of laptops. These machines would be produced in 2009 and beyond. In late November 2008, David Hill, Richard Sapper, Tom Takahashi, and Aaron Stewart, the human-factors-design specialist, led a three-day marathon of reviews in Yamato. Each morning, they'd settle down in a conference room and, at any given time, they'd meet with seven or eight of the Japanese designers.

They started with a tactical review of all of the products that had come out in the past year or were in the late stages of development. They spent about one hour on each machine, talking over what worked and what didn't. When X300's turn came, the designers were pleased with the way things had ended up. They liked the satiny rubberized paint on the outside and the shiny black hinges. The paint treatment made X300 stand out from black laptops made by other PC companies. The new coating on the keys felt good to the touch and was more durable than the previous one. The backlighting of control buttons made them easy to find on a dark airplane. The designers were pleased with the reengineered touchpad and keyboard. And they liked the way so many of the labels had been tucked away inside the battery bay.

Those reviews were just the warm-up for a deep discussion of the future of laptop design. Peter Hortensius, the head of the portable division, had ordered up a complete reappraisal of the ThinkPad product line, and Stewart was on the hook to write a 100-page report about the design issues. This reappraisal was something that the old-time IBMers were accustomed to. Every few years they'd do a "clean sheet" exercise, where they'd throw out all of their assumptions about how a ThinkPad should be engineered and rethink everything from scratch. At this point, the ThinkPad crew hadn't done one of these exercises in several years, but the X300 project got their creative juices flowing. Now they were dreaming up ideas that were even more radical than those that had launched the Kodachi project, including a completely new way of situating the display. Stewart wouldn't give me the details on what they had in mind. He didn't want to tip their hand to competitors. But one thing was clear: "Kodachi is serving as an inspiration for what comes next," he said.

All over the world, at the end of Kodachi's journey to market, engineering and design teams at dozens of tech companies, from Apple to Nokia and from Intel to Microsoft, were engaged in similar soul-searching exercises. The portable computer had come a long way since Alan Kay had first conceived it nearly forty years earlier. Laptops were light, compact, and powerful. They had been refined to the point of near perfection. Mobile phones were evolving into small portable computers—capable of handling e-mail, Web browsing, navigation, e-commerce, and more. Inventors were hard at work on a new generation of machines that would be smaller than conventional laptops but larger than smartphones. And, finally, after years of experimentation, electronic book readers were good enough to replace paper books. All of these devices would get better and cheaper over time, thanks to the miniaturization of microchips and the work of imaginative designers. But major challenges remained. When would voice and handwritten computing commands finally achieve their full potential? Would it be possible to provide people with a single identity code that would serve as their permanent and universal phone number and online address in all aspects of the digital world? And would portable computers ever become the smart digital assistants long dreamed of by visionaries from Kay to Palm's Jeff Hawkins and to Hewlett-Packard's Sam Lucente? Asked for his view of the future of portable computing, Lucente says: "Essentially, it's about the always-connected experience. Your information will follow you everywhere, and you can do anything from anywhere, and the device will change from a personal device to a work device depending on what's happening in your day. It will be like changing your shoes."

While there's a strong drive to try to combine features into a single, multipurpose machine, most people who are on the forefront of technology believe there's a plethora of devices in our future. Robert Brunner, the former Apple design chief who now runs Ammunition Group, carries a collection of electronics gear when he travels, including an iPhone, a laptop, a digital camera, and a Kindle e-book reader from Amazon.com. Each device is purpose-built, and the specialty items—the digital camera and Kindle—do one thing better than any general-purpose device could do it. The way Brunner sees things, successful design of portable devices will be based on a keen understanding of the limitations of humans. Our eyes, hands, and ears won't be changing much over the next few thousand years. Beyond that, the devices need to answer a basic human need in a way that resonates deeply with their users. "Designers have to look at design not just as the object," Brunner says. "A good design is an object. A great design is an idea. How does it connect with people? You want people to understand them and to covet them." Apple's especially good at this with its iPod music player, iTunes Web site, and iPhone smartphone. That's why the company itself matters to people. Once, Brunner asked a classroom full of students at Stanford University how many cared if Motorola, a leading maker of mobile phones, went out of business. Few raised their hand. What about Apple? Everybody raised their hand.

For some of the industry's wise men, the ultimate portable computer is the one that isn't. Instead of always carrying a device around, people might be able to get information, communicate, and express themselves via a variety of displays, networks, and input methods that are built into cars, stores, offices, airports—even bathrooms. "I think the computer should disappear," says design guru Donald Norman. "You should have the electronic tools for the task you're trying to accomplish. In some cases, they'll look like today's computers. In others, they won't look like computers at all." Norman believes it's essential for designers to think deeply about how people and machines can most effectively communicate with one another, so they understand words the same way, and so machines can begin to anticipate the wishes of their human masters.

Many of the people who were the pioneers of computing in the 1970s, 1980s, and 1990s continue to be the pioneers in the new century. Take John Ellenby. His GRiD Systems produced the first commercial laptop computer, the first pen-based computer, and the first mobile data network. And, after years of work, in late 2008 his vision of the mobile phone as the ultimate digital pointing device is at last taking hold not just in mobile-crazy Japan but in the United States as well. Using his GeoVector software and service, people with mobile phones equipped with Global Positioning System (GPS) systems and compasses can point their handsets at a building or historic site and get all sorts of information about what goes on there—via text, pictures, audio, and video. If they point to a train station, they can get schedules, and, soon, they'll be able to buy a ticket. The aim is to enable people to interact more deeply with the world around them. Ellenby has a vision of a new sort of device, World Surfer, which will stretch the imaginations of both designers and consumers. When you're at home, these gizmos will be your cordless phone and family messaging system. When you're away, they'll help you navigate with precise mapping and up-to-the minute information about weather, traffic, and areas with high crime rates. Sensors will alert you to chemical leaks, dangerous pollution, or allergens; they'll monitor your health and tell you when to take medication. Much of this capability will be provided via microelectromechanical systems, known as MEMS, which are essentially tiny machines built into bigger machines. A high-quality digital camera will automatically attach time and place information to each photo or video taken. World Surfer will know who you are, and it will understand the context of all of your communications and creations, and act or react appropriately. "The machine will be your guide, your helper, your recorder, and your entrée to the data behind the physical objects in the world. It will also be your friend," says Ellenby.

For Ellenby's vision to be fully realized, a tremendous amount of information will have to be gathered in digital form about each place, thing, and person. And it will have to be stored in data centers so it's instantly available to portable devices via data networks. Think of data centers as the factories of the info economy. Every day, in thousands of nondescript buildings in the hinterlands or in the basements of office towers, trillions of chunks of information coded in ones and zeros are moved, stored, and assembled into new shapes. Those electronic packets include millions of e-mails, Facebook pages, blog entries, and YouTube videos; vast quantities of electronic transactions; plus an ever-expanding universe of commercial data that needs to be stored, sliced, diced, and analyzed. Tech-market researcher IDC estimates that, each year, the digital world creates about three million times the information contained in all the books ever written. Some of this information will be so valuable that it makes financial sense for companies to collect it and make it available for a fee. Other information will be paid for by advertising. Much of it will be on public Web pages and will be easily searchable via Google or other search engines. But a lot of the data, especially the personal stuff, will have to be gathered by our computers, both fixed and portable, as we live our digital lives.

That's where the thinking of another of computing's pioneers comes in. Gordon Bell, a Microsoft researcher who was a key architect of Digital Equipment's minicomputers in the 1960s, is on a decade-long quest to record and store every significant bit of information about himself, including what he has heard, said, and seen. His project, called MyLifeBits, was inspired by Vannevar Bush's 1945 concept of Memex (a personal computer as an extension of our memory) combined with Bill Gates's goal of someday being able to store everything we have seen and heard. "I'm exploring the use of the computer as the ultimate surrogate or supplement to our brain," Bell says. He sometimes wears a digital audio recorder and camera around his neck. The camera, called SenseCam, was produced by Microsoft Research Cambridge Lab, and captures a photo every few seconds—triggered by changes of light or sensing the presence of a person.

Portable computing plays a significant role in his project, since much of what he sees, says, and hears takes place when he's away from his desktop PC. Bell believes that before long cell phones will come with 200 gigabytes of storage so they can collect this ocean of information when we're on the go—later uploading it into one of those vast data centers. "It's a quest to free one's life of information clutter by retaining and organizing a person's information for total recall, to supplement their memory, and to provide for digital immortality," says Bell. His motto: "Delete nothing."

One of the biggest challenges facing the creators of portable computers is the difficulty in using the natural interfaces between humans and computers—speech and touch. You can't simply speak to your portable computer or write on a touch-sensitive surface and expect it to understand everything you say or write with the level of accuracy you'd like. Getting machines to recognize handwriting has been a goal since the 1970s, and, while there has been progress, the technology is not yet good enough to go mainstream. Mitch Kapor, whose frustration with the hassle of getting his handwritten notes into his computer helped launch the pen computing craze of the early 1990s, is still frustrated. It turns out that trying to solve the handwriting recognition challenge with brute force, by adding more computational horsepower, hasn't provided a complete solution. Handwriting recognition requires a level of contextual understanding by the computer that scientists have not yet been able to figure out how to provide. "I predict that we still won't have a pen-based solution to the original problem of capturing my notes in the next twenty years," says Kapor.

The same goes for speech recognition. So far, speech is only useful in tightly controlled circumstances, but that's gradually changing. IBM Research, for instance, has developed speech-to-speech translation software that it provided to U.S. forces in laptops and PDAs for use in Iraq. A soldier speaks into a microphone attached to the computer. The software immediately converts what he says into text on the screen, translates it into at least two interpretations in Arabic, and then translates those interpretations back into English. The soldier picks the version that's truest to his intent. Once he has made his choice, the Arabic words are spoken by an automated voice. The person the soldier is talking to then answers using the same process. The conversation can move relatively quickly if both parties are familiar with the software, but it's far from natural. Still, you can see where this might go.

David Nahamoo, director of IBM's speech and translation technology, foresees the software being used by tourists. Rather than fumbling with a French or Italian phrase book on a street corner in Paris or Milan, Americans will be able to conduct complex and accurate conversations with locals—assuming they find patient Samaritans to help them out. Right now, since the technology requires quite a bit of computing power, it's limited to laptops and PDAs. But, in the future, much of the computing will be done in data centers and available via wireless networks, so people will be able to manage computer-aided translations on their mobile phones.

The hopes for being able to speak to computers were high in 1999 when Mike McCue and Angus Davis left Netscape Communications to start their own company, Tellme Networks. They dreamed of creating a parallel Internet to the one where people looked at text and pictures on Web browsers. Their notion was that people would pick up a phone, say what they want, and get it. Rather than PCs and browsers, they'd use their phones and voices to navigate the Net. McCue called his vision DialTone 2.0. Then came the dot-com bust, which stunted McCue's plans. Tellme switched its focus to business customers. When you call such companies as American Airlines, AT&T, and Verizon for customer service information, you're interacting with Tellme's voice-automation system.

But, now, McCue's dream of word-of-mouth Web services is finally coming true. Tellme, now an independent subsidiary of Microsoft, is out front in delivering consumer voice search services. Its Tellme By Mobile service, on mobile phones, makes it possible for consumers to ask for directions to a nearby store or office and hear them spoken by an automated voice. They can also instruct the phone to dial a number, or send and get short messages. By early 2009, the Tellme By Mobile service will be integrated into Microsoft's Windows Mobile operating system, so it will be part of a software package that's loaded on tens of millions of mobile phone each year. Speech commands are on the verge of going mainstream.

McCue sees the voice service becoming ever more powerful as mobile handsets get new capabilities, such as GPS. Your phone will know who you are and what you like—perhaps learning by monitoring how you interact with it. When you're in a city far from home and say, "Find a nearby restaurant," it will pair your tastes with what's available in the vicinity and offer you the best matches. "This is a complete transformation of how people use devices," says McCue. "It's the next user interface for the next wave of consumer computing, which is inherently mobile."

Developments like this are thrilling to Microsoft's Bill Gates. He has been a pilgrim on the portable computing journey practically from the beginning, and he has the blisters and calluses to show for it. But he claims he's not discouraged. "The pen has been tougher than I would have expected, but we're undaunted," he says.

One of the most encouraging signs he has seen involves his own 12-year-old daughter. Every child at Jennifer Gates's school gets her or his own tablet computer, equipped with a stylus, starting at age eight. Most of their school materials and textbooks are electronic, and they're stored on the school's Web site. The students download homework assignments and complete them on their computers. They use Microsoft's OneNote program, which allows them to gather and organize test, photos, digital handwriting, audio clips, and video recordings in a virtual notebook. Once Jennifer completes her homework, she can turn it in online, and Bill can later see the grade and comments the teacher puts on it— assuming Jennifer gives him permission. Says Gates: "She's not carrying textbooks around. She's just got that tablet machine. When you see how natural it is for these kids, you get a clear glimpse of the future."

But Jennifer Gates is one of the most privileged young people in the world. What about the billions of youngsters who have never even seen a computer—much less have a nifty laptop of their own? This is where portable computing could have one of its most profound effects over the coming decades. Laptops and cell phones have proved to be empowering devices for everybody from corporate executives to middle-school students in the United States, Western Europe, and the wealthy parts of Asia. For a 12-year-old girl in rural Cambodia or a sprawling urban slum in Brazil, a laptop or mobile phone equipped with an Internet browser could provide a window onto a world they hardly knew existed and a way to interact with that world. As educational tools, portable devices could help break a stalemate of poverty and disease that seemed immovable until very recently. If the designers of portables have learned anything in the past half-decade, it's that you can't design a machine for the wealthy of the West and expect to foist it on poor people elsewhere. Those devices are too expensive, too flimsy, and, in many ways, unsuited to the cultures of the developing world.

That realization came home to members of a Nokia design team when they were on a fact-finding trip to Mongolia in 2006.

In frigid Ulaan Bataar, they met a man who ran a mobile phone calling service. He stood outdoors. Beside him on a small metal table was an old-fashioned desktop phone, complete with a base station, curly cord, and handset. He had transformed it into a cell phone by installing radio electronics and a Subscriber Identity Module (SIM) card inside. The entire setup was wrapped in a form-fitting suit of furry yak hide. The phone was "mobile" because when somebody rented it to make a call, the proprietor would walk around holding the table as the person drifted around, talking, in the open air. While people waited to use his phone, he'd try to sell them cigarettes and candy.

The Skunk Works where Nokia's design strategists ponder the innovations that will be necessary for creating phones and portable computers for the next billion global consumers is in an unassuming place: a sun-bleached office park in the Los Angeles suburb of Calabasas, a stone's throw from the Ventura Freeway. There's no Nokia sign on the door. The designers got rid of the signs after they had too many visitors strolling in who wanted to buy a new phone. Eight designers here work with another six in Helsinki on the company's Design Strategy team. The group was formed in early 2008 to explore the larger themes surrounding mobile communications and to advise Nokia's top executives on the directions the company should take. "Design is now seen as a strategic element, not a tactical element. And it's very daunting as well as exciting," says John-Rhys Newman, a slim 38-year-old Welshman who defies the mores of car-crazy Southern California by often riding a bicycle to work.

On March 14, 2008, Newman led me on a tour of the Calabasas design center that echoed the tour that Lenovo's David Hill had given me in Morrisville nearly two years earlier. That's when Hill first showed me his concepts that ultimately led to Kodachi. Nokia's office had a high ceiling and big windows that let in lots of sunlight. Designers worked at tables around the sides, and the middle of the room was dominated by a curved wall covered with dark brown corkboard. Artifacts of the design team's four-year quest to change the way Nokia makes products were pinned on to it. On the far left end was a timeline scrawled on sheets of white paper tacked up horizontally. The timeline tracked the progress of a research project, code-named Positive Consumption, which they'd launched four years earlier. At that time, several of the Calabasas designers had worked on concepts that were supposed to shape the company's products three to five years out. Alastair Curtis, then the head of handset division design and now the corporate design chief, had challenged them to redefine the series of Xpress-on handsets, which had replaceable covers in various colors. The designers complied, but their project took an unexpected turn: they decided to explore the next wave of disruptions that they believed would sweep mobile communications. They had seen what Toyota's Prius hybrid vehicle had done to the auto business, and they believed environmental consciousness would also reshape the cell phone business. So their goal was to come up with technologies and strategies for environmentally sustainable products. The project yielded just one product, a biodegradable Xpress-on cover. But, for them, products weren't really the point. The design strategy group began to take shape. For the first time, instead of focusing on a pretty and useful object, the designers were crafting a principle.

A key date on the corkboard timeline was November 2006. That's when Positive Consumption was retooled as a project code named Homegrown. Some of the early research had awakened Newman to the immense power of Nokia. With a 40 percent share of the worldwide mobile handset market, and producing more than one million phones a day, the company was in a position to have a profound impact on the world. If Nokia made a design change that saved electricity or enabled an illiterate farmer in Tanzania to sell his crops at a better price, the multiplier effect was huge. What if the company made the environment and bridging the digital divide two of its most important strategic concerns? That became the Homegrown team's agenda. The project has since yielded a couple of prototype devices, including a charging adapter that shuts off automatically after an hour of charging (enough to charge most phones) and a shiny aluminum-clad phone made entirely of recycled or recyclable materials. The phone, code-named Remade, was shown publicly for the first time ever on February 13, 2008 by Nokia CEO Olli-Pekka Kallasvuo. He said Nokia was evaluating some of the concepts to see how they might influence future products.

But Newman's team is just beginning to scratch the surface of what it hopes to accomplish. Acquiring grassroots knowledge is an important step. In the past, Nokia sent ethnologists and consumer insights experts out into the field to see how people use mobile phones and miniature computers in their natural habitats. But now the strategic design team is conducting its own primary research. Photos from a recent field trip to Ghana were pinned on the middle section of the corkboard—including a picture of a discarded Nokia phone half-buried in red dirt and one of a young man evidently listening to a voice on a phone for the first time, with a look of wonderment on his face. On this trip, they learned how important it is in developing countries for handsets to be reparable. And they met a woman whose only way of communicating with her family in a remote village is to wait at a city bus station until she finds someone who is traveling there, and give that person a verbal message to pass along. "It brings home the importance of the affordability of the phone," said designer Duncan Burns, an Australian who looks like Beatle George Harrison's long-lost son.

The last collection of information on the Calabasas corkboard was an outline of Homegrown's six priorities. Only the top two were exposed. The rest were shielded from prying eyes by sheets of copy paper pinned over them. The ones that showed were revealing enough, though. The first was Remade, the prototype of a handset made of recycled materials. But the second was potentially even more impactful: an entirely new user interface for handsets designed to be usable by everybody from an illiterate farmer to a captain of industry. The aim was to make mobile communications much more easily accessible to billions of people who had never used a phone before. The lead designer for this project was Raphael Grignani, a Frenchman who had recently broken his leg in a snowboarding accident. He sat on a chair in a conference room with his splinted leg propped on another chair, wincing from time as he showed me a demonstration of how the new user interface (UI) worked. Earlier, he had shown the same demo to people in Ghana and San Diego—to get their input. "It's a user interface designed for everybody, whether in the U.K., Paris, or Uganda," said Grignani.

In preparation for this work, Grignani and his colleagues had erased all they thought they knew about how the user interface on a mobile phone should look and feel. Instead, they rethought communications from the ground up. People's lives are ruled by time, they figured, so they placed the date and time on a "horizon line" near the top of the display, and arranged all of the interactions the user had with the device, arranged in time sequence, on a list that started below the line. So the items on the list would include photographs, text messages, and the like. Above the horizon line, the designers set aside a space, labeled "Make New," for initiating actions—everything from calls to photos to calculations. Rather than extensively using icons—those mainstays of most computer interfaces—they relied primarily on simple word labels and pictures. Grignani, a confident 30-year-old, said the use of icons in the graphical user interface that Kay and his colleagues at Xerox PARC had come up with were not the right choices for handheld communicators. "They're abstractions," Grignani said. "People have to shift their brains. It's more natural to see a face and just press it to make a call."

At the time, Nokia was in the middle of a reappraisal of its user interfaces, and the Homegrown UI was one of the inputs. There's no telling if all or even just pieces of the interface will ever make it into commercial products. "We design without compromise, so what we come up with is an extreme," said Newman, adding later: "Perfection is what we're seeking, but we never get there."

And what of Alan Kay? I met him later on the same day I visited Nokia. He ran Viewpoints Research Institute in nearby Glendale, a nonprofit he set up to conduct research into the use of computers in education. Since leaving Apple, he had worked at Walt Disney Imagineering, the technology consulting group Applied Minds, and Hewlett-Packard. He also had part-time teaching gigs at colleges. Wherever he went he took with him his obsession with computers as tools for learning and creativity. (He calls the advent of Web browsers a "terrible setback" because they turn computer users into passive consumers of information rather than creators.) While he had long been recognized for his early contributions to personal and portable computing, since the turn of the century he had been collecting official accolades, as well, including three of technology's top prizes, the ACM Turing Award, the Kyoto Prize, and the Charles Stark Draper Prize. All the recognition didn't seem to have gone to his head. When we met at Ocean Avenue Seafood, a restaurant in Malibu overlooking the Pacific Ocean, he had the air of an affable college professor—with his comfortable sweater and unkempt graying hair and salt-and-pepper mustache. Even at 67, there was still a youthful aura about him.

But Kay was not content. He had written an essay in 2007, "The Real Computer Revolution Hasn't Happened Yet," arguing that the computing industry had not yet created a computer that was an intellectual amplifier for children. Instead of taking the ideas of tech pioneers of the 1960s and 1970s and building on them, the industry had instead focused primarily on mass production. "What happened is it turned into something like Levittown. The architecture had been done and the carpenters took over," Kay had told me during an interview a few months earlier.

When I asked him what computer had come closest to realizing his Dynabook dream, he was quick to answer: the One Laptop Per Child (OLPC) organization's XO Laptop. OLPC had been set up by Nicholas Negroponte, the long-time head of the MIT Media Laboratory, to create $100 laptops for disadvantaged children in developing countries. OLPC technologists, aided by volunteer programmers and designers, had produced a small green-and-white laptop that required very little electricity, could be used outdoors, and was equipped with "mesh" networking technology that made it possible for a whole village of children to be connected to the Internet via a single Net access account. The software had been designed from the ground up for networking and communications—with the child at the center of things. The idea was that if each child had a laptop of his or her own, which was to be used at home and at school, the machine could become an essential tool in the child's formal education and in his or her out-of-school thinking and interacting with others. The machines shipped with a program called Squeak Etoys, designed by Kay and colleagues, which made it easy for even young children to create presentations and Web pages, and to collaborate with one another on projects.

When Kay and I met, the first XO Laptops were being distributed to a handful of countries that had ordered them. The price of the machines, at nearly $200, was almost twice what Negroponte had predicted. It was clear that he would fall far short of his very ambitious goal of supplying 150 million of them to children through schools by the end of 2008. And critics were starting to pile on. But Kay held XO up as one of the first signs of true progress on the computers-in-education front in many years. "The wonderful thing is that it does exist, and it's causing all sorts of good pressures in all sorts of directions," he said. "Something is happening, and that's something all these businesses haven't been able to make happen in 25 years."

There's no mystery why the XO computer is so dear to Kay's heart. Negroponte and Kay have been close friends for decades, and Kay had advised Negroponte when he formed OLPC in 2003. On top of that, the Constructionist educational theories of another friend of theirs, Seymour Papert, a professor emeritus at the Media Lab, underlie both XO and Kay's Dynabook. Remember, it was after Kay visited Papert in Boston in 1968 that he got the idea for Dynabook. Papert took Kay to a school where students were experimenting with his Logo program on mainframe computers, and the discussion they had afterward inspired Kay. Papert had long argued that children learn best by doing, and in 1980 he published a manifesto arguing his case: *Mindstorms: Children, Computers and Powerful Ideas.* Sadly, in December 2006, Papert, then 78, was run down by a motorcyclist on a busy Hanoi street, and he suffered a serious head injury and memory loss. He had been in Vietnam for an educational conference, and, ironically, he had been talking with a colleague about coming up with an algorithm for analyzing Hanoi's chaotic traffic flow when the motorcyclist struck him.

When I met Kay in the Malibu restaurant, the Hanoi accident was on his mind. The reason: he couldn't recall the date in 1968 when Papert had opened his eyes to the possibilities of computers in education. Now, Papert couldn't help him remember. This mattered because Kay had come up with a scheme to actually produce a Dynabook prototype for the first time, and he wanted to unveil the machine on the fortieth anniversary of his trip to Boston. He called it a "stunt." The plan was to hold a commemoration at the Computer History Museum in Silicon Valley. "Because the actual Dynabook didn't happen, this will be what the Dynabook idea was, and what it could have been," Kay told me.

He remembered vividly the car ride back from the school, which was in Lexington, Massachusetts, to Papert's office in Cambridge. Papert was driving. Kay was in the back seat. Papert kept turning around and talking to him—not minding the traffic. It was a cold day, but no snow. The best Kay could figure, it had been October or November. That's the way it goes with events that become historical. When something is happening, you don't know how important it might become. You're just living your life. So you can't necessarily piece together all the details later.

Now Kay was piecing together the machine that might have been. He came up with the idea of making the Dynabook in December 2007, when he saw the anniversary coming. Most of the components he needed were readily available. He had asked Chuck Thacker, one of his former colleagues from Xerox PARC, to help him out with the motherboard. Wacom, a maker of pen tablets and displays, had shown a willingness to supply the stylus sensor. The folks at Applied Minds had volunteered to make the casing in their machine shop. He'd use the SmallTalk program he had created at PARC as the operating system, and Squeak Etoys would be the programming tool for kids. But some features called for in the Dynabook concept were still on the cutting edge of technology. The display was supposed to be an ultra-high-resolution screen that was capable of presenting crisp animation and enabling richly detailed drawing with electronic ink. He knew people at a display company, E Ink, which specialized in high-quality displays, including the one in Amazon.com's Kindle electronic book reader, but its current versions weren't good enough for a Dynabook prototype. But it turned out that the company had some technology on the drawing boards that might meet Kay's expectations, so he urged its engineers to try to produce a sample display for him based on their newest stuff.

What a journey portable computing had taken since Kay's visit to Papert in Boston! First, there was a decade of experimenting with the concept of personal computing itself. Then, as scientists at Xerox PARC and designers at Apple gave physical shape to their dreams, they produced machines that thrilled engineers and hobbyists. The miniaturization of electronics allowed entrepreneurs to produce ever-more-portable computers—machines for every kind of personal and business task. Graphical user interfaces made them ever easier to use. The Internet connected people to one another and to all of the wisdom and foolishness of the world. And ultraportable computers and smartphones put people in contact anywhere and any time at the touch of a finger.

As my meeting with Kay drew to a close, I asked him the ultimate question: looking back over the nearly forty years since he had conceived of Dynabook, was he pleased or disappointed with the progress that had been made in portable computing by two generations of inventors, designers, and entrepreneurs? He paused for a moment to consider, then picked his words carefully. "You have multiple perspectives," he said. "If you can get a large part of a utopian dream out there, you should be pleased. But if you're utopian, you're never satisfied." So much for perfection.

INDEX

ACKNOWLEDGMENTS

I want to thank the many people who helped me out as sources for information and anecdotes in this book, especially Deepak Advani, Robert Brunner, Rod Canion, Steve Capps, Anand Chandrasekher, Bruce Claflin, John Ellenby, Lee Felsenstein, Jean-Louis Gassée, Bill Gates, Tim Gitchell, Jeff Hawkins, Trip Hawkins, David Hill, Peter Hortensius, Jerry Kaplan, John Karidis, Alan Kay, Bert Keely, Hiroyuki Kinoshita, Andy Kozak, Jon Krakower, Mihal Lazaridis, Sam Lucente, John Medica, Bill Moggridge, John-Rhys Newman, Richard Sapper, Steve Sakoman, Ted Selker, Tomoyuki Takahashi, John Sculley, Aaron Stewart, Michael Tchao, Yang Yuanqing, and Yao Yingjia. Two PR people, Carol Makovich and Ray Gorman, were extremely helpful. My thanks to *Business-Week* colleagues who helped out with stories that later fed into the book: Kenji Hall, Tiff Roberts, David Rocks, and Jay Greene. Thanks to Mary Glenn, my editor at McGraw-Hill. Also, thanks to my wife, Lisa Hamm, who was the photo editor for the book.

ABOUT THE AUTHOR

Steve Hamm is a senior writer at *BusinessWeek* where he writes about information technology, globalization, innovation, and leadership. His *BusinessWeek* blog, GlobeSpotting, spans these four topics. Hamm previously worked for *PC Week*, the *San Jose Mercury News*, and the *New Haven Register*. He's the author of *Bangalore Tiger*, a book about the rise of the Indian tech industry, which was published in 2006 by McGraw-Hill. Hamm lives in Pelham, New York, with his wife, Lisa, a book designer, and his son, Daniel, a singer-songwriter and college student.